BERNARD-MARIE KOLTÈS:
SEVEN PLAYS

BERNARD-MARIE KOLTÈS: SEVEN PLAYS

Edited by

Amin Erfani

Martin E. Segal Theatre Center Publications

Frank Hentschker, Executive Director

Martin E. Segal Theatre Center Publications
New York, © 2022

All rights reserved. Except for brief passages quoted in newspaper, magazine, radio or television reviews, no part of this book may be reproduced in any form or by any means, electronic or mechanical, including photocopying or recording, or by an information storage and retrieval system, without permission in writing from the publisher.

Professionals and amateurs are hereby warned that this material, being fully protected under the Copyright Laws of the United States of America and all other countries of the Berne and Universal Copyright Conventions, is subject to a royalty. All rights including, but not limited to, professional, amateur, recording, motion picture, recitation, lecturing, public reading, radio and television broadcasting, and the rights of translation into foreign languages are expressly reserved. Inquiries concerning use of these translations should be addressed to Amin Erfani, aminerfani@gmail.com. Inquiries concerning performance rights should be addressed in advance, before rehearsals begin, to Arcadia Media, prof@arcadia-media.net, http://www.arcadia-media.net. For inquiries concerning global publishing rights and translations please contact Les Éditions de Muinut, 7, rue Bernard-Palissy, 75006 Paris, contact@leseditionsdeminuit.fr, http://www.leseditionsdeminuit.fr

Library of Congress Cataloging-in-Publication Data

Names: Koltès, Bernard-Marie, author. | Erfani, Amin, editor, translator.
 | Koltès, Bernard-Marie. Plays. Selections. English.
Title: Seven plays / Bernard-Marie Koltès ; edited by Amin Erfani ;
 [translated by Amin Erfani and 5 others].
Description: New York : Martin E. Segal Theatre Center, [2022] | Summary:
 "A collection of seven plays by the French playwright Bernard-Marie
 Koltès with introduction and additional archival material on three of
 the plays"-- Provided by publisher.
Identifiers: LCCN 2021058418 | ISBN 9781953892058 (paperback)
Subjects: LCSH: Koltès, Bernard-Marie--Translations into English. | LCGFT:
 Drama.
Classification: LCC PQ2671.O426 S49 2022 | DDC 842/.914--dc23
LC record available at https://lccn.loc.gov/2021058418

Christopher Silsby, Production Editor

Elsa Ruiz, Cover Photo

Christopher Silsby, Cover Design

Frank Hentschker, Supervising Editor

© 2022 Martin E. Segal Theatre Center

BERNARD-MARIE KOLTÈS: SEVEN PLAYS

Edited by

Amin Erfani

The Night Just Before the Forests

Battle of Black and Dogs

West Pier

In the Solitude of Cotton Fields

Tabataba

Back to the Desert

Roberto Zucco

CONTENTS

Acknowledgements ix

Introduction xi
Amin Erfani

The Night Just Before the Forests 1
translated by Amin Erfani

Battle of Black and Dogs 25
translated by Michaël Attias

    Notebooks to Battle of Black and Dogs 99
    translated by Michaël Attias

West Pier 111
translated by Marion Schoevaert and Theresa M. Weber

    Notes to West Pier 211
    translated by Marion Schoevaert and Theresa M. Weber

In the Solitude of Cotton Fields 217
translated by Amin Erfani

Tabataba 245
translated by Amin Erfani

Back to the Desert 253
translated by Andy Bragen

    A Hundred-Year History of the Serpenoise Family 333
    translated by Amin Erfani

Roberto Zucco 339
translated by Anna G.R. Miller

A Short Biographical Account 405
Amin Erfani

ACKNOWLEDGEMENTS

This collection would not have seen the light of day without the support and friendship of the author's brother, François Koltès, and Frank Hentschker, the Director of the Martin E. Segal Theatre Center at the CUNY Graduate Center. Translating Bernard-Marie Koltès is a work of love, and I am proud to share this love with the group of stellar translators who contributed to this collection. Particular gratitude is owed to Marion Schoevaert, along with Doris Mirescu and Robert Lyons who produced the New York Koltès Festival in 2003, at the Ohio Theater in SoHo, which was a major step in introducing Koltès in the United States. Importantly, I am grateful for the longtime friendship—and brotherhood, to use a Koltésian word—of Ismaïl Ibn Conner, an immense actor whose encounter with Koltès' dramatic work shook him to the core, leading him to found another major Koltès Project at the 7 Stages Theatre, in Atlanta, GA, that lasted from 2006 to 2012. A special thank you to the French Embassy in the United States and the FACE Foundation for supporting the stage productions of four of the plays included in this collections; and particularly to Nicole Birmann Bloom who has been a lifeline for stage productions of Koltès—and so many others—in the United States for many long years. My first foray into Koltès translation and stage production in Atlanta would not have happened without the trust and help of Carole Scipion. Professors Judith Graves Miller and Tom Bishop, in the French department at New York University, have championed French and Francophone theater including Koltès' work in the United States for decades, so much so that American exposure to that very different dramatic tradition would have been much poorer if it weren't for their work. I would like to express my gratitude for the friendship of Koltès biographer Arnaud Maïsetti, and also that of Christophe Bident without whom my academic journey into theater would have been a missed encounter. Nothing I do would come to fruition without the support of my wife and children. Thank you to Philip Boulay, André Petitjean, Jérémie Majorel, Florence Bernard, Karl Pollin, Stéphanie Boulard, the Department of French and Italian at Emory University, and the Languages and Literatures Department at Lehman College, CUNY. This book is very much indebted to Christopher Silsby for designing it and bringing it to completion, as well as to the help of Andie Lerner. Finally, this project benefitted from a grant from PSC CUNY, and the support of the School of Arts & Humanities at Lehman College, CUNY.

INTRODUCTION

> I like my job because it is inessential. Making theater is the most superficial, useless thing in the world, and as a result, you want to do it to perfection.
>
> Bernard-Marie Koltès

The most celebrated French playwright of the end of the twentieth century does not hide his disdain for the theater. He goes to plays only "two to three times a year." During his interviews at the height of his career, he confesses: "I cannot stand the theater. You get bored out of your mind ninety-nine percent of the time at the theater. Not to get bored, I need to be overcome by devastating and unquestionable beauty, and how many times does that happen in a lifetime?"[1]

It happened to Koltès on January 12, 1968, at the age of nineteen. In Strasbourg, a friend took him to a performance of *Medea*, by Seneca, starring the exiled Spanish actress Maria Casarès. This was no random performance, and its impact on Koltès was life-changing. Casarès was one of the most emblematic figures of the golden age of French theater. Still today, we can hear her voice alongside Antonin Artaud and Roger Blin in the notorious and censored recording of *To Have Done With the Judgment of God* (1947). Two years prior to Koltès' encounter with her, Casarès performed the larger-than-life role of the Mother in Jean Genet's revolutionary play, *The Screens*, also staged by Blin, which incited riots by right-wing activists at the Odéon theater in Paris. Eighteen years after the encounter between this mythical actress and the young man, who had not yet written a single line for the theater, Casarès would play the role of the Mother but this time in Koltès' 1986 play *West Pier* (*Quai ouest*).

After the performance of *Medea*, the ambivalent student in journalism at last found his life purpose. In a letter to his mother—who, in his eyes, was a quasi-saintly figure—Koltès writes about his life-changing decision, close to his twentieth birthday:

---

1 Koltès, Bernard-Marie. *Une part de ma vie : Entretiens*. Les Editions de Minuit, 2010, 144.

Here I am on the eve of putting myself at the service of Theater. I believe I understand the dangers, take stock of the "inconveniences." Even so, I happily take this risk, despite the abyss before me if I fail. If I fail, I will be nothing, no doubt, deprived of a "situation," a family, even a reason to live, and without any place in society. I know that. Even so, will I give up hope for a life lived to the fullest, a reason to live in the true sense of the term; will I give up on everything that I could give—no matter how small—to so many people?[2]

Despite his commitment to theater at a young age, he fails the admission exams to the coveted Comédie de l'Est, in Strasbourg, both in acting and directing. Rejected by the institution, writing will become his entree into the theater and, as the years go by, his weapon *against* it. He produces his first plays himself with a student group from the drama school he failed to get in through regular channels. Although not entirely original texts, his dramatization for the stage of great classics helps him find and nurture his own style in the early years. These texts include stage adaptations of the biblical poem the *Song of Songs* (*la Marche*, 1970), novels by Gorki (les *Amertumes*, 1970), Dostoyevsky (*Procès ivre*, 1971), and Salinger (*Sallinger*, 1977), as well as a rewriting of Shakespeare (*le jour du meurtre dans l'histoire Hamlet*, 1974). He does write three original texts, two for the radio (*Heritage*, 1972; *Voix sourdes*, 1974), and one for his own purposes as an aspiring director (*Récits morts*, 1973). These last three plays already demonstrate the process of maturation of Koltès' signature style: emphasis on poetic language, often through the form of monologues, unresolved tensions between characters, lack of emphasis on plot. Repudiating these early plays, Koltès later calls his groundbreaking monologue *The Night Just Before the Forests* (*la Nuit juste avant les forêts*, 1977) the true beginning of his dramatic work.

The Night Just Before the Forests is a single sentence that stretches over ten thousand words, presented between two quotation marks, without a final period, without stage instructions, and without naming the character. The text is by standard measures not a dramatic text, although written for the theater. The lack of any period or final punctuation postpones all dramatic conventions: plot, character, resolution, even transparent meaning. Instead,

---

2 Koltès, Bernard-Marie. *Lettres*. Les Editions de Minuit, 2009, 56, all translations in this introduction are by Amin Erfani, except when noted otherwise.

it puts the emphasis on rhythm and musicality. Compared by the author himself to a fugue by Bach, the contrapuntal monologue presents itself as a call, a demand, an ask by a seemingly homeless drunk man to a passerby. He approaches you to ask for a light for his cigarette, for money to buy coffee or beer, for a room to sleep at night, and most and foremost, for love. Revolutionary in many respects, and echoing Samuel Beckett's radical *Not I* (1972) while detaching itself even further from the theatrical apparatus, *The Night* subscribes to what Anne Ubersfeld calls a *quasi-monologue*: neither a soliloquy nor a long address to another character, it speaks directly to the audience who cannot reply, while begging for a response that would be in the form of love. *The Night* will be the last play Koltès stages himself, at the Avignon Festival in 1977, "a staging that wasn't really one"[3]: an actor, a table, and a chair. His self-proclaimed inauguration as a legitimate playwright is concurrent with the end of his short streak as a stage director. His relation with Patrice Chéreau, a couple of years later, will be increasingly shaped by the playwright's unrelenting desire to write *against* the expectations of his faithful stage director.

In the winter of 1978, at a friend's invitation, Koltès travels to Lagos, Nigeria. In his childhood, his mother often visited her missionary brother in Africa. Both filled the young Koltès with stories of idyllic nature and folklore. His trip to Lagos puts an end to his childhood illusions, and imbues in him a political awareness that will intensify as an adult. Upon his arrival at the airport, he witnesses a scene at first ordinary: a car bumps into another. But immediately three white policemen drag a black driver to the ground and beat him senseless. On the way from the airport to Lagos: bodies of dead black people laid alongside the road. At the construction site, managed by white French men and guarded by black men on top of watchtowers, he witnesses the everyday racism of the European toward the native Nigerians. He recalls in an interview that being himself a white man confronted to the European's violence: "I looked at the black people. I was ashamed of my people; but there was such a hatred gleaming in their eyes that I got scared, and I run back toward the white folks."[4] His biographer Arnaud Maïsetti notes that Koltès' experience in Nigeria was "an edifying mirror: in it Koltès looks at himself and what he sees is the appearance of a colonizer, although he would have liked to see himself as a brother to those black people."[5] Like

---

3   Maïsetti, Arnaud. *Bernard-Marie Koltès*. Les Editions de Minuit, 2018, 117.

4   Ibid., 137.

5   Ibid., 141.

Jean Genet, Koltès grows increasingly spiteful of his own skin color, the repressive history and the power structure it represents. Maïsetti reports that, one day, "in the morning, a workman died on the construction site, crushed by a machine and thrown into the sewers. Nobody cared. His name was Nwofia. Koltès didn't forget his name."[6] This horrific scene will become the premise of *Battle of Black and Dogs* (*Combat de nègre et de chiens*, 1978): a black man, Alboury, walks into a construction site to collect his brother who was killed and thrown into the sewers by a white racist engineer. Koltès understood that writing in the name of Africans would redouble the colonizer's violence. Instead, he presents Alboury as the colonizer's nightmare: one who answers the most human call for mourning, but who ends as a powerful and uncompromising avenger against white oppression. Maïsetti aptly points that for the author, "avenging reality is the purpose of writing."[7]

For Koltès like for Genet, writing is neither merely mimicry, eulogy, or an extension of lived experiences. It acquires instead a function as fundamental and primary as life itself. Embroiled in a complex relationship, one always competes with the other:

> Life is lived on the one hand and written in reverse, I mean by that the emotions, the things, the experiences I live and the people I mix with, from the moment I write them, I put them to death somehow. Besides, that is the problem, the only problem I am preoccupied with as a writer: when I experience something, when I meet someone, I know that one day or the other, I will use them as scapegoats (*ils vont me sévir en pâture*). . . I mean by that I will use them to write, if I may say so. . . and from that point on, I will do a work of death (*je ferai une œuvre de mort*), vis-à-vis those I've met. [. . .] And I feel on both sides, on the side of existence and on the side of writing, a drive to live each fully, and I know very well that is not possible.[8]

A second event that would change his life and impact his later work took place only months after that faithful January day, in 1968, when Koltès saw Maria Casarès on stage, a decade before his trip to Lagos. In the summer

---

6 Ibid., 146.

7 Ibid.

8 Bernard-Marie Koltès interviwed by Jacques Lemire (1981), in *Théâtre d'aujourd'hui n° 5. Koltès, Combats avec la scène*, [CD-ROM], Paris, CNDP/Ministère de la Culture et de la Communication, 1996.

of the same year, the twenty-year-old man makes a new unbreakable pact with himself. Shortly after moving from the town of Metz to the more bustling city of Strasbourg, he travels to Quebec for a three-month job at a summer camp for children. The life-changing encounter does not take place at his point of destination, but during the transfer between the plane arriving from France and the bus leaving for Canada: "New York is utterly indescribable, because everything is out of proportion [. . .]. A forest of skyscrapers and neon lights. [. . .] You suddenly dive in another world, another civilization, even stranger than the Arab world; it is ruled by blacks, by publicity; dollars, prostitution, and pornography are displayed for everyone to see, six-year-old kids walk by themselves in the streets. It is unforgettable."[9] At the end of his stay in Quebec, he hitchhikes all the way to Washington, DC, and stays two weeks in New York: he is in awe of Harlem. In a letter to a friend, he inscribes the second commitment to himself, one he will not break:

"I have found
my place
in this world:
New York
I will come back here
for a long time."[10]

Throughout his adult life, his obsession with the city grows. In his eyes, New York represents the inverse of Western cities, which he increasingly despises. His spite is particularly directed toward the European model, cities like Strasbourg or Metz. For him, Metz in particular is a "desert": growing up as a kid he witnessed, in 1961, bombings of local Arab cafés by the army-backed right-wing French militia, the OAS.[11] In contrast to the European urban model that segregates the minority population to the outskirts: "New York is truly like no other city in the world; it is like a big bag where they put everything that could not fit anywhere else."[12] Koltès is attracted to the diversity of the city's population, where minorities, in contrast to cities in Europe, constitute the majority of its dwellers. In a 1989 interview: "I didn't have the time to dream about Paris, I immediately dreamt about New York. And New York in '68, it was really a different world."[13] He clearly places himself in the New York landscape among the millions of outcasts

---

9   Koltès, *Lettres* 60-61.
10 Ibid., 84.
11 Maïsetti, 23.
12 Koltès, *Lettres*, 83.
13 Koltès, *Une part de ma vie,* 149.

who don't fit elsewhere. As the years go by, other urban landscapes—"spaces of marginality,"[14] such as Lagos, Salvador de Bahia, Lisbon—will become dim reflections of New York City.

Ever since that transfer on his way to Canada, the compulsion to return to the American megalopolis grows stronger: it will become the only place where his "urges and habits" are met. Although rarely speaking about his sexuality, in his personal letters or interviews, Koltès thrives in the gay liberation movement of the period. He spends time in the abandoned and derelict Hudson River piers, west of Manhattan, where the gay community basked under the sun in clandestinity. Of Peter Rabbit, a famed bar for black and white gay men, he writes in 1981:

> Peter Rabbit, a place I prefer to my bed, to my mother's belly, where wings grow under my feet [. . .]. There's always a splendid woman who does the vocals on blues songs, I sit there gaping at her, she winks at me and makes me fall off my chair. It is situated on the Hudson piers, and, drunk on Coke, on whiskey, on smiles, and on images from Jack London novels, I go by the water, there are warehouses on the right and warehouses on the left, nobody murders anybody there, the arms of the thugs are so soft they make you shiver, I shiver. [. . .] I am creating within myself urges and habits that won't be easily met elsewhere.[15]

The American megalopolis is not only the space for sexual liberation, it is equally the space for writing. Although, like for Jean Genet, writing requires a state of absolute solitude, unlike the former inmate, Koltès finds his solitude in large crowds, particularly while traveling to foreign countries where he barely understands the language. "You develop an astonishing relation with language in a foreign country. I write differently, for instance, in New York than in Paris. You take a particular pleasure because you are alone."[16] The anonymity of the crowd, and the effort required to communicate with foreigners, strip away the writer's native language of its pre-made idioms and stereotypes. The contact with the foreign language contaminates the writer's own language, turns it into something foreign in and of itself. "I find that the relation you maintain with a foreign language—while you keep inside yourself a 'maternal' tongue that no one else understands—

---

14 Ibid, 129.

15 Ibid., 445-446.

16 Koltès, *Une part de ma vie*, 77.

is one of the most beautiful relations you may have with language; and it is perhaps the same relation the writer has with words."[17] The becoming foreign of one's own native tongue is turned into a pre-requirement for writing. Writing, in these terms, presents itself as a form of translation of one's own *incomprehensible mother tongue*.

Beyond the crowded solitude of the megacity conducive to writing, New York also serves as a major source of inspiration for his work. His letters testify to the writer's increasing fascination: "I have seen things so beautiful, so beautiful—in Harlem, on the West Side, by the Hudson River; oh the nights of New York!—if I had enough talent to steal a piece of this beauty, I know I would be the *most accomplished* writer of the century!"[18] The city is inspirational mainly because this "bag" where exiled people meet from all over the world brings about "impossible" encounters. The site of these encounters is exemplified by the abandoned warehouses, almost crumbling down, alongside the Hudson River, in the '70s and early '80s, just a few years before the acknowledgment of the AIDS epidemic. We see them in the emblematic photographs by Alvin Baltrop, or the street art of David Wojnarowicz. In Koltès' experience, these decrepit structures serve as "a shelter for tramps, fags, drug deals, settling of old scores, and yet a place where cops never go."[19] These warehouses at the West End represent what Koltès idealizes about New York City: "a privileged corner of the world, like a mysteriously neglected square in the middle of a garden, where the plants would have grown differently, a place where normal order doesn't exist, but where a different order, a curious one, is created."[20] Not long after Koltès discovered this harbor for outcasts like himself, the second-time-elected mayor of New York, Ed Koch, "cleans up" the city in the early '80s, closing the bath-houses and destroying the abandoned West piers, all hubs for the gay community. Koltès is unforgiving and, once again, he uses his pen in retaliation.

In *West Pier* (1983), a corrupt tycoon turned bankrupt who is revealingly named Koch is driven by his secretary to an abandoned warehouse, in a decrepit neighborhood of an unnamed town by an unnamed river where cops never come. Koch is returning to the place of his childhood, where he grew up in a lower-class household, to commit

---

17   Ibid, 44.
18   Koltès, *Lettres*, 442.
19   Koltès, *Une part de ma vie*, 12.
20   Ibid.

suicide. The warehouse shelters a community of outcasts, rejects of society. They include a South American family of indigenous origin: the begrudged mother, Cécile, the father Rodolph, maimed by war, the son Charles originally named Carlos, and the daughter Claire. The other members of this destitute community are Fak, an Asian young man, and Abad, the most destitute of all, who keeps mute on stage. Abad is depicted as the most marginalized character and therefore imbued with an almost mystic authority. Although there are no such stage instructions in the play, Koltès adds in the appendix that Abad, by function, must be played by a black actor. Again like Genet, Koltès is emphatic about the privileged—if not quintessential—role of blacks in his plays. "They will inevitably be present, until the end, in everything I write."[21] This is as much an aesthetic statement as a political one, especially in a racially repressive France: "It is true that, today, the blood of our people is black and Arab [. . .]. There is new blood because of the presence of blacks and Arabs; there is no new blood in France's heartland, which is a desert; there, no life exists, and if anything happens, it is always thanks to immigrants."[22] The political reach of *West Pier* also pertains to France's theater scene. The play was originally commissioned by the Comédie-Française, the country's most prestigious state theater, which was unsurprisingly composed of only white actors. Knowing that the troupe would not be able to stage a play with a majority of non-white characters, Koltès drafts *West Pier*, consequently forcing the Comédie-Française to let the play be staged by his favored director, Patrice Chéreau.

Characteristically, *West Pier* is subversive not just in content, but also in form. The play purposefully exceeds the dramatic genre, drafted as a challenge for any stage director. Although written for the theater, the text is punctuated by a series of what Koltès calls "novel-like" monologues and quotations, which are intended for the reader rather than the spectator. It yearns to be a *total theater*, one that mixes tragic and comedic genres, but also brings theatricality beyond the stage and onto the page. In such an attempt, Koltès reveals that theater must not be exclusively a visual medium, limited to stage productions. In addition, he purposefully disrupts dramatic conventions, stating that the text must dispense with traditional stage interpretations. For instance, instead of playing realistic or psychological characters, Koltès requests in the afterword that the actor "must always say a text like a child with a strong need to piss, reciting a lesson: very fast, shifting from one leg to the other, and who, when he's finished, rushes off to

---

21 Ibid, 61.
22 Ibid, 126.

do what was on his mind all along."[23]

I referred from the outset to the playwright's distrust of conventional dramatic productions, which drives him to write, to some degree, *against* theater. Because of the advent of new media, and particularly the hegemony of cinema, he believes that "the theater will always be inferior to other technologies."[24] As such, for theater to survive as a legitimate and autonomous art, it must not rely on the visual appeal of staging, but on the power of the text: the incantatory impact of speech and language conveyed by the actor. "There's no need for staging (*la mise en scène*). These days, I am very upset with stage directors, I find that they complicate things. I like a good director who creates pretty lighting, a nice stage set, etc. But still, he's like a crab sitting on the theater, who wasn't needed for centuries and won't be needed again after a given point. The theater needs writers and actors, that's it."[25] In his interviews, Koltès is in fact not much more generous toward actors who, in the end like stage directors, must "be at the service of the text."[26] It is significant that Koltès' later plays, which brought him fame, were systematically published in a book format by les Éditions de Minuit way before their production. The text was therefore not influenced or changed by its stage productions. Contrary to most playwrights who write for the stage and often alongside directors and actors, his was not a script, but truly a piece of dramatic literature. *West Pier* was too massive to handle, even for a director like Chéreau: its reception was tepid. Instead of giving up on his protege, Chéreau immediately decides to stage Koltès' new text, one that will seal his reputation as the most celebrated French playwright of the late twentieth century.

In the Solitude of Cotton Fields (*Dans la Solitude des champs de coton*, 1985) lifts textual lyricism to a level unprecedented in modern theater. Once and for all dispensing with notions of psychological characters and dialogical speech, his language is driven by long rhythmical sentences within long consecutive monologues that convey a plethora of metaphors, blurring the lines between poetry, prose, and theater. Lacking stage instructions, except for character names, the Dealer and the Client, the text is the second literary work born out of Koltès' experience in New York.

---

23 Koltès, Bernard-Marie. *Quai ouest*. Les Editions de Minuit, 2011, 104, translated by Marion Schoevaert and Theresa M. Weber.

24 Ibid., 58.

25 Ibid., 143.

26 Ibid., 73.

It depicts one of those "impossible" encounters he had witnessed in the abandoned warehouses by the Hudson River. At the genesis of the text, Koltès recalls seeing an alleged drug dealer attempting to sell merchandise to a punk; but the punk soon realizes the dealer has no merchandise to sell and that, instead, he is begging for money. Chéreau subsequently stages this encounter primarily as a flirt between two men who refuse to openly admit their sexuality, speaking in innuendos. The literary power of the text lies in its ability to defy any definitive interpretation. The Dealer attempts to sell something to the Client, but stubbornly refuses to reveal his merchandise. The Client denies having any desire to buy, yet remains perplexed by what the Dealer might have to offer. In never revealing the object of transaction, Koltès builds the theatricality of the text on the tension between the two characters, as well as on the text's poetic language. He effectively does away with the most central element of a traditional play: plot. He prolongs the gesture he had already started with *The Night*, putting poetic and incantatory speech as the central—if not the sole—element of theater. He is the first to admit: *In the Solitude of Cotton Fields* is not written for the theater per se, "it strikes different cords."[27] He contends that the text is simply an intertwined alternation of two long monologues. As he puts it, the text may possibly be put on stage, but it was not necessarily conceived for the stage. Systematically writing against the traditional rules of theater, Koltès shifts the boundaries, redefines them.

As in the case of Abad, Koltès is adamant that despite the lack of stage instructions the Dealer must be played by a black actor. This expressed desire will rarely be taken into account in subsequent stage productions, even by Chéreau who decides to cast himself in the role of the Dealer, replacing the great Ivorian actor Isaach de Bankolé in the second production of the play in 1988. This decision becomes a major point of contention between the writer and his celebrated stage director. As explained in the afterword of *West Pier*, "blackness" serves as the "photonegative" of representational theater, to a great extent because European theater was predominantly white. The author's desire to have a black actor in his plays at any cost was as much an aesthetic as a political statement.

This expressed wish was never as publicly defended as in the case of a production of *Back to the Desert* (*Retour au désert*) in Germany in 1988. In general, Koltès' plays were first translated and produced abroad before being staged by Chéreau in France. It was so because—to both

---

27 Ibid., 75.

Koltès and Chéreau's dismay—the French institution of public theater and its stage directors are generally averse to risk, favoring classical texts over contemporary ones. On the other hand, foreign productions of Koltès' plays abounded, but lacked Chéreau's rigor. A German production in Hamburg resorted to *blackface* for the important role of the black paratrooper, then played by a white actor. Koltès was enraged and threatened to block the production. Even after his death, the Comédie-Française resorted to giving the role of Aziz, a character of Algerian descent, to a white actor, prompting the author's surviving brother, François, to fight the production in court.

Back to the Desert (1987) takes place in a provincial town east of France, reminiscent of Metz, this "desert" where Arab cafés were bombed by right-wing French activists in the '60s. A sister, exiled to Algeria by his wealthy French family, returns to the town with two mixed-blood children, to reclaim her part of the heritage from her brother. As usual, Koltès spares none of his characters from an inherent cruelty one toward another, building the theatricality of the play upon such tensions. But also characteristic of Koltès is his subversion of genre: this play appeals to the conventions of Boulevard theater, originally aimed at bourgeois sensibilities; but instead, its thematic aims at confronting the bourgeois public of private theaters to their own bigotry. For the first time, indeed, Chéreau produced a Koltès play in a private theater starring a renowned Boulevard actress, Jacqueline Maillan.

Although generally silent on his health, as he was drafting what will be his last completed play, *Roberto Zucco* (1988), Koltès knew he was losing the battle against AIDS. His writing was unrelenting and his anger was unforgiving. Quintessentially a Shakespearian character, Zucco is both a murderous anti-hero and an almost mystic figure. He was inspired by the notorious killer Roberto Succo, declared Public Enemy Number One in Italy, France, and Switzerland in 1988. Young and handsome, Succo became a media obsession after a series of gruesome murders, including of his father, mother, a doctor, and two policemen. Beyond terrorizing the public, his handsome mug shot monopolized TV screens, the front pages of newspapers, and covered subway-station walls. The public's fascination also stemmed from his ability to escape from the police and prisons shortly after being caught. Once, in front of news cameras and to the public's awe, he attempted an evasion on top of prison roofs, climbing on electric cables, and stripping to his underwear. It hasn't escaped many critics that Koltès' own features, in Elsa Ruiz' iconic photographs, bear an unsettling resemblance to that of Roberto Succo.

The play *Roberto Zucco* attempts one last time to extend the reach of theater, from references to *Hamlet* to scenes worthy of popular TV shows, from complex tragic characters to cartoonishly comedic ones, all punctuated by some of Koltès' most masterful signature monologues. In his last interviews, the playwright is not shy about his own fascination with the murderous character: "This man killed for no reason. That is why, for me, he is a hero. He completely matches the man of our century. [. . .] And the way he commits his murders brings us back to the great mythologies."[28] The genius of Koltès' depiction of Zucco stems from his understanding that he becomes myth only thanks to the public's gaze; his strength emanates from the media obsession created around him: "the admirative gaze that the others direct toward him, that's what turns him into a hero."[29] As the character Zucco explains, in the seminal scene of the underground subway station: "There are no heroes whose clothes aren't soaked in blood, and blood's the only thing in the world that cannot go unnoticed."[30]

By the time *Zucco* is drafted, Koltès has fallen out with Chéreau, since the director had already cast himself in the role of the Dealer, instead of a black actor, in the second production of *In the Solitude of Cotton Fields*. In sending his final completed work to the German director Peter Stein, Koltès creates a rift not just with Chéreau, but with the world of French theater, of which he had grown wary over the years. Stein's first production of *Zucco* occurs in 1990, after Koltès' passing.

For the first time, this collection provides American translations of Koltès' seven major plays to readers, artists and scholars. Despite the author's international status, "Koltès studies" and theatrical productions of his plays in the English-speaking world have been lagging in comparison to other major languages. There is no doubt that the tradition of American and British theater, more plot-driven and reliant on realism, psychology, and transparent language, vastly differs from the French, and even more from Koltès' work, which is heavily driven by poetic and invocatory language, often to the detriment of character and plot. Previous volumes of British translations have the merit of introducing the playwright's work to the English-speaking readership, artists, and audience. But there is the argument to be made that those translations also adapted Koltès' language to British and

---

28 Ibid., 109-110.

29 Ibid., 110.

30 Koltès, Bernard-Marie. *Roberto Zucco suivi de Tabataba-Coco*. Les Editions de Minuit, 2011, 37; translated by Anna G. R. Miller.

American sensibilities, producing psychologism and spoken language when the playwright's uniquely rhythmical and poetic style rigorously refrained from just that. As a result, a plethora of new translations, particularly in the United States, attempted to breathe a new life into Koltès' reception in the English-speaking world over the past few decades. American productions did not lack, however, even during Koltès' own life. In 1982, Françoise Kourilsky produced an early translation of *Combat de nègre et de chien* under the title *Come Dog, Come Night* with the Ubu Repertory Theater, at La MaMa Experimental Theatre Club. The production and its translation were poorly received by the public, the critics, and the author himself.[31] Later in 1995, Kourilsky attempted an American production of *la Nuit juste avant les forêts*, while Travis Preston staged *Roberto Zucco* in Chicago during the same year. But the first major introduction of Koltès in the U.S. happened in 1996, at the Brooklyn Academy of Music, with Chéreau and Pascal Greggory performing the third and most acclaimed staging of *Dans la solitude des champs de coton*. As the New York Times reported, the performance was accompanied by "simultaneous English translation, provided by earphones," under the mistranslated title *In the Loneliness of the Cotton Fields*. The intrigued critique in the New York Times also noted: "The play belongs to a revered tradition of declamatory theater, which is almost as old as French theater itself and is virtually unknown in this country." Despite this objective diagnosis, it is worth noting that Koltès' work holds a unique place in the said French tradition, and hardly assimilates to it. In 2003, stage directors Marion Schoevaert and Doris Mirescu, with Robert Lyons of the Soho Think Tank at Ohio Theater, created a massive Koltès/New York festival in the Off-Off Broadway, at the heart of New York's experimental theater. For Schoevaert, the dissident voice of Koltès acquired a singular meaning in post-911 America, at the dawn of the Iraq war and during the social and racial turmoil of the time. Koltès finally resonated with the American public, and the festival was positively received. For the New York Times, "The heat of the moment gives the productions a peculiar relevancy and power." Beyond its political impact, another New York Times critique noted that "Koltès now sounds like Dante speaking in the voice of Sam Shepard." Despite the festival's success, its translations were not given publication rights, because the second volume of the author's British translations was on its way. The lack of established American translations created a void, which artists around the country filled with their own new translations. A second major Koltès project took place in Atlanta, initiated by the actor Ismaïl Ibn Conner. Living

---

31 Maïsetti, 217.

in the American South, "alienated from the world as both an American and a person of African descent," Conner found a unique and intimate connection with Koltès' voice. The French director Arthur Nauzyciel first cast him in 2000, at the 7 Stages Theatre, for the role of Alboury in a collaborative translation of *Battle of Black and Dogs*. Following the production's positive reception, Conner and the 7 Stages launched a Koltès Project which lasted from 2006 to 2012, with François Koltès' support. The project created new translations and productions of Koltès, in collaboration with renowned French stage directors and American artists. Some of the translations in this collection are products of these two major projects.

Our common approach to the translations of these seven plays was not only to put the texts to the test of stage productions, but to account for the author's very singular approach to language and writing. As explained earlier, one would be mistaken not to consider Koltès' French as, itself, foreign to common speech. In fact, before subscribing to any dramatic conventions, particularly to psychologism and linguistic transparency, his signature style seeks to obscure them. It does so stylistically through an extremely rhythmical and singularly rigorous repetition of the same words, the same expressions, and the same motifs, in vastly different contexts, thus putting to test their semantic stability. Stripping the translation from those rigorous repetitions for the sake of transparency alone is, quite simply put, misunderstanding the heart of what is at stake in Koltès' writing. It would turn the translations into pale reflections of the original plays. There is in this author a certain belief that obscurity—not transparency or immediacy— is *fertile*, in particular when paired with rhythm and musicality. One might say that there are two aspects of language, one that relies on referential meaning ("*signification*"), the other that creates meaning ("*sens*") through musicality. As Koltès points out in an interview: "A word, in itself, has no meaning (*sens*). For meaning to appear, there needs to be an accumulation of words, a rhythm, a music; music produces meaning (*sens*), not an isolated word."[32] One sees this not only in his approach to writing, but also in his approach to translation. Describing his own French translation of Shakespeare's *Winter's Tale*:

> I tried to transmit the most obscure passages of *Winter's Tale* through a scrupulous, word for word, manic translation. The

---

32 Koltès, *Une part de ma vie*, 108.

long lyrical passages were the easiest to translate; but there are metaphors, short lines, uncanny allusions whose meaning and reason escape; I believe one must let them escape, not be hasty, not consult anything but the words themselves. Eventually, their meaning may not appear; not any more than in the English text; but consistency (*cohérance*) is key, it is more essential than a thousand things. Shakespeare doesn't explain himself, and in that regard, the translator must not explain either.[33]

Consistency and musicality over transparency and communication, these are not random criteria. In addition, as a way to avoid psychologism, or naturalization of language, we paid heed to another important dimension of the writer's style. Although Koltès toils to preserve poetic obscurity, his grammar is almost always impeccable and his choice of vocabulary adheres to the dramatic convention of decorum. Even the most outrageous insults are very often given a poetic turn. In fact, he performs a feat worthy of the greatest magicians: if his characters may sound aggressive, provocative, even at times vulgar, they almost always dispense with actual vulgar language and attack one another in the most perfect and poetic French. There is a natural tendency in translations of his work, and not just into English, to attribute more vulgar vocabulary and turns of phrase to his writing than what exists in the original text. We rigorously avoided doing so. But we also decided to change a very few number of terms that difficultly translate, not from French to English, but from one culture to another, and from a past period to ours. Those include, for instance, racial slurs such as the word "*nègre*" which may appear simply as "black," or as other declinations of its equivalent English, depending on the context and who is speaking. Another is the word "*camarade*" in *The Night*, referring to France's cultural acceptance of communism in the late '70s, translated in its antithetical American context as "brother" or "sister."[34]

---

33   Koltès, cites in Maïsetti, 303.

34   The French word "camarade" (comrade) as used in *la Nuit* has the same functional value as the word "*frère*" (brother) in Koltès' subsequent plays. Beyond its primary function of indelibly binding two people, it is a word that could be easily heard in churches, or among members of social or political organizations. But more importantly, the word "brother" as later defined by Koltès is paradigmatic of the relation staged between his characters, depicting both utter intimacy and incredible violence: "The provisory advantage of the word 'brother' over all other words that bind one person to another is that it is void of any sentimentality, any affectivity; or, in any case, you can easily get rid of them. It could be harsh, aggressive, fatal, almost uttered with regret. It also suggests irreversibility and blood (not the blood of kings, families, or races, quietly contained in the body and with no additional meaning or color or value than the stomach or the spinal cord, but instead the blood that is drying on the sidewalk)." Bernard-Marie Koltès, Prologue, Editions de Minuit, 1991, 121.

As a closing note to the introduction of these Koltès translations, I would be remiss not to mention—and draw the lessons from—the period when the playwright offered *Quai ouest* to the great Heiner Müller for him to translate into German. While making the offer, Koltès knew full well that the renowned post-Brechtian playwright—who readily accepted the assignment—did not read a word of French. Koltès defended his decision to the end, even after critics admonished Müller's final product for its many infidelities and mistranslations. In a 1986 interview with *Theater Heute*, Koltès insisted: "I don't speak a word of German, but I know I am right: this time, I didn't give my play to a translator, but to a writer. I think it is good that Heiner Müller inscribed his own voice into my play."[35] This approach is not in substance contradictory to Koltès' own "manic translation" of Shakespeare, as far as the goal is not simply to transfer signification between languages, but also to preserve the above-mentioned "fertile obscurity." And who is more apt than Müller to do just that? One must not either see a paradox in Koltès' own response to reading an "academic" translation of *Solitude*, writing to the translator: "The 'academic tradition,' as you say, is effective in that it is precise, and I prefer it by far—for Latin languages in particular—to the more interpretative work of ordinary translators."[36] What these two seemingly opposite approaches to translation have in common relates to what Koltès despises most in both translation and theater: *interpretation*. In French, the meaning of the word is manifold, and includes as much the act of pedagogical explanation as a performance on stage. To the "interpretative" method, Koltès associates psychological performances as well as explanatory translations. And, gladly, he would do away with both.

AMIN ERFANI

---

35   Koltès, *Une part de ma vie*, 108.
36   Koltès, *Lettres*, 515.

THE NIGHT JUST BEFORE THE FORESTS

Translated by Amin Erfani

"You were turning the street corner when I saw you, it's raining, one doesn't look one's best when it rains on the hair and the clothes, but anyway I dared, and now that we're here, I don't want to look at myself, I should dry off, go back down there and fix myself up—at least the hair, so I don't catch anything, but then I went down there a minute ago, to see if it were possible to fix myself up, but down there are the pricks, hanging out: all the time it takes for the hair to dry off, they don't move, they pack like a mob, they look behind their back, and I went up again—just the time to take a piss—in my wet clothes, I'll stay like this, until I find a room: the moment we settle down somewhere, I'll take everything off, this is why I'm looking for a room, because at home, impossible, I can't get in—not for the whole night though—, this is why you, when you were turning, right there, at the street corner, when I saw you, I ran, I thought to myself: nothing easier to find than a room for the night, for part of the night, if you want it so bad, if you dare ask, even with the wet clothes and the soaking hair, even with the rain that makes me go to pieces when I look at myself in the mirror—but, it's difficult not to look at yourself, even when you don't want to, so many mirrors are hanging all around here, in the cafés, in the hotels, they must be left behind one's back, like now that we're here, they are looking at you, me, I keep them behind my back, all the time, even at home, and even there it's full of them, like all around here, all the way to the hotels—one hundred thousand mirrors looking at you, you've got to look out for them, because I've lived at the hotel for almost all my life, I say: home by force of habit, but it's at a hotel, tonight though it's not possible, other than that, that's really where my home is, and if I get a hotel room, it's old habit, in three minutes top, I make it look like my home, with just the little things, almost nothing, make it look like I've lived there my whole life, look like my regular room, where I live, with all my little habits, with the hidden mirrors and close to nothing, to a point when, if all of a sudden it comes over someone to give me a room inside a house, to make me live there, or in an apartment just set up the way they like it, like those with families inside them, when I walk in there, I turn it into a hotel room, just by living there, me, because of old habit—they would give me some kind of cottage, like those in the stories, deep in the forests, with the big beams, a big fireplace, big furniture like you've never seen before, one hundred thousand years of old age, when I get in there, me, with nothing whatsoever and in no time, I make you a room that looks like those in the hotels, where I feel at home, I hide the fireplace behind the pile of furniture, I make the beams disappear, I change the taste of everything, I ditch all those objects no one ever notices anywhere, except in the stories, and that special smell, the smell of families, and old stone, and old black wood, and the hundred thousand years of old age laughing at you, that make you feel like you're a foreigner, that never let you think you're really at home, I ditch them all and old age with it, because I'm like this, I don't like things reminding you that you're a foreigner, but still I am a little bit of a foreigner, you must have noticed, I'm not really from here—they did notice, for sure, those pricks, packed behind my back, after I took a piss, when I was washing my ding-a-ling,—makes you think they're all pricks, those French, can't even imagine, because they've never seen anybody wash his ding-a-ling, except for us, it's old habit, my father taught me that, where I'm from you do this all the time, and me, I do it all the time after taking a piss, and when I was washing it, a minute ago, like I always do, by the sink downstairs, feeling all those pricks packed behind my back, I acted like I didn't understand, like a complete foreigner, who could understand nothing those pricks said in French, and I could hear them while I washed myself:—what's he doing, that weird foreigner?—he's making his ding-a-ling have a drink—how do you do that, make your ding-a-ling drink?—like I could understand nothing they said, and me, I keep doing it, cool and all, making it drink so those French pricks would keep wondering, packed behind my back, in front of the sink: how do you make your ding-a-ling drink, and anyway, how can your ding-a-ling be thirsty? then, when I was done with it, I cut through the crowd, still like a foreigner, who could understand not a word they said, this is easy for me, I'm not completely from here, I'm sure you've noticed this, those French pricks with no imagination got it right, and, despite all this, I ran after you the moment I saw you turn the street corner, despite all the pricks left in the street, in the cafés, in the basements of the cafés, here, everywhere, despite the rain and the wet clothes, I ran, not only for the room, not only for that part of the night for which I need a room, but I ran, ran, ran, so that this time, turning the corner, I don't find myself in a street empty of you, so that this time, I don't find only the rain, the rain, the rain, so that this time I find you, on the other side of the corner, and I dare shout: brother !, I dare grab you by the arm: brother !, I dare approach you: brother, give me a light, that'll cost you nothing, brother, this nasty rain, the nasty wind, this fucking intersection, there's nothing good in walking around here tonight, for you or for me, but I don't have any cigarettes, it wasn't completely for a smoke that I said: give me a light, brother, it was, brother, to tell you: this fucking neighborhood, this fucking habit of walking around here (way to approach people!), and you too, you walk around, your clothes soaking wet, taking the risk to catch any possible disease, I'm not asking you for a cigarette either, brother, I don't even smoke, it will cost you nothing to have stopped, no light, no cigarette, brother, no money (then you'd walk away!, twenty bucks don't make a difference, not tonight), and besides, I've got enough here to buy us coffee, let me treat, brother, instead of walking around in this strange light, so it costs you nothing that I've approached you—maybe I have my way of approaching people, but in the end, it costs them nothing (I'm not talking about a room, brother, a room to spend the night, because then the nicest guys have their mouths shut, you'd walk away! let's not talk about a room then, brother), but I have an idea to tell you—come, let's not stay here, we'll catch something, for sure—no money, no job, this doesn't make things easy (I'm not really looking for one, it's not really that), it's that, I've this idea, first, that I must tell you, you and me, walking around in this strange city with no money in our pockets (but I'll buy you coffee, brother, I've got enough, I'm not taking that back, not now), because on first impression, it's not the money, it's not you, or me, that keeps us nailed to the ground! so, me, I've got this idea, brother, for those like you and me with no money, and no job, and I'm not really looking for one anymore—it's just that having a job, for people like us, in the outdoors, with empty pockets, we don't carry a lot of weight, the slightest blow of wind would carry us away, no one could force us to stay on the scaffolds, except by tying us to it: a good blast of wind and we take off, light—, and me, working at the factory, never!, to you, it'll be hard to explain, even for me, it's hard to understand everything without mixing things up, but my idea, it's like—it ain't a religion, it ain't some foolishness you'd peddle to people one way or another and that'd change nothing, it ain't politics, definitely not a party or nothing like that, or like the unions that know it all, that've seen it all, and that let nothing escape them, and then to add my idea to this, there would be no room left, and it has nothing to do with that, no, my idea, it's not that at all, don't worry, brother: it's for our defense, only for our defense, because that is really what we need, to defend ourselves, right? maybe you think: not me, but then, let me tell you: maybe I'm the one who approached you, I'm the one who'd need a room tonight (no, brother, I didn't say I did), I'm the one who asked: brother, give me a light, but the one who approaches is not always the weak one, and I saw right away, from there, that you didn't look very strong, walking around all wet, not very tough at all, while me, despite all this, I'm resourceful, and me, I recognize those who aren't very strong, with one quick glance, because of their gait, especially, just the way they walk with those tiny steps, nervous, like you, with their back nervous, and the way they move their shoulders, nervous, something in their gait that doesn't fool me, with their face, too, made of little lines, not beat up or anything, but nervous!, like you: something on the face that doesn't fool me, almost nothing, even when they walk all swaggering, like pimps do, but pimps made of nerves, little punks who spread out, but who come straight from their mothers, and the whole top, like this, all swaggering like nothing's going on, under the rain, but me, I see right away this kind of nervousness, the kind that nobody can hide—because all that's nervousness, it comes from the mother, straight out, and their mother, those little punks, they can't hide her away, no matter what they do—me, instead, I'm like blood, hulk made of bones, and muscles, and all that comes from the father, nerves have never bothered me, because my father, it's the opposite, he was the tough type, the type that never got his nerves tangled up because of thinking too much, nothing disturbed him, a man made of bones, muscles, a man of blood, people could have called him: the terminator, and me too, they could call me: the terminator, and that really is why politics, and the parties, and the unions that exist today, and the cops, and the army, which are all political, they're not what I want, all that, it's way too tangled up because of the head, and with their head, they throw you back to the factory, and me, the factory, never!, but, anyway, they always end up throwing you back to the factory, but then the idea I'm telling you about, it's: a union on an international scale—it's very important, the international scale (I'll explain it to you, even for me, it's hard to understand in my head),—but no politics, only for the defense, me, I'm built for the defense, and for that, I'll give it everything I've got, I'll be the one who terminates, in my international union for the defense of those little punks who aren't very strong, sons who come straight from their mothers, who act like pimps full of nerves, who're swaggering and walking around, all alone, in the middle of the night, at the risk of catching any possible disease—that's exactly why, me, I see the uselessness of your mothers, see how useless your mother is: she gives you a nervous system, and then drops you, at any intersection, under the fucking rain, not tough enough, too trusting, because I see right away that you're too trusting, all small and nervous that you are, you trust everybody, but don't imagine that there are no bastards here, that they won't let you get it, me, I know we brush against them, and a minute ago, I fell on my face, they almost got me, too trusting like you, so now, I see them everywhere, they're here, they brush past us, the worst kind of bastards that you can imagine, and they make us live like this: me, I thought they were invisible, hiding up there, above the bosses, above the government, above everything, with faces of killers, rapists, embezzlers of ideas, with faces that aren't real faces like yours or mine, and they have no names: the clans of cheats, of gang-bangers in hiding, the unpunished and the vicious, cold, scheming, technical, the little clan of technical bastards who decide: to the factory and be quiet!, (and the factory, me, never!), to the factory and shut your mouth! (and what if my mouth, I open it?), to the factory, shut your mouth, and we get the last word—and they get the last word, the small group of fuckers who decide for us, from up there, plotting all together, scheming all together, technical on the international scale—the international scale! me, my idea, it's a union on the international scale: it's important, the international scale, I'll explain to you—, right now, we're screwed!, it's the factory, or becoming light, like you, like me, being carried away by the slightest blow of wind, because: what can we do, you and me, when they hold the government, the cops, the army, the bosses, the streets, the crossroads, the subway, the light, the wind, and when they can sweep us away from up there anytime they want? what can I do, me, against that, except my idea for a union?—you, you're too trusting, like I was before, but now, they're here, they're after us, they came down and they almost got me, because the worst sort of bastards imaginable come in strange shapes and in strange ways, ah, if only they came straight out, so we see everything on their faces, if we saw every time who we're dealing with, so we could throw punches, but the ways they come in, rubbing against us with faces that make it impossible to stay put, and you get the crap beaten out of you by the worst kind of bitches because you're too trusting—but how can we tell? me, I couldn't: if I could have imagined, I would have invented her like that, like she was when I approached her: not tall, not tough, all blonde, curly with golden glints, not too many curls and not too blonde, just enough to make you believe in it, and to make it impossible to stop running after her, and when I approached her: you've got a light, by any chance, sister, sorry, her eyes looking at you like you could have only invented them, the sparks in them exactly how I would have invented them, to walk on clouds, on a night when it's empty out and nothing's happening, but there are other nights, despite the rain, despite this nasty light and the night that get in the way of everything, where the girls walk the streets—not just one randomly, but many, one after the other, one more beautiful than the other, but not beautiful like you think, beautiful like it ain't possible, to make you go crazy, to make you hour after hour go even crazier, hour after hour girls that are even more impossible, you don't know when that's going to stop, it goes up, you start walking on clouds, nothing's left to imagine anymore, because there're girls like those marching before you!, and when you think it can't get better than that, that you can't go any crazier by looking at them, one like her shows up, who makes you drop everything to run after her, nothing you can do, but forget the rain and the lack of money that make you go to pieces, with this one, there's nothing you can do but run after her and approach her, and her hair, and her eyes below them, not tough looking and not too many curls: sister, sister!— and that's exactly when: sister! sister!—, when they expect you, when they're going to get you like a damn fool: if I had known that she was from the other side, that she was a bitch—come with me, kitty, tonight, we're chasing the rat—, if only she had kept her mouth shut, I would have never known what a mouth like hers could spit (before, when I used to work, I thought everybody, and the girls walking the streets at night, that deep down we were all the same, that you could talk to them, just a question of daring, everyone except the small gang of bastards with faces of gang-bangers, but now I think everybody's gone on the other side, and I will never again run after a girl till I go crazy, I will never go crazy again), she's the one who didn't recognize me, because of this light that makes us look so much like each other,—we'll chase the rat, kitty, and after that, you'll stay with me!—: she tells me this up close, in the strange café where she'd taken me (by the hand, hanging on to me, all ready to spend the whole night with me, and bring me to her room, she liked me, for sure, before I got upset listening to her shit, before she got upset because of what I said to her, we liked each other and all), because the next thing you know, she didn't know who I was—the new power, we're it, she said to me, and I must be part of it too—, me, I would have liked that, because of her eyes that make you walk on clouds, but the worst kind of technical and international crap has taken shapes like these, they've made everybody cross over to the other side, even the girls that ain't possible and would make you go crazy, if they didn't talk, but her, I got scared because of what she told me, the way she told it to me, and because I couldn't stop listening to her, she still didn't realize who I was, in that strange café—come with us, kitty—and I'd have gone with her, like a damn fool, if, just in time, it didn't come out of my mouth (louder even than what I would have wanted) who I was: sister, this is who I am, a foreigner myself, affiliate of the international union, and all the rest, now shut the fuck up or I'll smash your face,—and I'd have smashed her face, if she didn't have her friends around, the Friday-night rat chasers, the squad of kitties armed to the teeth, me, by myself, a foreigner against all of them, in what kind of shit did I get myself into like a damn fool?, with this light that got me confused, but what if, before all of this poured out of me, just in time, by force, out of my mouth, she had begun to sing?, if instead of spitting out all that (because she trusted me) she had said them to me in a song?, she could have sung whatever she wanted, I'd have given in, I'd have agreed to anything, just at the sound of her voice if she had sung, I'd have hidden my real identity, I'd have signed up for anything, the New Forces, the fascists, the royalists, Occident, all the rat chasers, the organized gang-bangers, international cheats, I'd have said to her whatever she wanted to hear, I'd have chased whoever she asked me to, because she was beautiful like it ain't possible, because of her promise, about us, after the chase, because she had made me drop everything and run, and if she had sung, she would have sung so beautifully!, what should I have done? shut my ears? if she'd brought her lips close to my ear, what should I have done?, run away? if she had put her hand on my lap, what could I have done? cut it off?—or: cut mine off? that's how they get to you, like a damn fool, so then, you've got to tie it to yourself, deny yourself even that, to make real sure you don't get fucked over! for us foreigners, brother, you have to deprive yourself from everything and be sure it's tied to yourself real tight: the big idea, in my idea for a union, is to keep yourself from getting a hard on, all the time, everywhere, as long as everything is under the control of the little secret clan, that's got its grip on the government, the cops, the army, the jobs, all the way to the little bitches with their curly blonde hair, and their ways, so not tough-looking it's unbelievable, but who have gone to the other side, like everybody else, keep yourself from getting hard and cumming, hold it in, no matter what, because that's when they're watching us and would fuck us over, with all the strength we have left and by all available means, until we have won, until my idea for an international union has finally won, and then everything will be ours, the cafés, the street, the bitches, the kitties, and their weapons, the whole planet and the whole sky, and it'll be the rats' turn to cum, brother, it'll be our turn, and me, the terminator, I, the one who's made of bones, of muscles and blood, deprived of everything from the beginning, forced from the beginning to hold it in, it'll be my time to throw punches, and I won't deprive myself of that, I'll look everywhere, where are they now, those who spat on me? and I'll find them all, because it'll be our time not to hold it in anymore, brothers: skin them, now, get hard, and cum, all you can, all that you've held in for so long, all over them, drown their killer faces, their beautiful and luxuriant faces, those who were cumming between themselves and commanded us for so long,—but I'd also say, if you come across someone, somewhere, walking around and around, shoulders spread out wide like pimps do, one of those nervous ones who come straight from their mothers, left out there at the street corner, without any defense, for no reason, rolling and turning around the way pimps do, then, let him go, don't hit him, don't touch him, he's still a child who needs to be defended,—and that's what my idea is, and this, make no mistake, this won't drag on any longer, even if now we have almost no money left, no work, and if I have no room to sleep for the night, and that you, you should not trust anybody, and if they ask you: who's the foreigner with you?, you answer: I don't know, I don't know, and if they insist, you say: I don't know him, he's someone who approached me in the street, when I turned at the corner, asking for a room to spend the night in, not even the whole night, before that, I'd never seen him, because I saw, from a distance, that you were only a child, a sort of a punk left out at the street corner, that the slightest breeze lifts you up and carries you away, and, when I run after you, once, twice, three times, there's nothing but an empty street and the rain, so, this time, I didn't want to lose you again, I didn't leave anything to chance, I was prepared: I kept the pricks from blocking my way, I was agreeing with them, I acted like I was listening to their bullshit, I agreed with all of them,—the bullshit they say, every night, when they're outside, despite this nasty rain and the sad light, are strange birds that exist nowhere except in the heads of pricks, and, if you want to agree with them all, you give your opinion, you invent colors, so, me, I invented, I hid from them that I was a foreigner by giving my opinion about everything, common problems, specific questions, fashion, politics, and I stood up, I stood my back against the wind, I always kept my back turned against the wind so I don't go to pieces before I approach you, and me, I thought to myself: there's nothing easier than feeling which direction the wind blows, than keeping them on my side so they don't stand in the way,—nothing could betray me, my foreigner's ding-a-ling, I kept it hidden, of course, held it tight, hand on the zipper, and I was holding in the urge to piss, not risking to betray myself, like this, by being distracted, by making it drink, because, then, they'd have recognized me, there'd be no hope left, a foreigner to all of them, but for the moment I stood well, under this strange light that reveals nothing, that turns all those talkers in the cafés and in the streets into brothers with the same looks and the same worries, and masks the one whose worries are from someplace else, a foreigner to all of them, my eyes secretly looking past them, and I kept my back against the wind like theirs, smiling and agreeing, half-drunk already with worries invented, I was thinking: mine is from someplace else and I must hide it, and, when I saw you, I ran, ran, ran, but no one stood in the way, I was prepared, I had stood on their side, I had listened to them hiding my differences, and now my escape catches them by surprise, I'm already at the corner of the street by the time they wake up, by the time they recognize me as a foreigner, chasing me down with their bullshit, getting prepared to take me by surprise someplace else, down there, in a minute, me however, I was already approaching you, I was saying: I saw you turning the street corner, sorry, I am half-drunk, I'm not looking my best, but I lost my room, I'm looking for a room just for tonight, for part of the night, because in a short time I won't be drunk anymore, I ask for five minutes,—so then I was saying that I was drunk and asked for five minutes, half my head filled with bullshit, the other half left for you whom I didn't dare look because of how mixed up I was, even then, with fashion, with politics, with money earned—when I worked, me, my money, it was a strange tiny bird that came in, that I locked in, and, the minute I opened the door again, it flew away all of a sudden and never came back, there was nothing left but regrets after it was gone, now, I don't work anymore—, but I couldn't resolve myself to look at the one whose arm I finally had tight under my grip: I ask for five minutes, to let the drunkenness go away, then we'll sit down, I'll buy coffee, I'll make him sit facing me, facing the mirror behind my back, forgetting all the rest, the nasty rain, the nasty light, the pricks hanging out and the gloomy colors they filled my head with, and I'll look at him, I'll dare, despite the hair still soaking wet, despite the clothes that won't dry off, I will wait despite having put the pieces back together the best I could,—I'm looking for a room for part of the night, because I can't find mine anymore: I wanted to ask this from you the moment I saw you at the street corner, I wouldn't have asked it for the world from one of those pricks I was hanging out with, though I didn't look like them (you must have noticed), but I was hanging out with them for a thousand different reasons, always keeping secret the other half of me searching for a room where I wouldn't be stuck with pricks, forced to hide that I was a foreigner, forced to talk about fashion, politics, money or eating food, all these French pricks with the same faces and the same worries, talking about eating even under the rain, their back against the wind and always talking about eating, and I was nodding, so that in a minute I could be free to run, run, run, I, the one who does not eat, the one who eats nothing, who becomes lighter and lighter every day, who gains no weight so that I can look for what I am looking for in hiding, passed the mob of eaters hanging out there, outside, in the cafés, I agreed, I agreed, I was intoxicated with all the eating they were talking about, feeling the wind on my back that made me sway, it would have lifted me up if I weren't discretely hanging on to those heavy eaters and their bullshit full of lead, the wind would have made me take off because I've become light, like the breeze makes you disappear at the street corners, when I saw you, once, twice, three times, I could see from a distance that you were still a child, so I dropped everything, the wind lifted me up, and I ran, feeling my feet barely touch the ground, as fast as you, nothing was standing in my way this time, to approach you at last: don't think, man, that I'm a fag, because I run, because I take you by the arm, and stop you, I talk to you without really knowing who you are, but I know you well enough the way it is, man, to tell you this—a girl on a bridge—that I can't keep for myself,—besides, would a fag dare approach someone when he's gone to pieces, with the clothes and the hair soaking wet? now, you see me like this, my head not really in the right place (but this will pass), and from the first glance, me, I could see that, you, you're the decent type one can talk to: I don't know her real name, the one she told me wasn't hers, so I won't say how she was either, no one will ever know who slept with whom, all night long, on a bridge, right in the middle of a city, there're still traces left, out there, in the stone: you're walking, one night, someplace, and by chance, you see a girl leaning right above the water, by chance you get closer, she turns to you, she says: me, my name's mama, don't tell me yours, don't tell me yours, you don't tell her your name, you say to her: where we go? she says to you: where would you want to go? we stay here, right? so you stay here, until early morning when she's gone, all night I ask: who are you? where do you live? what do you do? where do you work? when can I see you again? she says, leaning above the river: I never leave it, I go from one bark to another, from one deck to another, I go up the canal and come back to the river, I look at the canal boats, I look at the tide gates, I look for the bottom of the river, I sit at the edge of the water or I lean over, me, I can speak only standing on bridges or riverbanks, and I can love only there, in other places I am like dead, all day I am bored, and every night, I come again by the water, and we don't leave each other until daybreak—, so she ran off and I let her run off, without making a move (in the morning, on the bridges, it's full of people and cops), until noon I waited in the middle of the bridge, it's not her real name and I didn't tell her mine, no one will ever know who loved whom, one night, lying on the edge of the bridge (at noon, it's full of noise and cops, you can't stay, without moving, right in the middle of a bridge), so during the day, I wrote on the walls: mama I love you mama I love you, on every wall, so that it was impossible that she didn't read it, I will be on the bridge, mama, all night, the bridge of the other night, all day, I ran like crazy: come back mama come back, I wrote like crazy: mama, mama, mama, and during the night, I waited right in the middle of the bridge, and just when the day came back I started again on the walls, on every wall, so that it was impossible that she didn't run into it: come back to the bridge, come back just for one more time, just for one more brief time, come back for one minute that I see you, mama mama mama mama mama mama, but shit like a fool I waited for one night, two nights, three nights, and more, I searched through all the bridges, I ran from one to the next, many times every night, there are thirty one bridges, not counting the canals, and during the day I was writing, the walls were covered all over, it was impossible that she didn't read me, but shit, she didn't come, and she wouldn't come anymore, but I kept writing on the walls, and I kept going through all the bridges, there are thirty one bridges not counting the canals, and I never found her again, leaning above the water, and now, for me, these kind of stories, it hurts my morale, because it makes everything blurry when it goes too far, I know a woman who died because it went too far, it hurts my morale how many would die if it were easier, how many would go far if they knew the ways, if you weren't afraid of the ways, because you're never sure if you're going to drop dead, it can take a long time, and the day they invent a damn gentle way to drop dead, provide it to everybody, it'll be a massacre because of stories like this, which always go too far, a damn massacre, for sure, like that woman who dropped dead all right because she swallowed the soil, she goes to the cemetery, she digs by the graves, she takes the soil in her hands, the deepest soil, and swallows it,—these kinds of story, if you listen to yourself, if you let go, it turns you crazy—, because the soil at the cemeteries, the kind that touches the coffins: you, who make the dead turn cold, you, who've got the damn habit of turning everything so very cold at the deepest depth until no one makes it back, turn cold once and for all the crazy woman I am!—, who told her that this trick would work? to this crazy whore who swallowed soil until she dropped dead, in the middle of the cemetery where, me, I saw her,—that someone would tell her about that trick, it hurts my morale, some other old whore for sure, who's got the recipes—a damn massacre, and all gently!—but not everybody swallows soil, if they invented the ways (instead of soil, a little light powder, that you don't feel go down, and free for everybody, that makes you comfortable for when it goes too far) everybody'd turn cold with the tiniest story, because, if you let go, even the tiny ones, the smallest ones go far, and blur everything, but the one I'm telling you about, she was a whore, I saw her, one night, from the street, at a window on the fifth floor, and followed her from there, to the cemetery, could you believe that of a whore, even they go crazy, I'll show you, in a minute, the window, so me, now, I'm all for getting some and then taking off: does that work for you? correct !—taking off before she starts talking, or I act like I don't understand, or then she tells you all the things that hurt your morale, so me, I'm for getting some good: is that cool? ok!—, and then taking off, comfortable, just before the big speeches, besides, getting some a single time is enough to know all there is to know, I could live a hundred thousand years with a chick and not know anything more after three hundred thousand years than what I knew the first time we did it, that's why I am all for it: is that good? let's go !,—then taking off fast!, knowing all there is to know, thinking all there is to think, making my opinion about her, because, man, what do you think? how do you make an opinion about someone without having fucked her? one hundred years with her without fucking, and you still don't know anything, except the big speeches that turn you crazy, what do you know about her with the big speeches, if you don't know how she is before, if you don't know how she moves, how she breathes, if she starts talking and making up stories, or if, on the contrary, she really likes you, and she says nothing, holds it in, keeps everything secret just for you and for her, what do you know about someone if you don't know how she breathes after she fucked, if she keeps her eyes open or shut, if you don't listen, a long time, to the sound she makes and the time it takes for her to breathe, where she puts her face and how it is like now, the longer it takes for her to breathe and for you to listen to her breathing, without moving, the more you know everything about her, but the minute she opens her eyes, sits up, leans on her chin, looks at you, starts breathing like the others, opens her mouth where you see the big speeches getting ready to come out, so me, I'm for taking off, and: correct? correct!—, but that night, me, I was alone in the street with the whores, a Friday night when I still used to work and didn't work the following day, so I look up, and I see, at a window on the fifth floor, the head of a whore completely crazy-looking,— if you want to go there, we'll go see it, the window I'm talking about, me I never go there by myself, they hurt my morale, especially a night like tonight, it's not that I'm scared of Friday nights more than any other nights, it's the opposite, now that I don't work anymore, I miss how it was, the Friday evening and the night after, when you don't work the next day, when everybody holds up a tired face but doesn't want to let go, and gets all worked up, gets wild, everybody yells and talks about smashing the other's faces, down here, the guys yell a lot, but they take their time before smashing the other's face,—back home, we throw a punch on the spot, without yelling, we're not the type to be shy, but down here, they ask you miles of questions: you're looking for something? did you say something? why are you looking at me like that? why are you laughing? did you touch me?,—if you touch him, he asks you a mile long if you're touching him for real, before he smashes your face, me, I throw a punch on the spot without being shy and all, you better believe me, but that's where I am looking at, at a window on the fifth floor, the crazy-looking whore who opens her window, glances over her shoulder, she opens it slowly, disappears in the room and then comes back, with a look that's really completely crazy, and a big pile of clothes in her arms, we'll go in a minute to see where it was, if you're not too afraid, me I'm not, I throw punches if someone talks to me, then everyone in the street of the whores sees a pair of pants falling like a bag in the middle of the sidewalk, and a red jacket floating like a parachute, an underwear and a shirt all light like made of silk, that hang to the street lamp, the tie that swings around, everybody stares at the crazy looking whore who leans from the window, who watches the clothes falling and swinging—now he's naked, he's naked!—, this guy got himself a crazy one, that's what everybody thinks to themselves, on the street, looking at the sidewalk and what's left floating up on the street lamp like flags, who would have believed that of a whore, even the whores are getting risky, that's what everybody's thinking, doubting even the street of the whores, where to go? where to go? everybody thinks to themselves straightening up their collar, and they all turn away,—where to go, now, where to go, that's what they wonder, as though, from all the way up there, someone had traced for them on a map areas they should be in during the weekdays, and on Friday nights the doors open on the street of the whores or the rest, but if they don't: where to go, nowhere else, and, me, ever since I stopped working, all the series of zones the bastards traced for us, on their maps, and where they imprison us with lines drawn in pencil, areas for work during the weekdays, areas for motorcycles and those for flirting, areas for women, areas for men, areas for fags, areas for sadness, areas for chit-chats, areas for heartbreaks and those for Friday nights, areas for the Friday nights I've lost since I've mixed up everything, which I want to find again because of how good it felt, so good I don't know how to tell you, but, since, I don't work anymore and everything gets mixed up on their damn maps, every night I looked for the Friday night when I felt good, not having to work the day after, I fucked on a bridge, I prowled along foreign neighborhoods, lonely like you cannot say, you'll come with me so we go there together, you won't have to be afraid, I throw punches fast and without being shy, and on Friday nights, with their tired faces and their big mouths, the guys who get worked up are more scared than we are, they yell at each other for being scared, they throw punches to each other for being scared, they smash each other's faces for being more scared than we are in their fists, in their legs, in their mouths, scared that we look at them, scared that we don't look at them, scared that we laugh at them and that we don't think too much of them, scared of the other punks that look too much like them, and more scared even of those who don't look like them at all, you'll come with me, and I'll show you the window where the whore was looking at the clothes swinging around, then you see a guy, furious, his hair straight on his head, who walks full speed, with the whore's voice following him: he's naked underneath his coat!,—the guy who picks up his jacket, his pants, and looks at his shirt, furious, his underwear and his tie floating like flags at the top of the street lamp, everyone straightens his collar and wonders: where to go? where to go? the whore runs after the guy like a crazy woman, herself half naked, you see the guy get into a car, turn on the engine, and the whore holds on to the door, jumps on the hood: don't let him leave, don't let him leave!—and the guy, furious, who drives off anyway, everybody around walks off looking behind their shoulders and looking for where to go, where to go, good god, if even the whores, would you believe that of a whore, so she lets herself drop off the car, lies in front of the wheels, and the guy, furious, he honks, he can't do anything else but stop, he honks like a madman, but the whore's still lying in front of the car, everybody who's walking off straightening their collar: help, help, don't let him leave!—everybody's gone, except for some old whores, no doubt it was one of them who gave her the recipe: you go to the cemetery, the soil is used to turning cold the crazy men and the crazy women, who told her this trick worked? and now, it hurts my morale to go down that street, by myself, because I always ask: did you know that whore, dead from eating soil? they call me crazy, did you know the whore from the fifth floor? they call the pimps to come and get rid of me, but still, me, I saw her, dead, at the cemetery, and now thinking about it, pal, just thinking about it, it makes me sick, it makes me want to drink (if it wasn't a question of money), and take off and leave this place (if I knew where to go), and be in a room, pal, where I could talk, here, I cannot bring myself to tell you what I must tell you, we must go someplace else, with nobody around, no more this question of money and this nasty rain, comfortable, like sitting on grass or things like that, not having to move, with all the time you need, with the shades of the trees, and then I will say: this is my home, I feel good here, I lie down and ciao, but that, pal, ain't possible, have you seen a place before where they let you be comfortable, have you seen before that they let you lie down and ciao?, they never forget about you, pal, not to worry, they go after you, they bust your balls, they don't leave you alone, they have to make you move, they say to you: go here, and you go, go there, and you go there, move your ass from here, and you pack up your things, when I worked, I used to spend my time packing my things: work is someplace else, it's always someplace else you have to go to find it—no time to explain yourself, no time to walk on clouds, no time to lie down on the grass and say: ciao, your ass kicked they'll make you move out, work is over there, and again over there, farther and even farther still, to Nicaragua they'd kick you, comfortable, because those from countries like this one, they always get their asses kicked, comfortable, and they land here, no time to talk, no time to sleep, no time to walk on clouds, if you want to work, move out, then, if you let this happen to you: us, the pricks from here, we let our asses get kicked all the way to Nicaragua, and the pricks from there, they let themselves be pushed and land here, in the meantime the work itself, it is always someplace else, and never can you say: this is home and ciao (that's why, me, when I leave, I always have the impression of leaving a place that felt more like home to me than the place I land in, and when they kick your ass again and you leave again, the place where you go to, you'll be even more of a foreigner there, and so on: you're always more of a foreigner, you're less and less at home, they always kick you farther away, so you don't know where you're going, and when you turn around, pal, when you look behind you, it's always, always the desert), but let's stop for good and say: go fuck yourself, I won't move anymore and you're going to hear me out, if we lie together on the grass once and for all and take the time to explain ourselves, and that you, you tell your story and those whose asses got kicked from Nicaragua or wherever tell their stories, tell one another that we're all more or less foreigners but ciao, now, we listened to one another, we listen, chill, to everything we have to tell each other, so it's clear, and to me, it was clear, that they're laughing in our faces, me, I stopped, I listened, I thought to myself: I won't work anymore if they keep laughing at us, what is it good for if Nicaragua comes all the way here, and that I go all the way there, since all the other places it's the same, and when I was still working, I talked about my idea for an international union to all the kicked-asses coming from I don't know where who land here to find work, and me, I listened to the Nicaraguans talk about their home, back there, there's an old general who spends all day and all night at the edge of the forest, he is brought his food so he won't have to leave, and he shoots everything that moves, he is brought munitions when he runs out, they talk to me about a general with his soldiers circling the forest, back there, taking potshots at everything that flies above the leaves, at everything that appears at the edge, at everything they see that doesn't have the color of the trees or doesn't move like everything else, those people, they heard me out and I heard them out, and I thought to myself: every other place is the same, the more I let my ass get kicked, the more I will be a foreigner, those people they end up back here and I end up back there,—back there where everything that moves hides in the mountains, the lakefronts, the forests, while a general and all his soldiers travel over the mountains, search the lakefronts, circle every forest, and they take potshots at everything that moves, and at everything that doesn't have the same color or the same movement as stones, water, and trees, I listened to this and then I stopped, I won't move anymore, I say: here, this is my home, if there's no work, I won't work, if work turns me crazy and they get on my ass, I won't work either, I want to sleep, I want to explain myself once and for all, I want grass, the shade of trees, I want to shout out and be able to shout out, even if they must shoot me, because this is what they end up doing: if you don't agree, if you open your mouth, you must hide deep into the forest, and they terminate you with machine guns as soon as they see you move, but then to hell with it, at least I would have told you what I must tell you, here I can't bring myself to do it, but someplace else, in a room where we would spend the night, a part of the night, because I will leave before daybreak, before you're fed up with it, I will leave on time, before you wanted to take off, you, because if you're fed up with it, if you leave me hanging right in the middle, before I find the time, me, I'm not the sensitive type who would feel hurt by it (and you can do what you want), but I know the tough guys, you take the toughest bullies, no show-off or anything, who throw punches and who're not afraid of blood, not sensitive or anything (the tough type you hope won't notice you when they're worked up), well then, that type of guys, if like this, quietly, no fight, you make a tiny pinhole in their arm, so that they see, all of a sudden, a little drop of blood (of their own blood, quietly, when they're not worked up, for no particular reason), the toughest of the tough ones, they turn white, they pass out, their eyes start rolling because of next to nothing, so, me, I'm not the sensitive type, but, if you took off on the spot, besides, it's not only that, but that you think I'm worthless, because today you may think that, because today it's not working, I can't really be happy, not like the people here who always look happy, who're always ready to cum, me, there's always in the back of my head, all of a sudden coming back to me, stories about a forest where nothing moves because of the machine guns, or stories about a whore who's buried and nobody knows about her, while those from here they've got nothing in the back of their heads, ready to be happy, ready to have fun, ready to cum on anything, anywhere, anytime, not thinking about anything except getting some, all those French pricks ready to get some and cum between themselves and with nothing in the back of their heads that would block them, from cumming all over the place, cumming all over our faces, their nasty fucking cum, while, me, I've got those stories in the back of my head, I'm not saying it never works, just a guy who can never completely cum because of those stories, sometimes I even feel good, real good, like right now if you don't take off and if I have time, but in the back of my head, it's always sad like I don't know how to say it, also with the worry that you could be fed up with me (because today perhaps I'm worthless, but another day), and you could take off beforehand, then, I'm not the sensitive type (you can do whatever you want), but then I'd tell myself anything, I'd want to be like something that isn't a tree, hidden in a forest in Nicaragua, like the smallest bird that wants to fly above the leaves, surrounded by lines of soldiers with their machine guns, aiming at it, watching for any movement it makes, and what I want to tell you, it's not here that I can tell it, we must find grass where we can lie down, with the whole sky above our heads, and the shades of trees, or maybe a room where we'll have time, but if you think I'm only looking for a room, I'm not, I don't want to sleep, and there's nothing easier to find than a room for a night, sidewalks are full of people who are looking for a room and those who find a room, and if you think it's only to have a talk, it's not, I don't need someone like those pricks outside, I'm not like them, me, I'm a guy, instead of talking, or following a pretty girl to look at her, but only to look at her, why do anything but look at a pretty girl, and still I'm a guy, me, who instead of looking at a pretty girl, just walks, and this is all the hobby I need, my whole life I wouldn't mind if I walked around, ran from time to time, stopped at a bench, walked slowly or faster, without ever talking, but, with you, it's different, and this, from the moment I saw you, now I have to explain to you everything, because I've started, because you didn't take off and leave me hanging like a prick, even now that my face is all messed up, that my hair and clothes won't dry off, I wouldn't want to look at the mirrors behind my back, while you, the rain didn't even get you wet, the rain fell right passed you, the hours move right past you, that's when I was right and understood that, you, you are only a child, everything goes right past you, nothing changes you, nothing messes up your face, me, I stay away from mirrors and I can't stop looking at you, who do not change, and if it wasn't a question of money, I'd buy us beer—instead of coffee—and then we'd feel really good the whole way through, we would have a few drinks like I wanted it from the beginning of tonight, I've already had one, and another, or three or four or more, I don't remember how many anymore, all the cash that I wanted to blow, we would blow now, if it wasn't that they took it from me earlier, I had enough money for us to drink all the beers you wanted all night long and be ok, but they took it from me in the subway, a nasty trick like that, I have nothing left for the remainder of the night except the change I had in my front pocket, enough for two cups of coffee, and I ran after them, though, like I was looking for it, until they took it from me, and smashed my face too, in the subway corridor there were two thugs, with faces that don't fool you, thugs that are looking for something, that are going to do something, thugs dressed up and who're in good shape, I run after them and I think to myself: we can have a beer together,—those thugs who're dressed up so well I always feel like running after them and tell one or the other: give me your clothes, your shoes, your hair, your walk and your face, as they are without changing anything, me, I'll give you anything you want (and, if they gave it all to me, I wouldn't even turn back to see what I've become), they didn't even turn back, they had not seen me, I don't take my eyes off them and I get behind them on the first train thinking to myself: they will be my guests and we will grab some beer, we will spend the night together and nobody's bored to tears,—but meanwhile, I feel in my back one of the two putting his hand in the pocket of my pants, he pulls out my wallet, I don't move right away, I feel like I'm in shape, so I think to myself: man, no fighting, I'll talk to them and there's no reason it won't work, I turn around, and say: — ok, don't be pricks, you will be my guests and we will grab some beer, and then, we'll see what we'll do, together, we won't get bored to tears—, this one thug at my back looks at his buddy, they don't say anything like they didn't see me,—ok, don't be pricks, you give me back my cash, we'll have a good drink, we'll have a good talk, and we'll keep it going together—, they keep looking at each other, like they don't understand, and then, little by little, with the eyes, like this, they come to an agreement, they start talking, louder and louder, for everybody to hear, still not looking at me: what does he want, this guy? he wants to mess with us or what? what sort of a guy is this? why's he busting our balls?—they push me against the door: we take this fag down at the next stop and smash his face—, so me, I say to them: ok, give me back my cash, then, we're all good—, but they say: this fag, let him wait, then we'll smash his face—, nobody reacts, nobody believes the cash story, everybody believes the fag story, and they take me down at the first stop and nobody else moves, and when they finished smashing my face like a complete fag, and left with my cash (despite that I yelled and that nobody believed me), me, I don't move right away: whatever you do, man, don't get worked up, sit on the bench, don't move, stay there—, I look, that's it and it's all right: there's music, far away, behind my back, one who's got to be begging for money at the end of the corridor (it's ok, man, but whatever you do, don't move), right in front, on the other platform, sitting, a crazy old lady, dressed all in yellow, waving with smiles (I'm looking, I'm listening, it's still all right), on the guardrail, up there, there's a woman who stopped dead to catch her breath, right next to me an Arab is sitting down and he sings to himself things in Arabic (I think to myself: don't get worked up about it, man, whatever you do), and in front of me I see, I am sure that I see: a girl in a nightgown, her hair down her back, she passes in front of me with her fists closed tight, in her white nightgown, and, right in front of me, her face's all mixed up, she starts crying, and keeps on passing to the end of the platform, her hair tangled, her fists like this, and her nightgown, then, all of a sudden, me, I've had it up to here, this time that's it, I can't hold it in any longer, I've had it up to here, me, with everybody here, everybody with his own little story in his own little world, and all their faces, I've had it up to here with everybody and I want to throw punches, the woman up there hanging to the rail, I want to punch her, and the Arab singing his thing just to himself, I want to punch him, the coughed-up behind my back, at the end of corridor, and the crazy old lady right in front, I've had it up to here with their faces and with all this wreck, with the girl in the nightgown, at the other end of the platform, who keeps crying, and me, I'm going to throw some punches, man, I feel like beating up, the old ladies, the Arabs, the coughed-ups, the tiled walls, the subway trains, the conductors, the cops, punch the ticket-machines, the signs, the lights, this filthy smell, this filthy noise, I think about the gallons of beer I had already drunk and that I could still be drinking, until my belly can't hold it in anymore, I kept sitting with this urge to punch, until everything ends, until everything stops, and then, all of a sudden, everything stops for good: the trains don't come anymore, the

Arab turns silent, the woman up there stops breathing, and the girl in the nightgown, no one hears her sniffing anymore, everything stops all of a sudden, except the music in the back, and the crazy old lady who's opened her mouth starts singing with a voice that ain't possible, the coughed-up's playing it, back there, without being seen, and she sings it, they're answering back to each other and go together like it was rehearsed (a music that ain't possible, something of an opera or some shit like that), but so loud, so together, that everything stopped for real, and the old lady all in yellow, her voice fills up everything, me I think to myself: ok, I get up, I rush through the corridor, I leap up the stairs, I come out of the underground, and I run on the outside, I still dream of beer, I run, of beer, of beer, I think to myself: what a wreck, the opera arias, the women, the cold earth, the girl in the nightgown, the whores and the cemeteries, and I run and I don't feel myself anymore, I'm looking for something that looks like grass in the middle of this wreck, and the doves fly above the forest and the soldiers shoot at them, the coughed-ups beg for money, the thugs all dressed up chase the young rats, I run, I run, I run, I dream of the secret song of the Arabs between themselves, brothers, I've found you and I grab you by the arm, I need a room so bad and I am soaking wet, mama, mama, mama, say nothing, don't move, I look at you, I love you, brother, brother, me, I've been looking for someone who would be like an angel in the middle of this mess, and here you are, I love you, and the rest, some beer, some beer, and I still don't know how I could say it, what a wreck, what a mess, brother, and still the rain, the rain, the rain, the rain"

(1977)

BATTLE OF BLACK AND DOGS

Translated by Michaël Attias

Construction site run by a foreign company in West Africa, any country from Senegal to Nigeria.

CHARACTERS:
HORN, sixty years old, the boss.
ALBOURY, a black man who has mysteriously entered the site.
LEONE, the woman horn has brought over.
CAL, thirties, engineer.

PLACES:
The compound where the personnel live and where the machinery is stored, surrounded by fences and surveillance towers.
- *a clump of bougainvillea; a truck parked under a tree*
- *veranda, table, rocking-chair, whiskey*
- *the half-open door of one of the bungalows*

The site: a river runs through it, an unfinished bridge. A lake in the distance.

The calls of the Watchmen—tongue clicks and throat sounds, sounds of metal against metal, metal against wood, yelps, hiccups, short tunes, whistling—run along the barbed wire around the edges of the camp like laughter or coded messages and block out the noises of the bush.

The bridge: 2 huge white symmetrical structures, made of concrete and cable, come toward each other but never meet, from both sides of the red sand, in the vast emptiness of the sky over a river of mud.

"He named the child born unto him in exile, nouofia, which means 'conceived in the desert.'"

Alboury: nineteenth-century king of douilof (wolof), opposed white incursion. Toubab: common name for whites in certain regions of africa.

Translations from French into Wolof by Alioune Badara Fall and from Wolof into English by Professor Ousmane Kane.

"The jackal pounces on a half-eaten carcass, tears off a few mouthfuls, eats on the run, uncatchable and unrepentant a mugger on the loose and occasional cutthroat.

Doom was certain on either side of the Cape, and in the middle, a mountain of ice spelled death for the blind who struck ashore.

The she-lion, while slowly choking her victim, remembers, in the darkly meditative ritual of her bliss, love's transports."

I

Behind the bougainvillea, at dusk.

HORN: I knew I saw somebody, from far away, behind the tree.

ALBOURY: My name is Alboury, Sir. I'm here for the body. The mother went to the construction site to lay branches on his body, Sir, and it wasn't there, there was nothing there. And his mother's bound to wander in the village all night wailing if she doesn't get the body. Awful night. No one will sleep with that old woman wailing. That's why I'm here.

HORN: Sir, was it the village that sent you or the police?

ALBOURY: My name is Alboury, Sir. I've come for my brother's body.

HORN: Awful situation. Unfortunate fall. Unfortunate truck driving by full speed. We'll punish the driver. The workers are careless even though we give them specific instructions. Tomorrow you'll have the body. They must have taken it to the infirmary to fix it up and make it look good for the family. My regrets to them, and my regrets to you. It's an unfortunate thing.

ALBOURY: Unfortunate yes, and no. Had he not been a worker, Sir, the family would have put the gourd into the earth and said, "One less mouth to feed." It's still one less mouth to feed: the site is about to close. He wouldn't have been a worker for much longer. Soon, he would have become one more mouth to feed. It's not a misfortune for very long.

HORN: I've never seen you around here. Come have a whiskey, don't stay there behind that tree, I can barely see you. Come sit down at the table, Sir. Here, at the site, we congratulate ourselves on maintaining an excellent relationship with the police and the local authorities.

ALBOURY: There's been talk about you at the village ever since the site opened. I said, "Here is my chance to see the White Man up close." Sir, I have many things yet to learn, I said to my soul, "Run up into my ears and listen, run up into my eyes and miss nothing of what is there for you to see."

HORN: Your French is pretty impressive. I bet your English is too and whatever other languages you speak. You all have such a wonderful gift for languages. Are you a government official of some kind? You seem official. You also seem to know more than you let on. That's a lot of compliments.

ALBOURY: They can be useful in the beginning.

HORN: Strange. Usually, the village sends a delegation, we settle everything quickly. Usually, there's more pomp, but it's quicker: eight or ten people, eight or ten of the dead man's brothers. I'm used to speedy transactions. Sad thing about your brother. Here, you all call each other "brother". The family wants compensation. We'll give it to them of course, whatever they have coming. As long as they don't go overboard. But I'm sure I've never seen you before.

ALBOURY: I've only come for the body, Sir, and I'll leave as soon as I get it.

HORN: All right, the body, ok ok! You'll get it tomorrow. I apologize, I'm very tense, I have huge worries. My wife has just arrived. She's been unpacking for hours. I can't tell what she thinks. Having a woman here is very overwhelming. I'm not used to it.

ALBOURY: Having a woman here is very good.

HORN: I just got married, very recently. Very recently. In fact, I can tell you, it's not completed yet, the technicalities I mean. Marriage is overwhelming, Sir. I'm not at all used to this kind of thing, I get worried, and not seeing her come out of that room's making me nervous. She's in there. She's been in there putting her stuff away for hours. Let's drink some whiskey while we wait for her.

I'll introduce you, we'll have a little party, and then you can stay. But, come on over to the table. Barely any light over here. You know, my eyes are kind of weak. Come out, show yourself.

ALBOURY: Impossible, Sir. Look at the watchmen, look at them up there. They're watching the inside of the camp too, and, Sir, they're looking at me. If they see me sit down next to you, they'll get suspicious. They say, "Beware of a live goat in the lion's den." Don't be offended by what they say. More honor in being a lion than a goat.

HORN: But they let you in. Usually, you need a pass, or to represent some kind of authority. They know that.

ALBOURY: They know we can't let the old woman wail all night tonight and again tomorrow, she has to calm down, the village can not go without sleep. They know the mother will only be satisfied when the body's given back to her. They know why I'm here.

HORN: We'll bring it to you tomorrow. Meanwhile, my head's about to explode, I need a whiskey. Don't you think it's an insane thing for an old man like me to take a wife?

ALBOURY: Wives are not insane things. I've heard them say, "The best soup is made in old pots." Don't be offended by what they say, by the words they use, it's very honorable.

HORN: Getting married?

ALBOURY: Especially getting married. Just pay the price and tie her up good.

HORN: You're a smart man! I think she's coming. Come, let's talk. The glasses are on the table. But don't stay there behind that tree, in the dark. Come, join me.

ALBOURY: I can't, Sir. My eyes can't take this light, it's too bright. They blink and they blur. They're not used to the powerful lights you turn on at night.

HORN: Come, come, you'll get to see her.

ALBOURY: I'll see her from a distance.

HORN: Sir, my head is about to explode. What could she be unpacking, it's been hours! I've got to find out what she thinks. You know about the surprise? So many worries! I'm shooting off some fireworks at the end of the night. Stay around, this craziness is costing me a fortune. And, also, we've got to discuss the situation. We've always maintained an excellent relationship. I've got the authorities eating out of my hand. She's over there behind that door and I don't even know what she thinks. And if you're with the police, that's even better, I'd rather be dealing with them. Africa must be quite a shock for a woman who's never been out of Paris. And my fireworks, they'll blow you away. And I'll go see what they did with that damn corpse. (*He exits.*)

II

HORN: (*In front of the half-open door*) Leone, are you ready?

LEONE: (*From inside*) I'm unpacking. (HORN *comes closer.*) No, I'm not. (HORN *stops.*) I'm waiting for it to stop.

HORN: What?

LEONE: For it to stop moving. I'll feel better when it's dark. Evenings are the same in Paris. I get nauseous during the hour day turns to night. Babies too, they scream when the sun goes away. I have to remember to take my medication. (*She sticks her head halfway out the door and points to the bougainvillea.*) What do you call these flowers?

HORN: I don't know. (*She disappears again.*) Come and have a whiskey.

LEONE: Whiskey? Oh, my goodness, no, I can't, it's against the rules. That's all we need, you'd really see me then. Whiskey is absolutely against the rules.

HORN: Come anyway.

LEONE: I'm making a list of what's missing. Many things are missing, and many I'll never use. People said, "Take a sweater, Africa's cold at night." Cold, ooh wee! The scoundrels. Now, I'm stuck with three sweaters. I feel jittery, Pumpkin, I'm all woozy, and I've got the jitters. What are the other men like? People don't usually like me at first.

HORN: There's only one. I already told you that.

LEONE: Airplanes, I don't like them. I much prefer the telephone: you can always hang up. Not that I didn't prepare myself. I did. Like crazy. Listening to reggae all blesséd day long. It drove the people in my building nuts. You know what I just discovered when I opened up my suitcase? People in Paris smell. I knew it. I noticed it before, that smell, in the metro, in the streets, with all the people who brush up against you. It lingers behind them and rots. I can still smell it here in my suitcase. I can't stand it anymore. It's like the smell of fish or something frying or a hospital smell: once it clings to a sweater, a shirt or any old rag, forget it. And this one's even tougher. It's going to take me a while to air out these clothes. I'm so happy to be here. Africa, at last!

HORN: But you haven't seen anything. You won't even come out of this room.

LEONE: Oh I've seen enough already, enough to know that I love it. I'm not the visiting kind. Okay. I'm ready. As soon as I've finished counting up everything I'm missing or have too many of, and aired out all my clothes, I'll come out. I promise.

HORN: I'm waiting for you, Leone.

LEONE: No, don't wait for me, no, don't wait for me. (*Calls of the watchmen.* LEONE *half appears.*) What was that?

HORN: The watchmen, all night long they call out to each other so they can stay awake.

LEONE: That's awesome. (*She listens.*) Don't wait for me. (*She goes back in.*) Oh Pumpkin, I have something to confess to you.

HORN: What's that?

LEONE: (*Softly*) Last night, just before leaving, I took a walk across the Pont Neuf. And you know what? Suddenly, I felt so good, oh so happy, like I had never felt before, and for no reason. It's awful. Whenever I get that feeling I know something bad is coming. I don't like it when I dream of things that are too happy, or when I feel too good. I get upset, and I spend the whole blessèd day waiting for the bad thing. I've got backward intuitions and they never steer me wrong, Pumpkin, I'm in no hurry to come out of here.

HORN: You're a little high-strung. That's normal.

LEONE: You hardly know anything about me.

HORN: Come on, please, let's go.

LEONE: Are you sure there's only one man?

HORN: I'm absolutely sure.

LEONE: (*Her arm appears.*) You are letting me die of thirst. After I drink something, I'll come, I promise.

HORN: I'll go get something to drink.

LEONE: Just make sure it's water! I have to take my medication with water. (HORN *exits.* LEONE *appears, looks around.*) I am in awe. (*She bends down, picks up a flower of bougainvillea and goes back inside.*)

III

The veranda. HORN *enters.*

CAL: (*At the table, his head in his hands*) Toubab, poor thing, why'd you go? (*He weeps.*) What harm did I ever do to him? Horn, you know me, you know my nerves. If he's not back tonight, I'll kill them all, goddamn dog-eating bastards. They took him from me. I can't sleep without him, Horn. I bet they're eating him right now. I don't even hear him barking. Toubab!

HORN: (*Laying out the bowls for the dice game*) Too much whiskey. (*He brings the bottle over to his side.*)

CAL: Too much silence!

HORN: I'm putting fifty down.

CAL: (*Lifts up his head.*) On five numbers?

HORN: On each.

CAL: I'm out. Ten a number, not a cent more.

HORN: (*Suddenly looks at him.*) You shaved and you combed your hair.

CAL: You know I always shave at night.

HORN: (*Looks at the dice.*) Mine. (*He collects the money.*)

CAL: Matter of fact, I want to play with chips, for pleasure, for the sheer pleasure of the game. All you ever do is sit there and pick up the cash. The only pleasure you get, it's disgusting. Every man for himself and nothing for just the pleasure. A woman's going to bring some humanity around here. You'll make her sick in no time. Me, I'm into the playing of the game for its own sake, not just to pick up the cash. We have to start playing with chips. Women like to play with chips. Women bring humanity to the game.

HORN: (*Quietly*) There's a man here, Cal. He's from the village or the police, or even worse, I've never seen him before. He's asking for explanations. He won't say in whose name. But he wants them, and you're going to have to give them to him. Get ready. I'm not getting myself mixed up in this. Too much on my mind. I don't know a thing. I'm not covering you. I wasn't there. My job is done, goodbye. This time, you're going to have to answer on your own. And you can't even handle one fucking drop of whiskey.

CAL: But Horn, I had nothing to do with it, I didn't do a thing, Horn. (*Quietly*) This is no time to be turning on each other, Horn, we've got to stick together, we've got to stay tight. Look. It's simple. You make a report to the police, make one to management, sign it, done. I keep a low profile. Everybody believes you. All I have is my dog, nobody listens to me. It's got to be the two of us against them all. I'm not talking to this nigger. It's simple: I tell you the whole truth, and you deal. You know my nerves, Horn, you know them well. Better I don't see him. I don't want to see anybody anyway, not until my dog comes back. (*He weeps.*) They're going to eat him.

HORN: Fifty a number and not a cent less.

CAL: (*Puts down fifty francs. Bullfrogs croak nearby.*) The workers and I were looking up at the sky. The dog had caught whiff of the storm. One of the guys was walking across the site. And I see him. Right then, a violent thunderstorm breaks out. I yell, "Come, Toubab, come!" The dog lifts up his face, his hair sticks up. He's sniffing death. It gets him all excited, poor thing. Then I see him running towards the nigger over there, with the rain pouring down on him. "Come here, Toubab!" I'm calling out to him, poor thing. Then in the middle of all the noise and the lightning gone wild, I see one big bolt come down. Toubab's standing still. We're all looking. And we see the nigger fall. The thunder's loud. He's been struck down. Tons of rain are falling on top of him. He's lying down in the mud. Drifting over towards us comes the smell of sulfur, then the sound of a truck, from over there, bearing straight down at us. (HORN *rolls the dice*.) My little Toubab's gone. I can't sleep without him, Horn. (*He weeps*.) Ever since he was little, he's slept on top of me. He's always come back to me. Instinct. He'll never make it alone, Horn. Poor thing. I don't hear him barking. They ate him. At night, it was like having a bunch of fur rolled up in a ball on my stomach, on my legs, on my balls. That's how I got to sleep, Horn, he got into my blood. What harm did I ever do him?

HORN: (*Looking at the dice*) Twelve. (CAL *collects the money*.)

CAL: (*Winking*) Horn, you sure surprised me! All you said was "I'm going to the airport", and then you come back and you say, "My wife is here!" You scored! I wasn't even aware you'd found one. What suddenly got into you, old man? (*They place their bets*.)

HORN: A man should put down some roots before he dies.

CAL: Sure, old man, sure. (*He collects the money*.) Main thing matters is you picked the right one.

HORN: Last time I went to Paris, I said "If you don't find her now, you never will."

CAL: And you found her! You're quite a stud, old man! (*They place their bets*.) Be careful of the climate, though. It's been scientifically proven to drive women crazy.

HORN: Not this one. (CAL *picks up the money*.)

CAL: Make sure she wears the right shoes. I could lend her some. Tell her that, old man. Women are always worried about looking elegant but they know shit about African germs, the kind you catch with your feet, old man.

HORN: This one's no ordinary woman.

CAL: (*Winking*) Well, I intend to make a good impression on her. I'll kiss her hand on the right occasion. She'll think it's elegant.

HORN: I said, "Do you like fireworks?" "Yes", she said. I said, "I put on a show every year, in Africa, and this year will be the last one. Would you like to see it?" "Yes", she said. So I gave her the address and money for a plane ticket. "Be there in one month, time for the package from Ruggieri's to arrive." "Yes", she said. That's how I found her. The last show. I wanted a woman to see it. (*He places his bet.*) I told her the site was about to shut down and that I was leaving Africa forever. She said yes to everything. She always says yes.

CAL: (*After a pause*) Why are they giving up on the site, Horn?

HORN: Nobody knows. I put fifty down. (CAL *places his bet.*)

CAL: Why right away, Horn? Why with no explanations? I want to keep on working, Horn. What about all the work we did? Half a forest chopped down, 25 kilometers of road? A bridge still under construction? And the compound, and the wells to dig? All that time for nothing? Why don't we know, Horn, why don't we know anything about the decisions being made? And why don't you know?

HORN: (*Looking at the dice*) I win. (*Silence. Calls of the watchmen.*)

CAL: (*Quietly*) He's gnashing his teeth.

HORN: What?

CAL: There, behind the tree, the nigger, tell him to leave, Horn. (*Silence. Barking in the distance,* CAL *jumps.*) Toubab! I hear him. He's hanging around by the sewer. Let him fall in, I'm not moving. (*They place their bets.*) Little shit. He's hanging out and when I call him, he doesn't answer, he acts likes he's thinking about something. Is that him? Yeah. Think first, you mutt. I'm not fishing you out. He must've caught whiff of an unknown creature. Let him deal with it on his own. He won't fall. And if he does, I'm not moving. (*They look at the dice.* CAL *collects the money. Quietly*) Horn, I'm telling you, that boy wasn't one of the workers. He was just hired for the day. Nobody knows him, nobody will talk. So he wanted to leave, right? I say, "No, you're not leaving". Wants to leave an hour early. An hour's a big deal. You let him take an hour, sets a bad example. As I was saying, I tell him, "No." So then he goes and spits at my feet and walks off. Spits at my feet, another inch or two it landed on my shoe. (*They place their bets.*) So I call the other guys over, and I say, "You see that guy?" (*Imitating an African accent*) "Yes boss we see him." "See him walk across the site without waiting for the whistle?" "Yes boss yes boss no whistle." "What about the helmet, guys, you see him wearing a helmet?" "No boss, anybody can see he's not wearing a helmet." So I say, "Remember that. And he left without my authorization, right?" "Yes boss oh yes boss no authorization." And then, he fell. The truck was coming and I ask you, "Who was driving the truck? Why's he going so fast? Didn't he see the nigger?" Done! (CAL *picks up.*)

HORN: Everybody saw you shoot. You jerk-off, you can't handle your own fucking rage.

CAL: It's like I told you, it wasn't me. He just fell.

HORN: A gunshot. And everybody saw you get into that truck.

CAL: But the gunshot was thunder. And the truck was everybody going blind from the rain.

HORN: Maybe I didn't go to school, but I already know all the bullshit that you're going to say. You'll find out what it's worth. As far as I'm concerned, see you later jerk-off, this is none of my business. I'm putting down a hundred.

CAL: I'm in.

HORN: (*Slams the table.*) Why'd you have to go and touch it, goddamn it? The one who touches a corpse that's fallen to the ground is responsible for the crime, that's the way it is in this fucking country. If nobody'd touched it, there would've been nobody responsible, it would've been a crime committed by nobody, a passive female crime, an accident. The whole thing would've been simple. But the women came for the body and it wasn't there. It was nowhere. Jerk-off. They found nothing there. (*Slams the table.*) Deal with it. You're on your own. (*He rolls the dice.*)

CAL: When I saw him, I said to myself, "I'm not letting this one rest in no fucking peace." Instinct, Horn, instinct and bad nerves. I didn't know who he was. All he did was spit an inch or two from my shoe. But that's the way instinct works, "I'm not about to let you fucking rest in peace." That's what I said to myself when I looked at him. So I put him in the truck, I went all the way to the dump and threw him on top of the heap, "That's all you deserve. Done." And I went home. But I went back, Horn, I couldn't keep still, he was working on my nerves. I picked him back up from the top of the garbage heap and I put him back in the truck. I take him to the lake and throw him in the water. But then it started gnawing at me, Horn, knowing he was resting in peace at the bottom of the lake. So I went back, I got in the water up to my waist and I fished him out. There he was, back in the truck, and I didn't know what else to do, Horn. "I'm never going to let you fucking rest in peace, I'm not strong enough." I look at him and I say to myself, "This spook's going to destroy my nerves." And then it came to me, "The sewer, that's the solution. You'll never jump in there to fish him out." And that's how it had to be, Horn, so I could leave him the fuck alone and in peace, in spite of myself, for good, Horn. Now I can finally calm down, a little. (*They look at the dice.*) If I'd buried him, Horn, I would've dug him back up, I know myself. And if they'd taken him to the village, I would've gone out there to get him. The sewer was the simplest way to go, Horn, it was the best. It did actually calm me down, a little. (HORN *gets up.* CAL *picks up the money.*) And about niggers, old man, nigger-germs are the worst. Tell her that too. You can never forewarn a woman enough against danger. (HORN *exits.*)

IV

HORN: (*Joining* ALBOURY *under the tree*) I just found out he wasn't wearing a helmet. Like I told you, the workers are careless. My intuition was correct. No helmet: we're not responsible.

ALBOURY: Let me have the body with no helmet, let me have it just the way it is, Sir.

HORN: But that's what I came to tell you. I'm giving you an option. Either you're here or you're not, but don't stay in the dark, behind the tree. It's unnerving knowing somebody's there. If you want to come over to our table, please do, I'm not saying you shouldn't. But if you don't then I'm going to have to ask you to leave. I'll see you tomorrow in my office, we'll examine the situation. Actually, I'd rather you left. I'm not saying I won't offer you a glass of whiskey. That's not what I'm saying. So what's it going to be? Are you having that drink or not? You're not coming to the office tomorrow? Well? Sir, you've got to choose.

ALBOURY: I'll wait here for the body. That's all I want. And I say, "When I have my brother's body, then I'll leave."

HORN: The body, the body! The body wasn't wearing a helmet. There are witnesses. He walked across the site without his helmet. They won't get a penny, Sir, you tell them that.

ALBOURY: I'll tell them that when I bring back the body. No helmet, no penny.

HORN: Have some consideration for my wife, Sir. All these noises and shadows and shouting. Everything's so scary when you first arrive. She'll be used to it tomorrow, but this is her first night! She just got here, and if there's somebody there, behind the tree, that she sees or senses or she catches a glimpse of. You don't realize. She'll be terrified. You want to terrify my wife, Sir?

ALBOURY: No, that's not what I want. I want to bring the body back to the family.

HORN: Sir, you tell them I'll give the family a hundred and fifty dollars. And I'll give you two hundred. I'll give it to you tomorrow. It's a lot. But this will probably be the last person to die on this site. Anyway, that's it, now scram!

ALBOURY: I'll tell them. One hundred and fifty dollars. And I'll bring the body back with me.

HORN: Yeah, you tell them, go ahead. That's all they'll care about. One hundred and fifty dollars will shut their mouth. Believe me, they don't care about the rest. Ha! The body, the body!

ALBOURY: I care.

HORN: Scram!

ALBOURY: I'll stay.

HORN: I'll have you taken out.

ALBOURY: I won't go.

HORN: But you're going to frighten my wife, Sir.

ALBOURY: Your wife won't be afraid of me.

HORN: Yes she will. Somebody lurking in the shadows! You know what? I'm going to have the watchmen shoot you, that's what.

ALBOURY: Kill a scorpion, it always comes back.

HORN: Sir, Sir, don't get carried away. What are you saying? I've always maintained an excellent relationship. . . Am I getting carried away? You've got to admit you're pretty difficult. Impossible to negotiate with. You have to make an effort too. Well stay, stay if that's what you want. (*Quietly*) I realize the people in the Ministry are furious. But you have to understand, I don't take part in high-level decisions. I'm the tiny boss of a construction site, I don't decide anything, I'm not responsible. As a matter of fact, there's something they have to understand: the government places orders but it never pays. They haven't paid for months. The company can't keep sites open if the government does not pay. Do you understand? I realize there's much to be dissatisfied with: bridges that aren't finished, roads that go nowhere. But, hey, what can I do? What about all the money? Where does it go? The country's rich, why are the coffers of the State empty? Sir, no offence, but can you explain it to me?

ALBOURY: They say the government palace has become a place of debauchery where they bring champagne from France and expensive women—that all they do in the halls of the Ministry, all day and all night, is drink and fuck. That's why the coffers are empty. And that's what they tell me, Sir.

HORN: They fuck, look at that! (*He laughs.*) Ridiculing his own country's politicians. You know what? I like you. I don't like government officials. Actually, you don't look like one at all. (Quietly) If what you're saying is true, when are the young people going to start doing something about it? With these progressive ideas they bring back from Europe, when will they finally decide to get rid of all the filth, take charge, and create some order? Will there be a day when these bridges and roads are built at last? Show me the light. Give me some illusions.

ALBOURY: But they also say that what they bring back from Europe is a deadly passion, the automobile. It's all they ever think about and all they ever dream of. Day and night they play with it, waiting for it to kill them, they forget everything else. That's what they bring back from Europe. And that's what I've been told.

HORN: Automobiles, that's right, and Mercedes no less. I see them all the time driving around like maniacs. Breaks my heart. (He laughs.) You don't even have illusions about the youth. I like you. I'm sure we'll get along fine.

ALBOURY: I'm waiting to have my brother back. That's why I'm here.

HORN: But listen, explain something to me. Why are you so stuck on having your brother back? Remind me what this man's name was?

ALBOURY: Nouofia was the name he was known by, and he had a secret name.

HORN: But why is his body so important to you? First time I've ever seen anything like it. I thought I knew Africans, how they don't value life or death. I'm willing to believe you're especially sensitive, but, I mean, it isn't love that makes you so stubborn, is it? Love's a European thing, right?

ALBOURY: No it isn't love.

HORN: I knew it, I knew it. I've often noticed this lack of sensitivity. It shocks a lot of Europeans. Personally, I don't condemn. Fact is Asians are a lot worse. But why are you being so stubborn for such a little thing? I told you I'd give you compensation.

ALBOURY: Often what little people want is a very simple little thing. But this little thing, they want it. Nothing will change their minds. They'd willingly die for it. Even if you killed them, even dead, they'd still want it.

HORN: Who was he, Albuoy, and who are you?

ALBOURY: A long time ago, I say to my brother, "I can feel the cold." He says, "That's because there's a little cloud between the sun and you." I say, "How can this little cloud make me freeze when all around me people are sweating and burning in the sun?" My brother says, "I'm freezing too." So we warmed each other up. Afterwards, I say to my brother, "But when will this cloud disappear, when will the sun warm us too?" He says, "It won't ever disappear, this little cloud's following us everywhere we go, it will always be there between the sun and us." And wherever we went, I could feel it following us. With people all around naked and laughing in the heat, my brother and I, together we froze and gave each other warmth. And so, under this cloud that took the heat away from us, my brother and I warmed each other up, and we got accustomed to each other. If my back itched, I'd have my brother scratch it; and I scratched his whenever his back itched. Worry made me bite the nails on his hand, and he'd suck the thumb on my hand in his sleep. The women we took, clung to us. Soon, they were freezing too. We were all so close and tight under the cloud that we kept each other warm, we got so accustomed to each other, one man's shiver would ripple across from one end of the group to the other. Mothers joined us, and mothers' mothers and their children and our children, a multitudinous family from which not even the dead could be torn away, that's how close and tight we kept them under the cloud that took the heat away from us. The little cloud had risen, risen towards the sun, taking the heat away from a family that was getting larger and more accustomed to each other all the time. A multitudinous family made up of bodies either dead, alive or soon-to-be alive, each one more necessary to the other, as we watched the borders of the earth still warmed by the sun get further away. That's why I'm here, asking for my brother's body that was torn away from us. Because his being gone breaks the closeness that kept us warm, because even dead we need his heat to keep us warm, and he needs our heat to preserve his.

HORN: We're having difficulties understanding each other, Sir. (*They look at each other.*) I think however hard we try, living side by side will always be difficult. (*Silence.*)

ALBOURY: They tell me, in America, blacks go out in the morning, and whites in the afternoon.

HORN: Is that what they tell you?

ALBOURY: Yes Sir, and if it's true, it's a very good idea.

HORN: You truly think that?

ALBOURY: Yes.

HORN: No, it's a very bad idea. It's the other way around, Mr. Alboury, we have to be cooperative, we have to force people to be cooperative. That's what I think. (*Pause*) Listen, my dear

Mr. Alboury, I'm going to tell you something will blow your mind. I came up with this excellent project on my own time, I've never told a single person about it. You'll be the first. Tell me what you think. People make a mountain out of the three billion human beings on the planet. Well, I calculated that if you housed them all in forty-story-high buildings—we can figure out the architecture later, but forty stories not a single one more, that's not even as high as the tower in Montparnasse. And you put them in average-sized apartments, my calculations are reasonable. And all these buildings made up only one city, that's it, a single one, with streets ten meters wide, very decent. Well, this city, Sir, would cover exactly half of France, and not one square kilometer over. Everywhere else would be vacant. You can check my calculations, I've done them over and over, they are absolutely correct. You think my project's stupid? All that's left is to choose where to put this one city, and all your problems are solved. No more conflicts, no more rich countries, no more poor countries, everybody under the same banner, with the resources to be shared by all. You see, Alboury, I'm a kind of a communist myself in my own way. (*Pause.*) To me France is the ideal location: it's temperate, gets plenty of rain, everything there—the weather, the vegetation, animal life, risks of disease—in the right proportion. France is ideal. Of course, you could build it in the South where you get the most sun. But me, I like winter, a good harsh winter. Sir, you don't know what a good harsh winter is. Best thing would be to build the city lengthwise, from the Vosges to the Pyrenees along the Alps. Those who love winter could go live in the former region of Strasbourg, while those who can't stand the snow take their runny noses and their wheezing to the empty spaces from which Marseilles and Bayonne will have been eradicated. This brand-new humanity would have only one conflict left: a theoretical debate on the comparative charms of winter in Alsace versus spring on the Riviera. The rest of the world, Sir, that would all be reserves. Yes Sir, Africa vacant. We'd exploit its wealth, underground and on the earth, its solar energy, all without disturbing a single soul. Africa alone could feed my city for generations before we have to stick our noses in Asia or America. We'd make the most of our technology, bring over the least amount of workers in rotating shifts, super-organized, make it a kind of a civic duty. And they'd bring us back oil, gold, uranium, coffee, bananas, all you could want, with no Africans suffering from foreign invasions because they won't even be here. Yes, France would be beautiful and open to all the peoples of the world, all the different peoples mingling and carrying on in the streets. And Africa would be beautiful, empty, bountiful, free from suffering, breast-feeding the world! (*Pause.*) You think my project's funny? And yet, Sir, my idea is more brotherly than yours. Yes Sir, that's the way I think and that is the way I will continue to think.

(*They look at each other. The wind starts blowing.*)

V

The veranda.

CAL: (*Sees* LEONE *and yells.*) Horn! (*He drinks.*)

LEONE: (*Flower in her hand*) What do you call these flowers?

CAL: Horn!

LEONE: Do you know where I could find something to drink?

CAL: Horn! (*He drinks.*) What the fuck is he doing?

LEONE: Don't call him. Don't bother. I'll find some on my own. (*She walks away.*)

CAL: (*Stops her.*) You plan on walking around here in those shoes?

LEONE: My shoes?

CAL: Sit down. What's the matter, you afraid of me?

LEONE: No. (*Silence. A dog barks in the distance.*)

CAL: In Paris, they know shit about shoes. In Paris, they know shit about anything, and they don't care, as long as it's fashionable.

LEONE: They're the only thing I bought for myself, and this is what you tell me? Scoundrels. You know how much a little piece of leather like this costs! Saint-Laurent's Africa boutique no less. Expensive, these! Ooh wee! Crazy expensive.

CAL: They've got to come all the way up and support the ankle. With the right shoes, you can deal. Shoes are what's most important. (*He drinks.*)

LEONE: Yes.

CAL: If it's sweating you're afraid of, that's stupid. One layer of sweat dries, and then another, and then another. It creates a shell that protects you. And if it's the smell you're afraid of, well, smell develops instinct. Matter of fact, when you know their smells, you know people. Practical too, you can recognize their things, simplifies everything. Instinct, that's all.

LEONE: Oh yes. (*Silence.*)

CAL: Have a drink, why aren't you having a drink?

LEONE: Whiskey? Oh no, I can't. I'm on medication. And, anyway, I'm not that thirsty.

CAL: Thirsty or not, you've got to drink around here, otherwise you dry up. (He drinks. Silence.)

LEONE: I should sew on a button. That's me all over. Buttonholes are way beyond me. No patience, none at all. I always leave them for the end, and in the end, see: a safety pin. Even with the most elegant dresses I've made, in the end, I always use a safety pin. Bad girl, one day you'll prick yourself.

CAL: Me too. I used to spit whenever I saw whiskey. I only drank milk, nothing but milk, I'm talking gallons, barrels of milk. That was up until the time I started travelling. After that, hell, that powdered shit, that American milk, soymilk, not even a cow's hair goes into that milk. End up having to drink this shit. (*He drinks*.)

LEONE: Yes.

CAL: Lucky this shit you can find anywhere. Never been without it anywhere on the planet. And, believe me, I've traveled. Have you?

LEONE: Oh no, this is my very first time.

CAL: I may look young to you but, believe me I've traveled. I've been around. Bangkok, been there. Been to Ispahan, the Black Sea. Marrakech, been there. Tangiers, the Reunion Islands, the Caribbean, Honolulu, Vancouver. Check it out, Chicoutimi. Brazil, Colombia, Patagonia, the Balearic Islands, Guatemala, been everywhere. Ended up in shitty Africa, all over, Dakar, Abidjan, Lomey, Leopoldsville, Johannesburg, Lagos. And I'm telling you, Africa's the worst. But wherever you go, there's whiskey and there's soymilk. And no surprises, ever. And even though I'm young, still, I can tell you, once you've seen a bottle of whiskey, or a construction site, or a French company, you've seen them all. Always the same old shit.

LEONE: Yes.

CAL: Now I'm not saying that this company's the worst of them. Don't put words in my mouth. It might even be the best. They know how to take care of you, how to treat you right. Food's good, lodging's good, what can I say, it's French. You'll see. You won't hear me say a thing against it, remember that. (*He drinks*.) It's not like these shitty Italian companies, or Dutch, German, Swiss, or fuck knows. They're all over Africa now, turned it into a fucking dump. No, not ours. Ours is real proper. (*He drinks*.) Believe me, I wouldn't want to be Italian or Swiss.

LEONE: Oh yes oh no.

CAL: Drink this. (*He holds out a glass of whiskey*.)

LEONE: Where can he be? (*Silence*.)

CAL: (*Quietly*) Why'd you come here?

LEONE: (*Startled*) Why? I wanted to see Africa.

CAL: What's there to see? (*Pause*.) This isn't Africa. This is a construction site for public works, baby.

LEONE: Still, it's . . .

CAL: No. You interested in Horn?

LEONE: Yes, we're supposed to get married.

CAL: With Horn? Get married?

LEONE: Yes, with him.

CAL: No.

LEONE: But why do you always say . . . Where's Pumpkin?

CAL: Pumpkin? (*He drinks*.) Horn can't marry. You know that, right? (*Silence*.) He must've told you about. . .

LEONE: Yes yes, he told me.

CAL: He told you?

LEONE: Yes yes yes.

CAL: Horn's a brave man. (*He drinks*.) Stayed here for a month all alone with a couple of spooks. Here all alone, so he could watch the machinery during their shitty war. Nobody'd make me do that shit. So he told you everything, about his run-in with the looters, and his wound, Horn's horrible wound—and everything? (*He drinks*.) Horn sure likes to gamble.

LEONE: Yes.

CAL: No. What does he get out of it? What more does he have, do you know?

LEONE: No, I don't know.

CAL: (*Winking*) But what he's got less of, you must know that! (*He drinks.*) This story stinks. (*He looks at her.*) What you got he's interested in? (*Calls of the watchmen. Silence.*)

LEONE: I'm so thirsty.

She gets up and goes off under the trees.

VI

Red dust rises in the wind. LEONE *sees someone under the bougainvillea.*

Amidst the whispers and breaths and the flapping of wings which surround her, she recognizes her name, and she feels the pain of a tribal mark carved into her cheeks.

The harmattan, the desert wind which carries the sand, carries her to the foot of the tree.

LEONE: (*Nearing* ALBOURY) I'm looking for water. Wasser, bitte.[1] (*She laughs.*) Do you understand German? It's the only foreign language I speak a little. My mother was German, you know, purebred authentic German, and my father Alsatian. So, for me, it's very . . . (*She goes towards the tree.*) They must be looking for me. (*She looks at* ALBOURY.) But he told me there wasn't . . . (*Gently*) Dich erkenne ich, sicher.[2] (*She looks all around.*)

---

1 Water, please.
2 I'm sure I recognize you.

When I saw the flowers I recognized everything. I recognized these flowers, whose name I don't even know. But in my head, they were hanging just like that from the branches, and in my head, all the colors were already there. How about you, do you believe in past lives? (*She looks at him.*) Why did he tell me there was nobody else here? (*Agitated*) I believe in them, I do. Happy moments, so very happy, they come back to me, from far away, so sweet. Probably ancient. I believe in them. I know there's a lake. I lived on its shores once. It often comes back to me, in my head. (*Shows him a bougainvillea flower*) You never find these anywhere else than in the tropics, right? Well, I recognized them from way back, now I'm looking for all the rest, the warm water of the lake, the moments of happiness. (*Very agitated*) Once, I was buried under a little yellow stone somewhere, beneath flowers just like these. (*She leans towards him.*) He told me there was nobody else (*She laughs.*) and here you are! (*She moves away.*) It's going to rain, isn't it? Tell me, how will the insects survive the rain? One drop of water on their wings and they're kaput. What happens when the rain falls? (*She laughs.*) I'm so happy you're not French or anything. That way you won't think I'm an idiot. Besides, I'm not really French either. Half-German, half-Alsatian. You see, we're made for . . . I'll learn to speak your African language, yes, and when I speak it well and really know how to choose my words carefully, I'll tell you . . . things . . . important things . . . which . . . I don't know. I'm afraid to look at you now. You're so solemn, and solemn's just not me! (*She grows agitated.*) You feel the wind? When the wind spins like that, it's the devil spinning. Vershwinde, Teufel.[3] Pschttt, go away. When I was a child, they would ring the bells of the cathedral to chase away the devil. Are there no cathedrals here? Strange, a country with no cathedrals. I like cathedrals. There's you, so solemn. I like solemn. (*She laughs.*) Sorry, I'm a bad girl. (*She stops moving.*) I would so much rather stay here, the air is sweet. (*She touches him without looking.*) Komm mit mir, Wasser holen.[4] Silly me. I bet they're looking for me this very minute. I shouldn't be

---

3   Be gone, Devil!

4   Come with me get some water.

here, that's for sure. (*She lets go of him.*) Somebody's there. I heard . . . (*Quietly*) Teufel! Verschwinde, pschttt! (*In his ear*) I'll be back. Wait for me. (ALBOURY *disappears under the trees.*) Oder Sie, kommen Sie zurück![5]

CAL *enters.*

VII

CAL: (*Puts a finger to his lips.*) Not too loud, baby. He wouldn't be happy.

LEONE: Who? There's just us here.

CAL: That's right, baby, just us, that's right. (*He laughs.*) Horn's a jealous guy. (*Barking close by.*) Toubab? What's he doing so close? (*Grabs Leone's arm.*) Was there somebody here?

LEONE: Who's Toubab?

CAL: My dog. He barks when he sees a spook. You seen somebody?

LEONE: Did you train him?

CAL: Train him? I never trained my dog. It's instinct, that's all you need. But you be careful if you see something, let the animals fight it out among themselves. Run and come for shelter.

LEONE: What? If I see what?

CAL: A punch in the stomach or a knife in the back, that's what you'll get if you ask instead of run. I'm telling you, you see something, anything you haven't seen before or that I haven't showed you,

---

[5] Or you, come back!

you just run run run and come for shelter. (*Takes* LEONE *in his arms*.) Poor little baby! Me too, one day I landed here with a head full of ideas about Africa. The things you'll see, the things you'll hear! I loved how it was in my head. But nothing you see or hear is like you thought. I understand why you're sad.

LEONE: I'm not sad. I was just looking for something to drink, that's all.

CAL: Your name?

LEONE: Leone.

CAL: Is it the money you want?

LEONE: What money? What do you mean? (CAL *lets her go, he goes towards the truck*.)

CAL: This woman's got wiles. She's dangerous. (*He laughs*.) What kind of work did you do in Paris?

LEONE: I worked in a hotel as a housekeeper.

CAL: A maid. We make less than you think around here.

LEONE: I don't think anything.

CAL: We work hard and make nothing.

LEONE: No, I know you make a lot.

CAL: Now, where'd you get that, little maid? Do I look like I make a lot? (*He shows his hands*.) Do I look like I don't work?

LEONE: Just because you work doesn't mean you're not wealthy.

CAL: With true wealth, our hands wouldn't be damaged, that's true wealth. True wealth gets rid of everything, no effort, not a single one left, not a drop of sweat, not even the slightest movement you don't want to make. No pain. That's true wealth. But us?

Get that out of your head. They pay, sure, but not enough, not even close. The truly wealthy have stopped feeling pain entirely. (*Looking at* LEONE.) Horn, he must've gotten a lot of money, with that trouble he had during the war, that . . . accident. Never talks about it, must've been huge. You interested in the money, huh, baby?

LEONE: Don't call me baby. The words you use: spook, baby, the name of your dog. Don't give everybody dog names. No, I didn't go with Pumpkin for the money.

CAL: Then why?

LEONE: I went with him because he offered.

CAL: You would've gone with just anybody who offered, huh? (*He laughs*.) This woman has fire.

LEONE: Just anybody did not offer.

CAL: And you like fireworks, baby, huh?

LEONE: Yes, he told me about that too.

CAL: You like to dream, huh? And you'd like to make me dream, huh? (*Hard*) But I only dream the truth, I don't dream lies. (*He looks at her.*) This woman's a thief. (LEONE *jumps.* CAL *draws her back into his arms.*) I'm just having fun, baby, don't worry. We haven't seen a woman here for ages. I just wanted to have some fun with a woman. You must think I'm a savage, right?

LEONE: Oh, no . . .

CAL: But we sure would turn into savages if we let ourselves go. Just because we live in this pit I tell myself, doesn't mean we should let go. Me, for instance, I'm interested in a whole heap of things, you'll find that out. I love to talk, I love to have a good time, most of all I love to share ideas. Like, you know, I was a philosophy fanatic. But how the hell would that ever show around here? Africa's not what you think, baby. Old ones here stop us from bringing in the new ideas. No time between the company and the job. But I have ideas or I used to. When you're alone all the time, thinking and thinking and thinking, you start feeling the ideas deflate in your head, one after the other. As soon as you get one going, pop like a balloon, pop. You must've seen those dogs on your way here, all along the road, their bellies swollen up like a balloon, legs sticking up in the air. Thing that matters, though, is being able to share. I've always been curious. Music, philosophy. Troyat, Zola, Miller especially, Henry Miller. You come to my room and help yourself to my books, I have all of Miller, my books are yours. Your name?

LEONE: Leone.

CAL: When I was in college philosophy drove me wild. Miller especially, Henry Miller. Reading him really opened me up. In Paris, I was out of control. The greatest crossroads of ideas in the world is Paris! Yeah, Miller. When he has that dream he kills Sheldon with a gun and he's saying, "I'm not a polack!" You know?

LEONE: No . . . I don't.

CAL: No, you can't let yourself go when you come here baby.

LEONE: Leone.

CAL: This woman's holding out on me. (*He laughs.*) Don't do that. Be absolutely direct. Nothing keeps us apart, we're the same age, we're alike. I for one am absolutely direct. No reason to get uptight.

LEONE: No reason.

CAL: Anyway, we don't have a choice. We're alone. You won't find anybody here to talk to, nobody. We're in the middle of nowhere. Especially now that it's the end. Only me and him left. And Horn's not truly what you'd call educated . . . . And, he's decrepit.

LEONE: Decrepit! The words you use. I like talking with him.

CAL: Yeah, maybe, maybe not, but comes a time you need to feel some admiration. Admiration's very important. A woman admires education in a man. Your name?

LEONE: Leone, Leone.

CAL: So?

LEONE: So what?

CAL: Why Horn?

LEONE: What do you mean why?

CAL: You'd marry a man who's missing the most important . . . thing? You would do that, for money? This woman's disgusting!

LEONE: Let me go.

CAL: Come on, baby. I just wanted to see your face. This isn't my story anyway. You crying or what? Don't take it like that. Baby I understand you're sad. But look at me, am I sad? I've got all the reasons in the world to be sad, better believe it, and real reasons. (*Softly*) I'll lend you my shoes. All we need is you catching some filthy bug. I know we've almost turned into savages. Here, the world is upside-down. That's no reason to cry. Look at me. I've got more diplomas, I'm more qualified and more educated than Horn, but I am under him. You think that's normal? Everything's backwards over here, but look at me, baby, do I get upset? Do I cry?

LEONE: That's Pumpkin. (*She gets up.*)

CAL: Don't move. A thief's gotten into the compound. It's dangerous.

LEONE: You see thieves everywhere.

CAL: A spook. The watchmen let him in by mistake. You see him one second, that's it, and then ha! right in your belly, ha! in your back. Get in the truck.[6]

LEONE: No. (*She pushes him away.*)

CAL: It was only to protect you. (*Pause.*) Baby you've got the wrong idea about me, I know. We haven't seen a woman here since the site opened. So to see one, to see you, it's turning me inside out. Hard for you to understand, coming from Paris. But it turned me inside out to see you. I wish I was different. Right away I knew there could be some attraction between us. But the way I am is never the way I want to be. Still, I'm sure we could be attracted to each other. I've got instinct when it comes to women. (*He takes her by the hand.*)

LEONE: I must be turning all red, oh.

CAL: You've got fire in you, I can see that right away. I like a woman who's got fire. Baby, we're the same. (*He laughs.*) This woman is very attractive.

LEONE: The women here must be so beautiful. Oh, I feel ugly! (*She gets up.*) Pumpkin's here.

CAL: (*Joining her*) Don't be such a priss, little maid. I've got instinct when it comes to certain things.

LEONE: (*Looking at him*) We're so ugly! He's here, I can hear him, he's come looking for me. (CAL *grabs her tight. She manages to escape him in the end.*)

CAL: Priss!

LEONE: Scoundrel!

---

6 K. seems to use *camion* (truck) and *camionnette* (van) indiscriminately throughout the play. Here within the same scene, he suddenly switches to *camionnette*. I've kept truck throughout the play for continuity and to avoid confusion. I imagine he imagines a pick-up truck.

CAL: Paris, the biggest whorehouse in the world!

LEONE: (*From far away*) Verschwinde, verschwind!

CAL: Shit! (*Pause.*) When you haven't seen a woman for a long time, you feel like . . . when you do . . . everything will explode. And then, nothing. Nothing at all. Another night, wasted.
(*He goes off.*)

VIII

At the table, the bowls are set up for the dice game.

HORN: The word is balance. Just like with nutrition: the right proportion of proteins and vitamins; the right proportion of fats and calories; balancing the food groups; organizing the appetizers, main courses, and desserts. To construct a good fireworks display, you need balance: color arrangement, knowing what blends, the right proportion in sequencing the explosions, the right proportion for the height of each launch. I tell you, constructing the balance of the whole and the balance of each individual moment is a real brain-buster. But you'll see, Cal, you'll see what me and Ruggieri can do with the sky, you'll see!

CAL: (*Stops playing abruptly.*) This is a stupid fucking game.

HORN: Stupid? What's stupid about it?

CAL: I think it's stupid.

HORN: Jesus I don't know what there is to think about.

CAL: That's just it, no thinking, nothing.

HORN: So what more do you want, Jesus? There's just two of us, I don't know, what else can two people play? Maybe it's not complex enough for you. We could make it more complicated, you know. I know some variations. You set up a bank, say you can only bet on . . .

CAL: No, this fucking game's even more stupid if it's complicated.

HORN: So you won't play.

CAL: No I don't want to. I think we get stupider every time we play.

HORN: (*Pause.*) Jesus. I just don't understand.

CAL: (*Head between his hands*) Pop!

HORN: What?

CAL: What I'm saying is every time we play this game it burns a synapse. (*He hits himself on the head.*) I can feel it right here.

HORN: What's the matter with you? They play it everywhere. In all the sites. And I've never heard of anybody stopping right in the middle of a game and saying, "It burns a synapse." What synapse? Jesus! You neither, I've watched you play this game for months and . . . Would you rather I go find her and we have us a game of . . .

CAL: No no no, not poker, no!

HORN: Oh playing cards too, that's . . .

CAL: Even more fucking stupid.

HORN: So anybody plays cards is stupid? Centuries people've been playing cards all over the world they've been fucking stupid and nobody knew it until you came along? Jesus!

CAL: No no no, I don't want to play anything ever again.

HORN: So what're we supposed to do?

CAL: I don't know. Not be fucking stupid.

HORN: Ok, fine. (*They sulk.*)

CAL: (*Pause.*) Now that is the sound of Africa. It's not the tom-tom, or the millet grinding. No. It's the fan above the table and the sound of card-games or dice. (*Another pause, very quietly.*) Amsterdam, London, Vienna, Krakow . . .

HORN: What?

CAL: Cities of the north I wish I knew . . . (*Pause, they pour some drinks.*) I'm putting five hundred on the ten.

HORN: With or without a bank.

CAL: No, no, keep it simple.

HORN: I'm in. (*They roll the dice.* HORN *pushes aside the bottle of whiskey.*) You just drink too much.

CAL: Too much? Absolutely not. I never get drunk, never.

HORN: What the fuck is she doing, Jesus, where is she?

CAL: How should I know? (*He collects.*) The other way around, drunk people've always made me sick. That's the main reason I like being here. I get disgusted when I have to look at a drunk. That's why I'd love it, yeah, I'd love it if on the next site . . . (*They place their bets.*) I could've been stuck with one of these guys who gets wasted every night like on some construction sites. I know they're around. I could've been, yeah, I could've. (*The dice roll.*) You could ask to have me with you on the next site. You pull enough weight, old man, you've got seniority in the firm. They'll listen to you, old man.

HORN: There isn't going to be a next site, not for me.

CAL: Sure there is, you know that, old man. You know that for a fact. You see yourself in a little house in the south of France with some woman whining and a little garden? You'll never leave Africa, old man. (*He collects.*) It's gotten under your skin. (*Pause.*) Don't go thinking I'm trying to flatter you but you have leadership in the bones. You're the kind of boss people get attached to, that's a fact. People get used to having you as their boss. That's what a good boss is. I'm used to you. You being my boss is a part of nature, I'm not even aware of it anymore, no argument there. At the job, when they say boss this or boss that, I always tell them, "Wait a minute, I'm not the boss, Horn is the boss." What am I? Nothing. Nothing. Not ashamed to say it. Without you: I am nothing. Whereas nothing scares you. Not even the cops scare you. I'm the opposite. Without you, well . . . I'm scared and I'm not ashamed to say it. And when I say scared, I mean really scared. I see a spook cop I run, that's the way it is. I see a spook that's not a cop I shoot. Nerves. With fear it's all about your nerves, you can't do a thing about it. I'd panic in front of a woman, old man, you know I would. You see I need you. (*Softly*) Everything's gone rotten here. The site's not what it was. People go in and out. If you and me split up, on top of everything else, we'd be all alone. (*Softer*) Don't you think it was a stupid fucking thing to do bringing a woman here? (*Even softer*) What about the spook, isn't that why he's here, because of the woman? (*They place their bets.*) We've got to stay like the fingers on one hand, that's what I think. Just the idea of ending up on some other site having to look at a bunch of fucked-up losers night after night, I tell you I want to start shooting, that's what. (*They look at the dice.* CAL *collects.*)

HORN: (*Stands up.*) What the fuck is she doing? Jesus!

CAL: One more game, boss, one last one. (*Smiling*) A thousand on the ten. (*He places the money.* HORN *hesitates.*) Come on, an old gambler like you, old man. You're not going to back out now? (HORN *places his bet. They roll the dice.*) Wait. (*They listen.*) He's saying something.

HORN: What?

CAL: Behind the tree. He's still there, and he's saying something.

They listen. The wind suddenly drops. Leaves tremble and cease. Dead sound of bare feet running on stone in the distance. Fall of leaves and spider webs. Silence.

IX

ALBOURY *squatting under the bougainvillea. Enter* LEONE. *She squats facing* ALBOURY, *at a distance.*

ALBOURY: Man naa la wax dara?[7]

LEONE: Wer reitet so spät durch Nach und Wind . . .[8]

ALBOURY: Walla niu noppi tè xoolan tè rekk.[9]

LEONE: Es ist der Vater mit seinem Kind.[10] (*She laughs.*) See I speak foreign too! I'm sure we'll understand each other in the end, I am sure of it.

ALBOURY: Yow dégguloo sama lakk waandé man dégg naa sa bos.[11]

LEONE: Yes yes keep on talking just like that, you'll see, I'll get it in the end. What about me? Do you understand me? What if I speak very slowly? No reason to be afraid of foreign languages. On the contrary. I've always believed that if you look at people long enough and carefully enough when they speak, you understand everything. It takes time, that's all. I speak foreign to you and you speak foreign to me, soon we'll be on the same wavelength.

---

7 May I tell you something?
8 "Who rides so late through the night and wind . . ."
9 Or should we stay silent and just look at each other.
10 "It is the father and his child."
11 You don't understand my language but I understand yours.

ALBOURY: Wax ngam dellusil, maa ngi nii.[12]

LEONE: But go slowly ok? Otherwise it won't work.

ALBOURY: (*Pause.*) Dégguloo ay yuxu jigéén?[13]

LEONE: Siehst, Vater, du den Erlkönig nicht?[14]

ALBOURY: Man dé dégg naa ay jooyu jigéén.[15]

LEONE: . . . Den Erlenkönig mit Kron und Schweif?[16]

ALBOURY: Yu ngelaw li di andi fii.[17]

LEONE: . . . Mein Sohn, es ist ein Neberlstreif.[18] It's coming, see? Of course, grammar takes more time. We'd need a lot of time together to make it perfect. But even with mistakes . . . Main thing is to have some basic vocabulary. Not even that, the main thing is the tone. Actually not even that. It's enough just to look at each other and not say a word. (*Pause. They look at each other. A dog barks far away. She laughs.*) I can't not say anything. We'll stop talking when we understand each other. My problem is I don't know what to say. Usually I'm a chatterbox. But when I look at you . . . I'm in awe. And I like to be in awe. Now you. It's your turn to say something, please.

ALBOURY: Yow laay gis waandé si sama bir xalaat, bèbèn jigéén laay gis budi jooy te di teré waa dëkk bi nelaw.[19]

LEONE: More, more, but slow.

---

12 You asked me to come back, here I am.
13 Didn't you hear the cries of the women?
14 "Father, don't you see the Erlking?"
15 Yes, I hear the cries of the women.
16 ". . .The Erlking with his crown and train?"
17 Cries that the wind carries here.
18 "My son, it's the mist."
19 It is you that I see, but in my mind, I see another woman, crying and not letting people sleep.

ALBOURY: Jooy yaa ngimay tanxal.[20]

LEONE: (*Quietly*) You're the only one here who looks at me when he speaks.

ALBOURY: Dégguloo jooyu jigéén jooju?[21]

LEONE: Yes yes, you see I really wonder why I even came. They all frighten me now. (*She smiles at him.*) Except for you. But that's just it. I don't know how to say anything in your language. Not yet. Nothing, nothing, nothing. (*Deep silence broken by two watchmen who brutally and abruptly call out to each other; then it's silent again.*) Too bad. I'd like to stay with you some more. I feel so horribly foreign.

ALBOURY: Lan nga ñäw ut si fii?[22]

LEONE: I think I'm starting to understand.

ALBOURY: Lan nga ñäw ut si fii?[23]

LEONE: Oh yes, I knew it would come.

ALBOURY: (*With a smile*) Are you afraid?

LEONE: No.

Suddenly the red sand and the yelps of a dog are swept up in a whirlwind that flattens the grass and bends the branches, while from the ground, there rises, like rain falling up, a swarm of frantic and suicidal moths veiling all brightness.

---

20 The cries disturb me.
21 Do you hear that woman crying?
22 What did you come here for?
23 What are you doing here?

X

At the table

CAL: Wasted a whole evening, a whole evening spent waiting. Tonight is strange, right? This game we keep on starting and stopping, the woman we're waiting for who's now disappeared. Later some fireworks. Here's some fireworks right now, African-style: exploding dust of dead bugs.

HORN: (*Examining an insect.*) Strange. Hasn't rained. Usually it's after the rain they come out. I'll never figure out this fucking country.

CAL: Wasteful, I call that wasteful. That woman doesn't even give a shit about you. She's probably somewhere crying in a corner, doing who knows what. I'm not surprised. Soon as I saw her, I smelled it, instinct. I don't mean to upset you, old man, really I don't. It's your money, sure it is, do whatever you want, it's yours, yours alone. Buy yourself whatever pleasures you want, old man. But, when it comes to pleasure, don't count on women, not in this life. Fuck women. We just count on us, just us. And tell them once and for all, we get more pleasure from a job well done—that's something you won't deny, old man. That's real pleasure, that's solid, no woman's ever as good. A real solid bridge made with our own hands and our own heads, a real straight road the rain season won't wash away, yeah, that, is pleasure. Women, old man, never get it right when it comes to a man's pleasure. That's something you won't deny old man. Right? I know you won't.

HORN: I don't know, maybe. Yeah, maybe you're right. I remember the first bridge I built. That first night, after we put down the last beam, gave it the last tweak. Hell, it was the night before the inauguration. I remember I stripped myself naked. I wanted to spend the whole night lying stark naked right on that bridge. I almost broke my neck ten times, walking up and down the whole night, touching it all over, damn bridge. I'd be climbing along the cables, sometimes I'd see it all at once all white, moon above, mud below, I remember how white it was.

CAL: But you're leaving this one unfinished! That is wasteful.

HORN: Well, that's something I can't do anything about.

CAL: I should've followed my first idea and worked in oil. Yeah, oil was my dream. Oil has nobility. Look at how the oil guys look at us. They know they're the top of the heap. Oil's always fascinated me. In fact, I'm fascinated by anything that comes up from under the ground. Now bridges make me sick. We who work in the public works, what are we compared to the oil guys? Miserable nobodies, less than zeros. We work the surface, we're boring, everybody sees us and knows everything about us, you don't need qualifications to get hired. What kind of men work here? Men who pull and push and carry and drive shit around. Donkey-men, elephant-men. Beasts of burden. All of us. A dumping-ground for men with no qualifications. Whereas in the oil business, ha. Six or seven qualified men, and look, old man, look at the fortune that goes through their hands! I'm a beast of burden too. I've turned into one. Even though I have the qualifications! Even though what I really need is for all of my strengths to be employed. At night I can see the flares from the refinery over there, I could watch them for hours

HORN: (*Places his bet.*) Play.

CAL: My heart's not in it old man, it's just not. (*Quietly*) Horn, you're really going to dump me, that's the idea right? Say it, old man, say it. You're dumping me, right?

HORN: What?

CAL: Have the watchmen shoot him down. Shit, we've got the right!

HORN: Don't worry about it. Play. Stop worrying.

CAL: Why'd you even talk to him? What'd you have to say to each other? Shit, why don't you have him taken out!

HORN: This one's not like the others.

CAL: I knew it. You're getting screwed. I'd really like to know what you were saying to each other. Anyway, you're dumping me. I knew it.

HORN: Jerk-off. Can't you see that in the end I will fuck him and that'll be that?

CAL: You will fuck him?

HORN: I will fuck him.

CAL: I still think what you're doing with that nigger is weird.

HORN: Jesus Christ, who's the one responsible around here?

CAL: You are, old man, I'm not saying you're not. It's just. . .

HORN: Whose job is it to fix other people's fuck-ups? Whose burden is it to be making all the deals, knowing all the moves, everywhere and all the time, from one end of the compound to the other and in the site, from morning till sundown? Who's got to keep it all locked up in his head all the time, from every single part of every single truck to every last bottle of whiskey in stock? Who's got to plan it and judge it and drive it all day and all night? Who's got to be the cop, the mayor, the chief, general, big daddy, ship captain?

CAL: You do, old man, sure you do, it's all true.

HORN: And who's had it, had it all the way up to here?

CAL: You, old man.

HORN: It's true, I may not have any qualifications but I'm still the boss.

CAL: Look, I didn't mean to upset you, old man, I was just saying something that passed through my mind, you know, it was weird, Horn, you talking to that nigger like it was normal, it was weird that's all. But if you say you're going to screw him, well then that means you're going to screw him.

HORN: It's practically done already.

CAL: (*Pause.*) Still, you're a weird guy. Come on let me fire him up, it'll be quicker.

HORN: You're not doing anything. I'm doing.

CAL: Your methods are weird.

HORN: Jesus, don't you know any other ways of defending yourself than shooting off your gun? Me, I use my mouth. I've learned to talk and make words serve my purpose. Maybe I didn't go to school but politics are something I know how to use. Only move you know is shoot your pistol, and then what? You're pretty happy somebody's there to get you out of the mess and watch you cry. Is that all you learn at engineering school is how to shoot your gun? Didn't they teach you how to talk? Wow! Great school! Now you all just go ahead and do what you like, shoot your guns off all over the place. You'll come crying, you'll come crying. This is the last time, I'm leaving when this is over. It's all yours after that.

CAL: Old man, don't get upset.

HORN: You are the wrecking-crew. Is that all you learned in your fancy schools? Yes, gentlemen, keep on going, don't stop using those goddamn fucking wrecking-crew methods! All of Africa will loathe you, not love you. But in the end, you won't get shit, nothing, not a thing. Got a big mouth, a pistol in your pocket, an inclination towards fast money at any cost, well, gentlemen, I'm here to tell you, when time's up you won't get a thing, not a thing, nothing! You don't give a shit about Africa, do you, gentlemen? All you care about is you taking the most you can and making sure you don't give a thing. Well in the end, won't be anything left, nothing, over. And the Africa that we knew, gentlemen, you fucking bastards, will have been destroyed, completely destroyed by you!

CAL: Horn, I don't want to destroy anything.

HORN: You don't want to give Africa your love.

CAL: But I do, I love it. Otherwise, I wouldn't be here.

HORN: Play.

CAL: My heart's not in it, old man. Knowing there's a risk, right here, right in the middle of the compound, that a spook's going to stick his knife into something, it fucks with my nerves, old man. What I think, is he's come out here to take advantage of the situation and start a riot. That's what I figure.

HORN: You don't figure shit. He wants us to be in awe of him. It's all politics.

CAL: Well then, it's the woman, like I thought all along.

HORN: No he's got something else in mind.

CAL: Mind, what mind, what else are you going to find in a spook's mind? I got it, Horn, you're dumping me.

HORN: I can't dump you, jerk-off.

CAL: And you'd prove it was an accident, Horn, you'll prove it?

HORN: An accident, sure, why not? Who's saying it wasn't?

CAL: I knew it. Best we stay tight. Tight we screw them all. I get it now. You talk so you can fuck him better. It certainly is a method, I won't deny that. But still you better watch out, old man. With methods like that, you might get some lead in your belly.

HORN: He isn't armed.

CAL: Still, still, you should still be careful. Those motherfuckers do karate. Tough mothers. Might find yourself horizontal before you even say a word.

HORN: (*Points to two bottles of whiskey.*) I have my weapons. This kind of whiskey nobody stands up to.

CAL: (*Looks at the bottles.*) Beer would've been just fine.

HORN: Play.

CAL: (*Places his bet sighing.*) What a waste.

HORN: But while I'm talking to him, you find the body. Don't argue, I don't care how but you find it. Go, I need it. Otherwise we've got a whole village on our ass. Find it before daybreak, otherwise I will dump you, for good.

CAL: No, it can't be done, no way. I'll never find it. I can't.

HORN: Find one, any one.

CAL: How? How can I?

HORN: It can't be very far.

CAL: No! Horn.

HORN: (*Looks at the dice.*) I win.

CAL: Your methods are bullshit. (*Slams his fist into the bowls.*) You're an asshole, a real asshole.

HORN: (*Gets up.*) Do what I tell you. Otherwise I dump you. (*Exits.*)

CAL: That asshole dumps me I'm fucked.

XI

The site, at the foot of the unfinished bridge, close to the river, in half-darkness, ALBOURY *and* LEONE.

LEONE: You've got great hair.

ALBOURY: The way it's told, our hair turned curly and black when the ancestor of all Negroes, who'd been abandoned by God and the whole of mankind, found himself alone with the devil, who'd also been abandoned by all. The devil reached and touched his hair as a sign of friendship. That's how our hair got burned.

LEONE: I love stories about the devil. I love how you tell them. You've got great lips. Actually, black is my favorite color.

ALBOURY: It's a good color for hiding.

LEONE: What's that?

ALBOURY: The song of the bullfrogs. They're calling for it to rain.

LEONE: And that?

ALBOURY: The vultures' call. (*Pause.*) And that is the noise of an engine.

LEONE: I don't hear it.

ALBOURY: I do.

LEONE: It's the sound of water. Something else is making that sound. How can you be sure? There are so many sounds.

ALBOURY: (*Pause.*) You heard it now?

LEONE: No.

ALBOURY: A dog.

LEONE: I don't think I hear it. (*Dog barking in the distance.*) Little runt, not much of a dog, you can tell by its bark. It's some mutt, he's far away, you don't hear him anymore. (*Barking.*)

ALBOURY: He's looking for me.

LEONE: Let him come. I like them, I like to touch them, they won't attack you if you like them.

ALBOURY: They're mean animals. They can smell me from a distance, they run after me to bite me.

LEONE: Are you afraid?

ALBOURY: Yes, yes I'm afraid.

LEONE: Of some little runt we can't even hear anymore?

ALBOURY: We frighten the chickens. It's only right the dogs should frighten us.

LEONE: I want to stay with you. Why would you want me to go with them? I quit my job, I quit everything. I left Paris, ooh wee, I left it all. What I was really searching for is somebody to be faithful to. I've found him. Now I can no longer move. (*She closes her eyes.*) I think I have a devil in my heart, Alboury. I don't know how I caught him but he's there, I feel him. He's touching me inside, and already I'm burned all over, all turned to black inside.

ALBOURY: Women talk so fast. I can't follow.

LEONE: Fast, you call that fast? When it's all I've thought about for at least an hour. An hour thinking about it, and I can't say it's something serious, well thought-out, and permanent? Tell me what you thought when you first saw me.

ALBOURY: I thought, "Here's a coin somebody dropped in the sand. Right now, it shines for no one. I'll pick it up and hold it until somebody comes to claim it."

LEONE: Hold on to it, nobody will come to claim it.

ALBOURY: Old man told me you were his.

LEONE: Pumpkin. Are you worried about Pumpkin? My goodness, poor Pumpkin, he wouldn't hurt a fly. What do you think I am for him? A little company, a little whim, because he has more money than he knows what to do with. And me who doesn't have any, wasn't it awesome luck to meet him? I must be a bad girl to have such luck. My mother, oh if she knew, she'd give me one of those looks, she'd say, "Naughty girl, that kind of luck only happens to actresses or hookers." But I'm neither of those, and it happened to me. And when he offered that I join him in Africa, yes I said yes, I'm ready. Du bist der Teufel selbst, Schelmin![24] Pumpkin is so old and so kind. You know. He doesn't ask. That's what I love about old people. They usually love me too. Often, they smile at me in the street, I feel good, like I'm with them, close to them. I feel their vibrations. Do you feel the vibrations of old people, Alboury? Sometimes, I can't wait to be old and kind. We'd sit and talk for hours, we wouldn't need anything from anyone ever again, never ask for anything, nothing to fear, nothing bad to say about anybody, far away from cruelty and unhappiness, oh Alboury, why are people so harsh? (*Light sound of a branch breaking.*) How calm it all is, how sweet the air. (*Branches breaking, muffled calls in the distance.*) It feels so good to be here.

ALBOURY: For you, but not for me. This place is for white people.

LEONE: Wait just a little bit longer then, one more minute. My feet are hurting. These shoes are awful. They cut into your ankles and your toes. That's blood, isn't it? Look at that. Crap. Three little pieces of bad leather just so you can tear up your feet and pay through the nose for it. Ooh. I'll never have the strength to walk for miles with these on.

ALBOURY: I will have held on to you as I long as I could. (*Sound of the truck, close-by.*)

---

24 You are the devil himself, my little joker!

LEONE: He's getting close.

ALBOURY: It's the white man.

LEONE: He won't hurt you.

ALBOURY: He'll kill me.

LEONE: No!

They hide. We hear the truck come to a halt. The headlights illuminate the ground.

XII

CAL, *rifle in his hands, covered in black mud.*

HORN: (*Suddenly appearing out of the darkness*) Cal!

CAL: Boss. (*Laughs and runs toward him.*) Oh boss, am I glad to see you.

HORN: (*Making a face*) What'd you come out of?

CAL: Shit, boss.

HORN: Jesus, don't come near me, you'll make me throw up.

CAL: But boss, it was you who said do whatever it takes to find him.

HORN: So? Did you find him?

CAL: No, boss, nothing, nothing. (*He weeps.*)

HORN: You covered yourself up in shit for nothing? (*Laughs.*) Jesus, what a jerk-off!

CAL: Don't laugh at me, boss. It was your idea but when it comes to doing whatever it takes, I'm always on my own. It was your idea, and now I'm going to catch tetanus because of you.

HORN: We're going home. You're completely drunk.

CAL: No, boss, I want to find him. I've got to find him.

HORN: Find him? Too late, jerk-off. By now he's floating away in some river. And it's going to rain. It's too late. (*Goes towards the truck.*) The seats must be in a hell of a fucking state. Jesus, it stinks.

CAL: (*Grabs him by the collar.*) Man, you're the chief, you're the boss, chief. You've got to tell me what to do now. Hang on to me, tight! I don't know how to swim, I'm drowning, old man. Better watch it, asshole, don't make fun of me.

HORN: Watch your nerves. Don't get excited. Cal, come on. You know I'm not making fun of you, you know that. (CAL *lets go of him.*) What the hell happened to you anyway? Now we're going to have to disinfect you.

CAL: Look at how I'm sweating, fucking hell, look at that. It won't dry. You don't have a beer? (*He weeps.*) You don't have a glass of milk? I want to drink milk, old man.

HORN: Calm down. We're going back to the compound. You've got to wash yourself, and it's going to rain.

CAL: Can I kill him now, huh, can I kill him?

HORN: Don't talk so loud, Jesus.

CAL: Horn!

HORN: What?

CAL: Am I a son of a bitch, old man?

HORN: What're you talking about? (CAL *cries*.) Cal, listen son.

CAL: All of a sudden, I saw Toubab right in front of me. He was looking at me with his little thoughtful eyes. Toubab, my little dog! I say, "What're you dreaming of, what're you thinking?" He grunts, his hair sticks up, he starts walking along the sewer, slowly. I'm following him. "Toubab, my little dog, what's on your mind? Did you smell somebody?" His hair sticks up, he lets out one short bark, and jumps into the sewer. I'm saying to myself, "He smelled somebody." I go in after him. But I didn't find a thing, boss. Just shit, boss. That's the place I threw him in, but he must've gotten away. I can't go looking in every body of water in the region and dredge the lake to find the corpse, boss. And now Toubab's gotten away too. I'm alone again and covered with shit. Horn!

HORN: What?

CAL: What am I getting punished for, old man? What did I do wrong?

HORN: You did what you had to do.

CAL: So can I kill him now, old man, can that be what I have to do?

HORN: Jesus, don't yell, you want them to hear you in the village?

CAL: (*Loading his rifle*) This is the perfect place right here. Nobody around to see anything, nobody to come claiming or crying. Motherfucker, I'll put you in the fern you'll disappear, baby your life's not worth a dime around here. Now I'm feeling all hopped up again, I'm getting hot, old man. (*He starts sniffing.*)

HORN: Give me that rifle. (*Tries to grab it from him.* CAL *resists*.)

CAL: Watch it, old man, watch yourself. Maybe I'm not good at karate, maybe I'm not good with a knife, but with a rifle, man, I'm awesome. Awesome, awesome. Even with a pistol or a machine gun, come up against me your life's not worth a dime.

HORN: You want to have the whole village on your ass? You want to have to do some explaining to the police? You want to keep on fucking up? (*Quietly*) Do you trust me? Do you or don't you? Let me take care of this. Don't let your nerves get the best of you, son. Got to stay cool when you handle these things. Believe me, we'll have this situation resolved by daybreak. (*Pause*.) I don't like blood, son, not one bit. Never been able to get used to it, never. Makes me jump out of my fucking skin. I'll talk to him one more time, and this time, believe me, I'll get him. I've got my own secret little ways. What'd been the use of being in Africa for so long if I didn't get to know them better than you do, know them inside-out? If I didn't get to have my own little ways against them, the kind they can't do anything about, huh? What's the use of shedding blood when we can just let things take care of themselves?

CAL: (*Sniffing*) Woman-smell, nigger-smell, fern-smell craving for it. He's here, boss, can't you smell him?

HORN: Stop the act.

CAL: Can't you hear, boss? (*Barking*.) Is that him? Yeah, that's him. Toubab! Come here, little dog, come here, don't ever go, come let me touch you, honey, let me kiss you, you little fucker. (*He weeps*.) I love him, Horn. Horn, what am I getting punished for, why am I such a son of a bitch?

HORN: You're not a son of a bitch!

CAL: Yeah well you're a stupid asshole, a stupid fucking asshole, boss. Sure I'm one, sure I am, from now on, that's what I decided. I'm a man of action. You just talk and talk, all you do is talk. What if he doesn't listen to you, huh, what if your secret little ways don't work, huh? Fucking hell, they won't work! Lucky I am a son of a bitch, lucky somebody is, otherwise there'd be no action. Stupid fucking assholes are useless when it comes to action. Me, a spook spits at me I blow his brains out, shit, as I should. It's thanks to me they don't spit on you, not cause you talk and talk and you're a stupid asshole. Me, he spits, I blow his brains out. Be glad. Cause another inch it was on our foot. Cause five inches higher, it was on our pants, and a little higher than that it would've been in our face. What would you have done then if

I hadn't done something? You'd be talking, talking right? With a gob of spit all over your face? Stupid fucking asshole. Cause they spit all the time around here, and what do you do? You act like you don't see. They open one eye and spit, open the other and spit, spit when they're walking, spit when they're eating, drinking, when they're sitting, lying down, standing, squatting. Between every mouthful, every drink they swallow, every minute of the day. It ends up getting all over the sand of the site and the paths, gets inside, turns it to mud, and when we walk, our boots, poor things, they sink in. For what is spit made of? Who truly knows? Certainly liquid, just like the human body, ninety percent. But what else? Ten percent of what else? Who can tell me? Can you? Spook spit spells a dark threat against us. If you collected all the spit of all the niggers of all the tribes in Africa for just one day—dug trenches where you'd make them spit, and canals, dikes, the waterworks, dams, aqueducts. If you collected all the streams of spit the black race of the entire continent has spit out against us, it would submerge all the dry land of the whole planet in a dark threatening sea. There'd be nothing left but seas of saltwater and spit all mingled. Only niggers'd be left to float, on top of their own substance. That is something I can not allow to happen. I want action, I am a man. When you're done talking, old man, when you're done. . .

HORN: First you let me deal. If I don't manage to convince her. . .

CAL: Oh, oh boss.

HORN: But you've got to calm down first. You've got nerves like a woman, Jesus, calm down.

CAL: Oh, oh boss.

HORN: Cal, listen son . . .

CAL: Fuck you. (*Barking in the distance.* CAL *shoots off like an arrow.*)

HORN: Cal! Come back here, it's an order, come back here!

Sound of the truck starting. HORN *stays.*

XIII

Branches break. HORN *turns on his torch.*

ALBOURY: (*In the shadow*) Turn it off!

HORN: Alboury? (*Silence.*) Come on out and show yourself.

ALBOURY: Turn off the light.

HORN: (*He laughs.*) Man you're nervous! (*He turns off his light for a moment.*) Sure got a voice on you. Might scare somebody.

ALBOURY: Let me see what you're holding behind your back.

HORN: Ah ha, behind my back, huh? Rifle or pistol? Guess the caliber. (*Takes two bottles of whiskey out from behind his back.*) Ah ha! That's what I'm hiding. You still have doubts about my intentions? (*He laughs, turns the light back on.*) Come on, relax. I wanted you to have a taste. These are my best bottles. You've got to admit, Mr. Alboury, I'm the one who's making all the first moves. You'll have to remember that, when we go over everything. You don't want to come to me, so I come to you. In friendship. Believe me, in the pure spirit of friendship. What can I say, I worry, I mean I wonder, about you. (*He shows him the whiskey.*) This'll help you loosen up around me. I forgot the glasses, hope you're not a snob. Anyway, whiskey's much better from the bottle. The aroma doesn't escape. That's how you recognize a real drinker. I want to teach you how to drink. (*Quietly.*) Is your conscience perfectly at ease, Mr. Alboury?

ALBOURY: Why?

HORN: I don't know. It's just that you keep looking around.

ALBOURY: The other white man is looking for me. He's got a rifle.

HORN: I know I know I know. Why do you think I'm here? He won't do anything while I'm here. Say, I hope you won't mind drinking out of the same bottle as me? (ALBOURY *drinks*.) Excellent, glad to see that if nothing else, you're not a snob. (HORN *drinks*.) Let it go down slow. Give it time to yield its secret. (*They drink*.) So I heard you were a karate champ. Are you really a champ?

ALBOURY: Depends on how you define champ.

HORN: You won't say a thing! But some day when we have time, I'd love it if you taught me a couple moves. I should tell you right away, I'm pretty suspicious of the Oriental techniques. Good old boxing! Have you ever done any good old traditional boxing?

ALBOURY: Not traditional, no.

HORN: Well then how do you expect to defend yourself? One of these days, I'll teach you a couple moves. I used to be real good. I even fought professionally, when I was young. Boxing is an art you never forget. (*Quietly*.) Calm down. You don't have to worry. You're my guest, and I consider hospitality sacred. You're practically on French territory, you've got nothing to be afraid of. (*They go from one bottle to the other*.) I'm looking forward to knowing which one you like better. Says a lot about a man's character. (*They drink*.) This one definitely has a very definite edge. You feel how edgy it is? Whereas the other one rolls, unquestionably. Little marbles, thousands of little metallic marbles. Right? How do you feel about it? This one is definitely edgy. And, if you take the time, you can feel ridges, ridges all along the edge that give you a light scratchy sensation in your mouth, right? Well?

ALBOURY: I don't feel the marbles, or the edge, or the ridges.

HORN: Really? You don't? But they are indisputably there. Try again. What's the matter, are you afraid of getting drunk?

ALBOURY: I'll stop before I do.

HORN: Oh great, yeah, excellent, applause.

ALBOURY: Why'd you come here?

HORN: To see you.

ALBOURY: To see me? Why?

HORN: To have a look at you, talk a little, waste my time. Friendship, pure spirit of friendship. For some other reasons too. Why, is my company a drag? Didn't you say you would enjoy learning a few things?

ALBOURY: I've got nothing to learn from you.

HORN: More applause. Right on. I was pretty sure you didn't think much of me.

ALBOURY: Only thing I learned from you, in spite of you, is that there's not enough room in your head and in all your pockets to hide away your lies, they always show in the end.

HORN: Excellent. But that, on the other hand, is not true. Try me. Ask me for something, anything just so I can prove that I'm not deceiving you.

ALBOURY: Give me a weapon.

HORN: Except for a weapon! Jesus you've all gone nuts with the pistols!

ALBOURY: He's got one.

HORN: Too bad for him. Enough about that jerk-off. He'll end up in jail, even better. Anybody who got rid of him would be doing me a favor. To tell you the truth, Alboury, he's the cause of all my problems. Get rid of him for me I won't lift a finger. You ought to tell me the truth too. What do the people above you intend to do?

ALBOURY: There are no people above me.

HORN: So then why do you pretend you're part of the secret police?

ALBOURY: Doomi xaraam![25]

HORN: Oh, you'd rather keep on playing hide-and-seek? Whatever. (ALBOURY *spits on the ground*.) No reason to get angry.

ALBOURY: How can a man keep knowledge of himself amid all your words and betrayals?

HORN: When I say to you, Alboury, "Do whatever you want I'm not covering him anymore", I am not telling you a lie, you can believe me. I'm not maneuvering.

ALBOURY: It's a betrayal.

HORN: A betrayal? What am I betraying? What are you talking about?

ALBOURY: Your brother.

HORN: No, please, none of that African talk. What this man does is none of my business. His life is not connected to mine in any way.

ALBOURY: But you're the same race, aren't you? Same language, same tribe, aren't you?

HORN: Same tribe, sure, if you say so.

ALBOURY: Both masters here, aren't you? Isn't it the masters who open up the sites and close them down with no fear of punishment? The ones who hire and fire the workers? Aren't the masters the ones who stop and start the machines? Aren't the two of you both the owners of the trucks and the machinery? The brick cabins and the electricity, everything here, aren't you, both of you?

HORN: Sure, if you say so, yes, as far as you're concerned, yes. So?

---

25 Bastard!

ALBOURY: So why are you afraid of the word brother?

HORN: Because, Alboury, the world has changed in the last twenty years. And what in the world has changed is what makes the difference between who he is and who I am, between an insane bloodthirsty murderer on the loose, and a man who came here with an entirely different spirit.

ALBOURY: I don't know what your spirit is.

HORN: Alboury, I used to be a worker myself. Believe me, I wasn't born a master, you know. When I came here, I knew from experience what it was to be a worker. That's why I've always treated my workers, black or white, the same way I was treated when I was a worker. That's what I meant by spirit. Knowing that if you treat a worker like he was an animal, he'll take his revenge like an animal. There's the difference. Now, don't blame me for the fact that workers here and everywhere else are unhappy. That is their condition, I can't do a damn thing about it. That's how I earned my living. Just by chance, do you believe there is a single worker in the world who can say, "I am happy"? Matter of fact, do you believe there will ever exist in the entire world a single human being who can say, "I am happy"?

ALBOURY: What do workers care about the sentiments of masters, and blacks about the sentiments of whites?

HORN: You're a tough one, Alboury, I'm realizing that. You don't consider me a human being. Whatever I say, whatever gesture I make towards you, whatever idea I express, even if I show you what's in my heart, all you see in me is a white man and a boss. (*Pause.*) Does it really matter in the end? Doesn't prevent us from drinking together. (*They drink.*) Strange. I keep on feeling like you're not really there, like there's somebody behind you. You seem distracted! No, no, don't tell me anything, I don't want to know. Drink. Are you drunk yet?

ALBOURY: No.

HORN: Good, congratulations. (*Quietly.*) I've got a favor to ask you, Alboury. Don't tell her anything, don't tell her what brought you here, don't talk about corpses or any of those things, they're disgusting, don't try to indoctrinate her, don't tell her anything that might make her want her to run away. I hope it's not too late. Maybe I shouldn't have brought her here, I know. But something bit me, that's the way it is. I knew it was madness but it truly bit me all of a sudden and now, no, she shouldn't be made afraid. I need her. I need to feel her around. I barely know her, I don't know what her desires are. I'm letting her be free. Knowing she's around is enough for me, I'm not asking for anything else. Don't make her run away. (*He laughs.*) What can I say, Alboury, I don't want to die alone, like an old fool. (*He drinks.*) I've seen a whole lot of dead people in my life, a whole lot of them. And I've looked into their eyes, dead people's eyes, a whole lot. And every time I see a dead person's eyes, I tell myself: everything you want to see, you better buy it right away, you better be ready to spend your money quick quick. Otherwise, what's it there for? I don't have any family. (*They drink.*) Goes down smooth, doesn't it? I see you're not afraid of alcohol, that's good. Still not drunk yet? You're tough. Show me? (*Takes his left hand.*) Why do you let just this one fingernail grow so long, why? (*He stares at the nail on his little finger.*) Is it a religious thing? A secret? I've been worrying about this nail for an hour. (*He touches it.*) Must be an awesome weapon if you know how to use it, one hell of a dagger. (*Quieter.*) You use it when you make love? Ah, poor Alboury, if you're not suspicious of women either you're in trouble. (*He looks at him.*) But you're not saying a word, you're keeping all of your little secrets. I'm sure deep down you haven't thought much of me from the start. (*Suddenly takes out a roll of bills from his pocket and holds it out to* ALBOURY.) There you go, son. Like I promised. Five hundred dollars. It's the most I could do.

ALBOURY: You promised me Nouofia's body.

HORN: The body, yes, the damn body. We're not going to talk about that again? Nouofia, that's what it was. And you said he had a secret name? What was it again?

ALBOURY: It's the same one for all of us.

HORN: That doesn't tell me much. What was it?

ALBOURY: I'm telling you: the same for all of us. That is the only way to say it. It's secret.

HORN: You're too dark for me, I like things to be in the clear. Come on, take it. (*He holds out the bills.*)

ALBOURY: That's not what I want from you.

HORN: Let's not go overboard, Sir. One of the workers is dead, fine. It's a serious matter, fine. I don't want to belittle the thing, not one bit. But this kind of situation will happen anywhere, any time. You think workers in France don't ever die? It's serious but also it's normal. It's part of the job. If it hadn't been him, it would've been somebody else. What do you think? It's a dangerous line of work. We're all taking risks. Actually they're not even that extreme. We're not exceeding the statistics, we haven't gone past the limit. Let's be clear. Work has a cost. All societies sacrifice something of themselves; all men sacrifice something of themselves. You'll find out. You think I haven't sacrificed anything? It's the law of the world. Doesn't stop the world, does it? You won't keep the earth from turning, will you? Good old Alboury, don't be so naïve. Be sad, I can understand that, but not naïve. (*He holds out the money.*) Here, take it.

LEONE *enters.*

XIV

Increasingly frequent lightning.

HORN: I was looking for you Leone. It's going to rain. You don't know what it's like here when it rains. Give me another minute then we'll go home. (*To* ALBOURY, *quietly*) You're just too complicated for me, Alboury. All your thoughts are tangled up in your mind, they're opaque and indecipherable like the bush is, like all of Africa is. Tell me why did I love it so much? Why did I want to save you so bad? Makes you think everybody here goes insane.

LEONE: (*To* HORN) Why do you make him suffer? (HORN *looks at her.*) Give him what he wants.

HORN: Leone! (*He laughs.*) Jesus! (*To* ALBOURY) Listen to me, the body of this worker is lost forever. It's floating away somewhere, the fish and the vultures are feasting on it right now. Give up, that's it, you'll never get it back. (*To* LEONE) It's going to rain. Come Leone. (LEONE *goes toward* ALBOURY.)

ALBOURY: Give me a weapon.

HORN: No, Jesus, no. I won't have any killing around here. (*After a pause*) Be reasonable, both of you. Leone, come. Alboury, take this money and go before it's too late.

ALBOURY: If Nouofia I've lost forever, then I must take the life of the murderer who took his.

HORN: Thunder and lightning, boy, take it out on heaven and get the fuck out of here, get the fuck out, for good, now scram! Leone, come here!

XV

LEONE: Say yes, Alboury, say yes. He's even offering to give you some money, he's kindly offering you money, what more do you want? He came here to fix things, it's true. Well then, fix things we must, since we can. What's the use of wanting to fight for something that's lost all meaning when someone is kindly offering to fix everything and give you some money too. The other one is crazy, now we know that, we just have to be careful, and remember, there's three of us, we should be able to stop him from doing bad things and hurting people, it's easy as falling after that. They're nowhere alike. This one is kind, he comes to talk but you refuse, you clench your fists, you stay stubborn, ooh! I've never seen anybody so stubborn. Is that how you act when you want something? My goodness, this one really doesn't know how to go about getting what he wants. I know, if you let me. I would certainly not clench my fists and look all warrior-like and stubborn, ooh wee! No, war is not how I want to live, I don't want to fight, or be trembling all the time, or be unhappy. I want to live, that's all, peacefully, in some little house, wherever you want, but peacefully, all of us. Oh I don't mind being poor, I don't care about that, or having to go far for water and eat from the trees and the whole kit-and-caboodle. I'm willing to live on absolutely nothing, but not to kill and fight and be stubborn and clench my fists oh no, why be so harsh? Or maybe I'm not even worth a half-eaten corpse, maybe I'm not even worth that! Albuory, is it because I have the misfortune of being white? But you, Albuory, could not possibly be wrong about me. I'm not really white, no. Oh I'm so used to being what you're not supposed to be, being a nigger too wouldn't cost me a thing. If that's what it is, Albuory, if it's about my whiteness, I spit on that a long time ago, I threw it away, I don't want it. Were you not to want me either . . . (*Pause.*) Oh black is the color my dreams are made of, black is the color of my love! I swear when you go back, I'll go back with you. When you say "Home", I will say "My home." When you say "Brother", I will say "My brother", I will call your mother "Mother"! Your village will be my village, your language my language, your earth will be my earth, and even when you sleep, I swear even when you die, I will be there with you.

HORN: (*From a distance*) Can't you see he doesn't want anything with you. He's not even listening.

ALBOURY: Demal fale doomu xac bi![26] (*He spits in* LEONE*'s face.*)

LEONE: (*Turning towards* HORN.) Help me, help me.

HORN: What? You throw away your dignity right under my nose for this guy and I should help you? You think you can treat me like a

---

26 Go away far from here, out of my sight, bitch's daughter!

piece of shit and I'm not going to react? You think all I'm good for is to pay and pay that's it, and I'm going to let myself be treated like a piece of shit? Tomorrow, Jesus yes tomorrow, you're going back to Paris. (*Turns to* ALBOURY.) As for you, I could have them shoot you down for trespass. Where do you think you are, at home? You think I'm a piece of shit? You think we're all a piece of shit? You're lucky I don't like to spill motherfucking blood. But you better drop those airs you put on why don't you, and wish you never showed up. You thought you could just waltz in here and seduce a French woman, on French property, right under my nose, and not pay the consequences? Scram. I'll let you deal with the people in your village when they find out you tried to seduce a white woman and blackmail us. I'll let you figure out how to get off the premises without running into the other guy, he's begging for a chance to skin you alive. Scram, disappear, you're ever seen on this compound again, you'll be shot down by the police if necessary, like a common thief. I'm washing my hands of your fucking carcass.

ALBOURY *has vanished. Rain starts to fall.*

XVI

HORN: As for you, please don't start having a fit now. That's all we need. Oh no, no don't, I can't stand tears, they make me jump out of my fucking skin. Stop that, I'm begging you, have some dignity. Well, I sure won't be getting any more bright ideas, what a fool! Stop it. Stop, stop it, please, show some dignity. People will hear, the slightest noise carries miles around. We must be a sight to behold, I swear, what a wondrously rich image of us you give. If you could only see yourself. Be quiet! Let's go. I don't care how just be quiet. Don't breathe a minute, do whatever, take a big gulp, it'll work, it works for hiccups, just stop it. Here, drink some. (*He throws her the bottle.* LEONE *drinks.*) More, don't skimp, have some dignity, not enough of it around. Where the fuck is Cal with his truck? Cal! Jesus. You, I'm asking you, please. The guy's probably hanging around getting off on watching this disgraceful, undignified scene. You sure make white people look good. What a bright idea I had, Jesus. Leone, I'm begging you, I can't stand it. (*He's walking in every direction.*) I don't feel well, this time it's bad, really bad. (*Stops abruptly next to* LEONE. *Quietly and very fast.*) Please, what if . . . what if we left, huh? Dropped the site right now, would you . . . (*He takes her hand.*) Don't leave . . . stop crying . . . don't leave me alone. I've got enough money, we could leave without notice, Cal would take over, and in a couple of days we'd be in France or somewhere else, in Switzerland or Italy, at Lake Bolsena or Lake Constance, wherever you want. I've got enough money, plenty of it. Don't cry, don't cry, Leone, with you I . . . Say yes. Don't leave me, I'm feeling really bad now, Leone, I want to marry you, that's what we said wasn't it? Say yes!

LEONE *has straightened herself. She shatters the whiskey bottle against a rock, and quickly, while looking off into the shadows where* ALBOURY *has vanished, she takes a piece of glass and carves deep into her cheeks, without uttering a cry, similar marks to the tribal scars on* ALBOURY's *face.*

HORN: Cal! Jesus, Cal! Blood. It doesn't make any sense. Cal! There's blood everywhere.

LEONE *faints.* HORN *runs shouting towards the headlights approaching.*

XVII

At the compound, near the table. CAL *is cleaning his rifle.*

CAL: I can't do anything when it's bright. Nothing. Nothing. The watchmen would see me, they would testify. They might go to the police, I don't want to have anything to do with the police. They might run to the village, I don't want to have the village on my ass. I can't do anything, it's way too bright.

HORN: The watchmen won't do anything. Believe me they're happy to have a job, they hang on to it. Why risk it by going to the police or to the village? They're not moving. They'll see nothing hear nothing.

CAL: They let him in one time, and now this time, behind the tree, that's him again, I can hear him breathing, I don't trust the watchmen.

HORN: They didn't see him come in, they might have fallen asleep. Haven't heard them in a while. They won't do anything. They're asleep.

CAL: Asleep? You must be blind, old man. I can see them. They can see us, their eyes are half-shut but I can tell they're not sleeping and they're watching. One just shook a mosquito off his arm. That one's scratching his leg. Look, one guy just spit on the ground. Everything's too bright, I can't do a thing.

HORN: (*Pause.*) Maybe if the generator broke down.

CAL: It would have to. It has to. I can't do anything otherwise.

HORN: No, let's wait until morning: We'll put a call out over the radio and send the truck into town. Let's go, I'm setting up the mortars.

CAL: You're what?

HORN: The rockets, the flares: all my gear for the fireworks.

CAL: The sun is going to rise Horn! She's shut up in the bungalow, she won't come out to watch. She doesn't even want anybody taking care of her wounds. If she catches tetanus we're stuck. Funny kind of woman, now she's marked for life. She was cute, too. Funny. And you . . . So who do you plan to show your fireworks to, old man?

HORN: Me. I'm going to show them to me. I'm doing it for me, I bought them myself.

CAL: And what am I supposed to do? We've got to stick together, old man. We've got to fuck him up for good, now.

HORN: I trust you to do it. Just be careful, that's all.

CAL: Except now I'm cold, and I have no idea of what I'm supposed to do.

HORN: One black skin or another is the same isn't it? The village wants a body. We'll have to give them one. They won't let us have any peace until we give them a body. We wait any longer they'll be sending out two of their boys, we won't be able to do anything then.

CAL: They'll see it's not the worker. They can tell each other apart you know.

HORN: He won't be recognizable by anybody. If you can't recognize the face, who can say "That's him", or "that's somebody else!" Just the face is what's recognizable.

CAL: (*Pause.*) I can't do anything without a rifle. I don't like fighting up close, these motherfuckers do karate, they're tough. And if I use a rifle, old man, they'll see where it hit, a hole in the face that's a mark. They'll see it and we'll have the police on our ass.

HORN: So best thing is we wait until morning. Best we do everything by the rules, kid. We'll talk to the police and settle it best we can, by the rules.

CAL: Horn, Horn, I can hear him breathing. What can I do, what am I supposed to do? I don't know anymore. Don't dump me.

HORN: A truck ran him over. Who's to say "It was a rifle struck him down", or "It was lightning, or "It was a truck", who? A bullet hole doesn't look like much after a truck's gone over it.

CAL: I'm going to bed. My head is killing me.

HORN: Jerk-off.

CAL: (*Threatening.*) Don't call me a jerk-off, Horn, never again, jerk-off.

HORN: Cal, son, your nerves. (*Pause.*) What I meant is we let this one go back to the village, there'll be two or three coming back, you get two or three of them in front of you, forget it! While the other way, we could have his body brought to the village and say "This is the guy the lightning struck down yesterday at the site, see, a truck ran over him." Then everything comes back to order.

CAL: But then they'll ask about this one. They'll want to know what happened to him.

HORN: This one's not a worker, we don't have to account for him. Never seen him. We don't know anything. Well?

CAL: Just like that, cold, it's hard to do.

HORN: When there'll be a bunch of them and the watchmen start letting everybody in, what do we do then? Huh?

CAL: I don't know, what do I know? You tell me, old man.

HORN: Better kill the fox than preach to the chicken.

CAL: Yes boss.

HORN: In fact I made him go soft. That boy's dangerous no more. Can barely stand. Drank like a fish.

CAL: Yes boss.

HORN: (*Quietly*) Do it clean, middle of the face.

CAL: Yes.

HORN: Afterwards, with the truck, do it clean.

CAL: Yes.

HORN: Be very very careful.

CAL: Yes boss, yes boss.

HORN: Cal, son, you see I decided not to stay until the end.

CAL: Boss!

HORN: Yes son, that's how it goes. I'm sick of it, you know. I don't understand Africa anymore, probably needs other kinds of methods, I just don't get it anymore. So when it'll be time for you to liquidate, Cal, Jesus listen to me: don't hide anything from management, none of your bullshit, say everything, get them to be on your side. They're capable of understanding anything. They can fix anything, anything. Don't deal with the police. They have to talk to management. Nothing exists outside of the management of the firm you work for, remember that.

CAL: Yes boss.

HORN: It will be day in two hours. I'm starting the works.

CAL: What about the woman, old man?

HORN: She's going with the truck in about an hour. Never want to talk about it again. She never existed. We're all alone. Goodbye.

CAL: Horn!

HORN: What?

CAL: It's too bright, it's way too bright.

HORN *lifts his eyes towards the towers and the watchmen who are absolutely still.*

XVIII

In front of the half-open door of the bungalow.

HORN: (*Speaking into the room.*) A truck's going into town with some papers in a couple of hours. It'll honk. Be ready. The driver's excellent. In the meantime it would be dangerous for you to be outside. Lock yourself up in your room and don't go anywhere, ignore whatever you hear until you hear the honk. I'll be at work already when you leave. Goodbye. See a doctor when you arrive. I hope he'll be able to fix your face, yeah maybe a good doctor could make you presentable again and fix it. I have to ask you not to talk too much when you get back. Think what you will but don't hurt the firm. Whatever else it gave you hospitality. Don't forget that. Don't do it any harm. It is in no way responsible for what happened to you. I'm asking you this as a . . . as a favor. I've given it everything I had. For me, it's everything, everything. Think what you will of me but don't bring any harm to the firm, otherwise it would be my fault, yeah my own fault. You can do me this favor. You're going back with a plane ticket paid for with my money. You accepted the ticket that brought you here. Now you have to accept the one that'll take you back. Well, so . . . Goodbye. I won't see you again. We won't ever see each other again. No. (*He exits.*)

LEONE *appears in the doorway suitcase in her hand. Her face is still bleeding. Suddenly, the light goes out for a few seconds, and we hear the sound of the generator starting up again.*

CAL *appears.* LEONE *hides her face with her arm and keeps it there the whole time he stares at her.*

XIX

The lights black out a few more times, interrupting CAL.

CAL: Don't worry, don't worry, baby, it's the generator. Those big machines are difficult to operate. Seems like there's going to be a blackout, these things happen, Horn must be trying to fix it, don't you worry. (*Comes near her.*) I washed myself. (*He sniffs.*) I don't think I smell anymore. I put on after-shave. Do I still smell? (*Pause.*) Poor baby. I can imagine it won't be easy to find any work now, huh? Especially not in Paris. That's a bitch. (*Pause.*) Must be snowing in Paris right now, don't you think? You're right to go back. Matter of fact, I knew you would. I knew he'd make you sick in the end. I still don't get what you saw in him, in Horn. When I first saw you from a distance, when you just arrived, you were all red, beet red! With that elegance women have in Paris, that chic, so glamorous and fragile! Now look at you . . . Horn, what a stupid asshole! You don't show children what's in the basement or in the gutter. He should've known that. You let them play in the garden or on the patio but you block off the way to the basement. But despite everything, baby, you brought us some humanity, to us who work here. In the end, I can understand Horn, that old dreamer! (*He takes her hand.*) As for me, I'm glad I got to know you, baby, I'm glad you came. You probably think badly of me. Probably. I have no way of knowing. But why should I care what you think? You're going back to Paris, we'll never see each other again. Probably, you'll say bad things about me to your girlfriends, for a while, and probably, as long as you have any memories of me, they'll be bad, and in the end, they'll be gone, you won't remember me at all. Anyway, I was happy to share some ideas with you. (*He kisses her hand.*) Now, when are we ever going to see a woman, a real woman like you again, baby? Have fun with a woman, when? When will I ever see a woman again in this hole? I'm wasting my life in this hole. I'm wasting what elsewhere would've been the best years of my life. Being alone, always alone, you forget how old you are. When I saw you, I remembered. Now I have to forget again. Here, what am I? What will I always be? Nothing. It's all for the money, baby. Money takes everything away from us, even the knowledge of how old we are. Look. (*He shows his hands.*) Do these look like a young man's hands? Have you ever seen what an engineer's hands look like in France? But then what's the point of being young if you don't have money, right? In the end I wonder, I really wonder, why I keep on living. (*The lights black out for good this time.*) Don't worry. It's just a blackout. Don't go anywhere. I have to go. Farewell, baby. (*After a pause.*) Don't forget me, don't forget me.

XX

FINAL VISIONS OF A DISTANT ENCLOSURE

The first blossom of light explodes briefly and silently in the sky above the bougainvillea.

Blue streak of a rifle barrel. Dead sound of bare feet running on stone. A dog's groan. Torch lights. A whistled tune. Sound of a rifle being loaded. Fresh breath of wind.

A sun made of many colors covers the horizon and falls with a soft muffled sound, raining down in little flames over the compound.

Suddenly, ALBOURY*'s voice: out of the blackness a warrior's secret call bursts forth, and, carried by the wind, it spins and rises from the clump of trees to the barbed wire and from the barbed wire to the towers.*

The intermittent illumination of the fireworks provides the lighting, and muffled explosions the accompaniment, for CAL*'s journey towards* ALBOURY*'s motionless silhouette.* CAL *points his rifle high towards the head. Sweat rolls off his forehead and his cheeks. His eyes are bloodshot.*

From that moment onward, a cryptic dialogue between ALBOURY *and the heights on all sides grows out of the blackness between the explosions. A calm indifferent conversation; short questions and answers; laughter; an indecipherable language that reverberates and grows, spins along the barbed wire and vertically fills the entire space, rules over the dark and resonates once more over the petrified compound, in a final series of sparks and exploding suns. The first shot hits* CAL *in the arm; he drops his rifle. The watchman on top of one of the towers lowers his weapon; on the other side, another watchman raises his.* CAL *is hit in the belly, then in the head; he falls.* ALBOURY *has disappeared. Blackout.*

The day slowly rises. Cry of vultures in the sky. Empty whiskey bottles float and bump on top of open sewers. A truck honks. Bougainvillea flowers sway; each petal reflects the dawn.

LEONE: (*Far away, we can barely hear her voice, it is covered with the noises of the day; she leans towards the chauffeur.*) Haben Sie eine Sicherheitsnadel? mein Kleid geht auf. Mein Gott, wenn Sie keine bei sich haben, muss ich ganz nackt. (*She laughs, climbs into the truck*), stark naked! nach Paris zurück.[27] (*The truck drives away.*)

Near CAL's *corpse. His shattered head is crowned with the corpse of a white dog baring its teeth.* HORN *picks the rifle up from the ground, wipes his forehead and looks up towards the deserted towers.*

END OF PLAY

---

27 Do you have a safety-pin? My dress is coming apart. My God, if you don't have one, I'll have to go stark naked . . . back to Paris.

NOTEBOOKS
FOR
BATTLE OF BLACK AND DOGS

Translated by Michaël Attias

HOW ALBOURY FOUGHT AGAINST THE FIRST DOG

I wondered, "Will I be frightened by a dog?" A white stain in the night was he, running towards me and towards you, Nouofia, barking like a host of demons. One moment, his voice sounded fierce like a tiger's, the next squeaky, like that of a mouse. I could neither say, "He is huge and I must flee," nor, "He is so small one kick will send him back to meet his forbears," for a small dog's voice can be fierce and a large one's squeaky. Meanwhile the little white stain ran, and still I knew not whether to flee or fight; still I stayed and looked, I stayed and wondered, for the wind had risen anew and my soul was with you, Nouofia. By then the time to flee had past, and at last I came to know the size and strength of my enemy.

We were face to face, and his breath, short and quick, had supplanted in my ear the long breathing of the wind. At last we measured each other with our eyes, and I saw that he was small, small as a scorpion—the white stain did not grow when it ran towards us from the horizon. So bloodshot were his eyes and quick his breath that I lost all desire to send him off with a kick waltzing back to the tiny domain of his tiny forebears. My desire now was to laugh; every hair on his body stood stiff, and I asked him, "Is this how you get hard, Toubab?" But he was poised to pounce and I barely had time to ask myself, "Is it my big toe he'll bite or will he go for my thigh?" I wondered, "Where is it you wish to die, little doggie?" But I had misjudged the strength of his legs and of his viciousness. In one pounce he was at my head, and it was my head he bit and clawed with tooth and nail. He sucked my blood and dug his face and paws so deep into my hair and scalp and the bones of my head that I had to struggle to tear him off and finally squash him like an errant bug.

And then I showed him forth, Nouofia, soul, father, brother and son of my race. I held him out in my hand to you so you could see the first corpse. To you Nouofia, who was conceived in the desert and who died in the desert, I shall bring others, many others. For to the dead of my race does the toubab's death belong, and with his the death of all that is his, his women, boys, his properties and his dogs, Xac bi déllul si xac yi!

MY FIRM, BY HORN

She's my true family, if I have one it's got to be her. Good old corporation, Jesus, I've worked for her so long she knows me inside out by now, whereas I'll never get done knowing who she is. But I know that you hit one snag and lo and behold, she's there! How do they do it? Jesus, spread out the way she is, all over the world, with sites everywhere, Africa, Asia, the Middle East, America, how many thousands of men working for her? And you always feel like you're the only one she has to take care of. The brains, Jesus, the brains they must have on high, I don't want to know whoever's in control, no, I'd rather catch glimpses, here and there. But the one head controlling all of this—maybe from Paris, who knows—I'd rather not have anything to do with her. She must hit hard when she decides to, Jesus. I think about it sometimes; not often but I do. I say to myself, hell a brain like that . . . I'm not afraid of men or riots, I'm not afraid of big mouths, weapons, or wild animals; I don't even give a fuck about the war. At war, everybody's in the same boat, everybody has the same chances. But what chance do you have against a head that can keep thousands of sites, from one end of the world to the other, in her head, every last machine, truck, coin, every man like you were the last one, always, and all the way down to the whiskey bottle she knows is right where it is, all the way to the cigarette I am smoking and that she knows I'm smoking? That's the one thing that, whenever I think about it, Jesus, I get scared.

HORN AND THE WORKING-CLASS

Believe me, Mr. Alboury, I've never liked the bourgeois. You're looking at a real prole. I'm probably more one than you are, I have no family and I've worked ever since I was a child. How do I like the bourgeois? One by one or all at the same time, you bet. But I feel the same about proles, don't like them either—I mean one by one I don't. Which is to say, I don't like anybody, taken separately. I've known plenty of people and all I know is proles smell, white, black, old or young, makes no difference. I have the right to say that, I was one, I was the real thing. They stink and I don't like the smell even if it's my own. I like the smell of machines or motor grease better. I've known more than my share of proles, I wouldn't give a cent for any one of them, no way, but that never stopped me from fighting the big shots and being union. But I spit on proles. Take a sixteen-year old guy his first day in a factory . . . you know what they made me do when I was sixteen? First three months they'd give me a chunk of metal this thick, Mr. Alboury, you ever worked with metal? They'd say to me, "Flatten it." Wasn't the boss who told me to, huh, wasn't a big shot; they don't give a fuck about that. No, a prole told me to, "Make it flat, pal." And when I'd gotten all sweaty hammering it good and flat and thin as my finger, they'd throw it in the junk heap, sir, give me another one and better shut the fuck up. And the point of all that? To break the worker; that's how they say it yeah: break him in, break him down. Workers break each other down so they can all look the same. A prole on his own is as sick-minded as a boss is; but without the wealth it's even more disgusting, sir, and all the more unforgivable.

WORKERS' GRAVES

The women cover the bodies of dead workers with branches and palm fronds to protect them from the sun and the vultures. By day, when the site is active, trucks drive over them, and, at night, the women come back to lay new branches. After a few days and a few nights, the branches and flesh mingle and form little mounds that dissolve and gradually merge with the earth.

LEONE

Upon her arrival coming down the airplane ramp, threads of spider webs land on her face and a heat on her shoulders that is thick as mud. She sees eagles circle the sunless and cloudless sky, she sees black hawks perched on top of a swollen corpse, obese and white from putrefaction, floating gently down the river—she stifles a small cry and hand over her mouth, lets out:

Ooh, what a tiny grain of sand we are!

LEONE SEES SOMEONE BENEATH THE BOUGAINVILLAE

All of a sudden, I want to make something for you, but "Fragile!", don't move, let yourself go, I see it already in my mind's eye. I'll measure you up and down you'll barely notice, I sew fast, my needle work is lightning quick. I want to take this Black and clothe him, take this shadow and brighten it. Give me your stillness one second only. I want to gather these bits of mauve, turquoise, purple, these tiny flowers, crimson, scarlet and vermilion, and sew them all by hand. I'll carve to shape, flare the sleeves, alter at the hip. Whip-stitched collar to waist, fringed at the edges and hemmed. I'll cover the back with bees' nests and do the shoulders in spider-stitch. I'll glide the neck and drape you in devil-stitch. I want to envelop you in my fancies and braided embroidering, I want to robe, adorn, and saturate you. Black, O most beautiful color, if you let me I'll dye your breast-pocket with moss and line it with orchids and thorns, gently, lovingly, you'll barely notice, I'll embroider your name in gold against earth shadow!

NOUOFIA'S MOTHER

When Nouofia's mother learned of her son's death on the White Man's construction site, she decided, against all warnings, to risk a journey there, so she could lay branches on the body and protect it from the birds. Nevertheless, as a precaution, she painted her face white so that Death prowling in the vicinity would not recognize her for who she was.

CAL, REVERIES OF AN INSOMNIAC ENGINEER

Too many nights, one every twenty-four hours, whatever you do. And long, they're way too long with all the nameless creatures that creep and dwell in the dark as we do in the daylight which is our natural element, theirs is night, they hide behind trees, along walls, low in the grass, up in the palms, and on moonless nights, hidden behind along the inside nothing there at all, night is enough. Yet can anybody know the number and the size, the intent and the goal, of all that creeping or not has as its natural element, night? By day then it is that one must stalk, pursue, catch, kill, slaughter, exterminate and pulverize anything recognizable as a potential threat.

Catch a spook at high noon and cut him up in four with a good machete, and each piece again in four makes sixteen pieces. And, before night comes, when they're harmless, cut each of the sixteen pieces again in four. That'll make sixty-four pieces of neutralized spook, and then again each piece cut it up in four and four and four, and again once more, until you now have sixteen thousand three hundred and eighty-four little pieces, all black, tiny, and harmless; now divide the earth into the same number of parts and bury in each one, as far down as you can, one little nigger-bit. Will I finally be able to sleep then?

What I believe is that from each of the sixteen thousand three hundred and eighty-four parts—four to the seventh power—of the sleeping world, a whole new spook will arise, huge and powerful, an even more fearsome motherfucker! I believe this is how they reproduce.

When will I sleep with no worry and no nightmares?

LEONE

Upon her arrival, in the car that picked her up at the airport, she looks out at the Africans on the side of the road, in the markets, sitting in front of their houses; busy, or sluggish, angry, laughing; while Horn sitting next to her wipes his forehead:
Crazy what a little sun will do to a man!

THE SITE, LIT BY LIGHTNING

An inverted field out to infinity—where plants grow their roots upwards towards the sky and bury their foliage deep. A small panicky white dog scrambles between the legs of an enormous buffalo that huffs and puffs and tramples the ground, while everywhere around gurgling mud bubbles up between clumps of smoky black earth.

THE CONTEMPT FOR MONEY AMONG THE OLD COLONIALISTS, ACCORDING TO HORN

Guys back then did with their money what you're supposed to do, Jesus, they knew how to spend! I remember one, a fine lush, at the cabaret in town, wanting to buy the piano. He lays out the cash but the doorway's too small and the piano can't get through, so he has it chopped down the middle, takes out the pieces and throws them in the sea. Another one, his wife cheated on him, she loved lingerie, so he buys up all the women's lingerie that the one merchant, who comes through every six months, has in stock; puts it all in a big heap and burns it in the town square; let's see you dress now. I remember another guy, he'd stay drunk four straight months out of the year and keep anybody else drunk who wanted to at his expense, until he'd blown all of his money. In the end, his body blew out too, he'd earned too much. Yes, that's all that money is good for.

THE COLONIALISTS' DREAM OF THE COUNTRY HOME, ACCORDING TO HORN

They all dream of France, but they all stay. They all talk about a house in the French countryside, and spend years drawing the blueprints, but you couldn't drag one of them out of here even if there were two of you. Sure, they bitch, sure they do, but I know one thing: wherever there's cash, once a person gets a taste, no kick in the ass will ever make him budge from his spot. And in Africa, there is cash to be made. So with all their talk of France and the countryside, I've never gotten a single postcard from any one of those dreamers.

CAL: YET ANOTHER NIGHTMARE

Africa is all sex. Everything is concentrated in the reproductive organs. Look at avocado pits, look at the fruits and the plants; it's horrible, it's disturbing to me.

When I got near the corpse, I took a good luck; and I saw that dead, even dead, even completely dead, the motherfucker had a hard-on!

CLICHES ABOUT HUNGER

HORN
  A Negro is never hungry and is never sated. He can eat a lot or very little, any time of the day or night, or go without eating anything at all for a long time. Don't base your opinion on European eating habits; a Negro doesn't experience hunger or satisfaction the way a European does; he eats what's there when it's there. And you can be sure he makes the most of every bit of food he ingurgitates.

CAL
  A spook? Hungry? Just look at them: they're twice as big and strong as we are!

WHAT ARE WOMEN THINKING? LEONE WONDERS.
  When I look at two people, one black one white, man or woman, one rich one poor, I say, "What are women thinking?" There had to have been a woman to give her teat and listen to their bawling without squashing either of them under her heel. And yet the little shrews must know that when they make one or the other, it'll have to be either a bully or a bullied. Which one's better? Can they tell me? And yet they keep right on producing massive quantities of them, knowing full well, silly shrews, that they're either feeding a bully who will start by bullying them first, or bringing somebody up for the bully to beat on. Spare me all the possible combinations, mixtures of white and female, rich and negro, poor and white, negro and male, they're no better: half bully–half bullied, they spend their lives split down the middle beating themselves up until there's nothing left. As for the women who hit the jackpot and do not shudder to produce a white male, and rich too while they're at it! Or the others, who nurse and cuddle the unspeakable: a black female poor as a church mouse, what in the world are they thinking? I tell you, they're the ones who should be squashed under a heel.

HORN ON AFRICANS

Who'll get Africa in the end, the Americans or the Russians? Noone knows, but who really cares? Africans certainly don't. And they're right not to. Africans have healthy minds and unsullied skulls, exactly what we do not. Let me explain: what makes them laugh, and what makes us laugh? I believe why you laugh is the best indication of how healthy your mind is. And what puts a smile on a European's face? Word games, references, quotes, things so complicated I'm not sure even I can understand them anymore . . . But with an African, all it takes is rain, three drops fall on their shoulders and they go nuts; it tickles. And if it pours, they're rolling on the floor, they're dying. That's what I call clear, healthy, unsullied minds. When it rains in Paris, well . . . I for one have learned from them how to enjoy such things. What I get pleasure from is watching them in the morning by the river when they wash. When they're all soaped up, head to foot, all white and covered with suds, they dive in, and . . .and I when see the water rinse them, and they come out, laughing so much, I can't help laughing too and enjoying it myself. I ask myself, "Who will win in Africa, who will lose?" Nobody knows. But they will never suffer. They'll go on laughing, squatting in the sun and waiting. Something else I learned from them, the pleasure of doing nothing for hours, thinking nothing, staring off into nowhere . . .

LEONE'S CONCEPT OF REINCARNATION

My personal belief is that in your first life you're a man like that horrible guy, Cal; men like that understand so little, they're stupid and thick, it has to be their first life, the scoundrels! I believe that only after many ridiculous and limited lives as a man, brutal and brawling as all men's lives are, can a woman be born. And only after many lives as a woman, many useless adventures, many unfulfilled dreams and many tiny deaths, only then can a Negro be born, in whose blood flow more lives and deaths, more acts of brutality and failure, more tears than in any other blood. And as for me, how many more times will I have to die, how many more useless memories and experiences will I have to stack up within me?

When is the life I will finally fully live?

CAL'S EMOTIONAL STATES

Cal never suffers nor does he ever feel happy. Nevertheless, sometimes a sweet, calm and peaceful world stretches out before him, and sometimes the universe is one wasteland after the other, prey to onslaughts of heat and hideous storms.

A VISION OF DAWN

Above the compound and the village, a heavy colored fog produced by the evaporation of an entire night's worth of dreams mingling above the roofs, by alcohol and loathing, cooked and vaporized through the pores of the skin and the breathing of sleepers, by human heat.

CAL:

So faint two soiled fingers might have traced them, two creases go from the outer edge of each eye to the cheek's hollow; and very deep-set, vertical, a dimple almost, on the right side close to the lips, is a wrinkle.

In his innermost self: a large green bird flies over the prairie, holding in its claws a puppy with women's eyes, and its panting close to the ear.

LEONE:

One around each eye, two wrinkles only, two perfect identical circles.

In her innermost self: at an age when it is difficult to tell a girl from a boy, a child lies in the grass and carries on its face and in every part of its body the burden of a sadness much older than its years.

HORN:

One reads the age of a tree when it's cut: with him too, one counts the slow deposit of wrinkles around his eyes and mouth, the furrows.

In his innermost self: an old woman, unknown, all dressed in black, face in shadow, comes regularly every night and sits by his side until morning, never saying a word, never making a sound; he could swear he doesn't know who she is.

WEST PIER

Translated by Marion Schoevaert
and Theresa M. Weber

The end of all flesh arose in my spirit.
- Genesis

I would like to see the shade and tree where I can rest my head.
- Burning Spear

An abandoned neighborhood of a large western port city separated from downtown by a river. A deserted warehouse on the old pier.

MAURICE KOCH, *sixty.*
MONIQUE PONS, *forty-two.*
CECILE, *sixty.*
Her daughter CLAIRE, *fourteen.*
Her husband RODOLFE, *fifty-eight.*
CHARLES, *their son, twenty-eight.*
A young man nicknamed FAK, *about twenty-two.*
An unnamed man in his thirties who, in the beginning, Charles called "ABAD" *two or three times.*

At the dawn of a snowstorm, two years before—Charles was warned, by the workers he passed every morning boarding the ferry at the pier, of a strange and disturbing presence lying along the outside walls of the warehouse. He went there and spotted some kind of mound, dark and immobile, half-covered by snow, looking vaguely like a dead or sleeping wild boar. He approached it. When he was two yards away, the form suddenly stood up, tall, large, trembling, bright-eyed and with a cap of snow on its head; it spoke a few unintelligible words, so unintelligible they made Charles laugh. Charles caught the final sound, probably English, possibly Arabic (a sound which he temporarily used to name the creature). Then, because he was in an excellent mood, he took it by the arm, led it into the warehouse, and found a spot where the stranger could be sheltered from the snow. He arranged some cardboard boxes to keep him warm, and after watching him burrow into them, emitting an intense steam along his entire body, Charles walked away whistling and returned home.

He stopped to orient himself. Suddenly he glanced at his feet.
His feet had disappeared.
- Victor Hugo

Facing a wall of darkness.
The sound of an idling car engine nearby.

(MONIQUE *enters.*)

MONIQUE: Now what? Which way? Where? How? Jesus Christ! This way? There's a wall. We can't go any further. No, it's not even a wall, it's nothing; maybe a street, a house, maybe the river, a wasteland, a big disgusting hole, I can't see anything, I'm exhausted. I can't go on. I'm hot, my feet hurt, I don't know where to go, Christ!

If suddenly, out of nowhere, someone or something came out of this black hole. What do I do? What do I do if some guy, a couple guys, a thousand guys showed up all around me? Sure, I could act natural, but here, right now, dressed like this! I'd look like a fool! I hear something. I hear some dogs. This place is full of wild dogs crawling through the rubble. I should have tried to bring the car up here. Maybe with the headlights on, at least we could see what's crawling around on the ground.

It's a wall Maurice. We can't go any further. Tell me, what do we do now? What hole do you want us to fall in?

(*Enter* KOCH.)

KOCH: I know exactly where I am.

MONIQUE: Exactly, oh really, you are so smart. Exactly. Hooray. Figure it out yourself then, since you know everything so exactly. After all, I'm not your mother, I'm not your wife, I'm not your nanny, I don't have to risk my neck for your whims.

KOCH: You don't have to risk anything Monique. Go home.

MONIQUE: You want me to leave? I have the car keys.

KOCH: I'll find my own way back.

MONIQUE: You? The way? Your way? What way? Jesus Christ! You can't even drive. You don't even know left from right. You would have never found this damn place without me. You are absolutely incapable of doing anything by yourself. I'd like to see you find your own way back.

KOCH: I'll call a cab.

MONIQUE: Oh really. A cab. Hooray. Do you see a phone here? Do you? Just wait for a car to pass by. Go ahead. Wait. Jesus Christ! We are lost in this disgusting hole and you're talking about a cab.

KOCH: There's a ferry that crosses to the new pier twice a day. I remember very well where it departs. It comes at six. I'll take it.

MONIQUE: What about me? What should I do? I can't leave you alone here, I can't leave without you because I'm the one who knows how to drive; I'm the one responsible for bringing you here, and you can't do anything by yourself, with your freaking boat that might not even exist anymore. Really, look like a fool. They could at least leave the streetlights on; we could see something. There's something slippery on the ground and I don't know what it is. You know, in my family, I was notorious for my ability to see clearly in the dark, they even quit locking me in the basement to frighten me. But I've never seen this much darkness before. I should never have left the keys in the car. That would be the icing on the cake if someone goes and steals it. Christ! It would take hours to get out of this place on foot with no lights or street signs. Besides, I think someone is watching us, Maurice, I'm sure of it.

Pause. Sound of car engine in the distance.

There used to be street lights here; it was a normal, vibrant middle-class neighborhood, I remember it very well. There were parks with trees; there were cars; cafes and shops; there were old people crossing the street, children in strollers; the old warehouses were used as parking lots and flea markets. It was a neighborhood for artists and retired people, an ordinary and innocent world. It wasn't that long ago.

But today, Christ! Doesn't matter who, the most innocent person who gets lost here in the middle of the afternoon could be slaughtered in broad daylight, their body thrown into the river without anyone even thinking to look for them here.

And why? Because rents are too low. They should have encouraged the landlords to raise the rents; they should have been forced to raise them, even if they didn't want to. The roaches, the rats and the roaches, have infiltrated this place like conquering soldiers; the landlords have left the walls cracked, the broken windows haven't been replaced, the old people died; so finally the merchants were forced to flee the neighborhood; and today all these buildings, miles of streets lined with buildings aren't worth a cent, not a nickel to anyone, nothing at all, nothing. It's disgusting. God knows what lives here now. God knows what's watching us.

Pause. Silence.

Let's go, Maurice; you aren't saying a word anyway and I don't intend to talk to myself all evening; the engine is running, let's go. (*Silence.* KOCH *moves further toward the darkness.*) Don't go over there, Maurice, the ground is slippery and you're not wearing proper dress shoes. (*Long silence.*) Maurice, Maurice, this world is not for the living. (*Silence.* KOCH *has disappeared into the darkness.*) Where are you? I can't see anything. I can't hear anything. The engine! I can't hear the car anymore.
    Don't leave me alone. Don't leave me alone.

We hear the crash of water against the rocks.

    Maurice!

A sudden break in the clouds briefly illuminates the huge facade of the warehouse and the deserted highway upon which falls a hushed rain of leaves; then darkness returns, leaving the sound of water lapping against the walls.

MONIQUE: Jesus Christ!

****

Inside the warehouse. Entrance faces the highway.

(*Enter* KOCH *who leans against the doorway.*)

KOCH: Would you please be so kind as to help me across this warehouse and take me to the river bank, where there's a good view of the new port, where the ferry leaves. I'm too clumsy to cross it alone; and could you help me find two stones to put in my pockets? I promise that's all I'll ask.

Please forgive my intrusion; I'll make as little noise as possible. Please believe I am innocent of whatever you may be imagining, of anything anybody would suspect, naturally, at seeing a man in this state, here and now, and with who-knows-what intention. I'm sure a thousand things are running through your head, a thousand reasons, which are all wrong. You must believe me.

It's true, I don't have the proper shoes to walk in this place and my memory is not good enough to lead me in the darkness. Everything is so different. Actually, I definitely need someone to help me across; maybe then, there'll be enough light for me to find the stones myself; then I'll thank you and we'll leave it at that.

The problem is money, cash, coins, bills, it's been a while since they passed through my hands, it's been a while, you know, since coins, bills were carried around—like in the Middle Ages I guess, but I don't know anything about History—I keep enough for a drink or to buy some cigarettes, but since I quit smoking and very rarely drink alcohol, I carry credit cards. I'd like to leave you my credit cards, if you know how to use them. I know it isn't easy, but if you do know how, then, good for you. I don't give a damn. (*He takes a few steps into the half-light, puts his wallet on the ground and backs up again.*)

It's not far from here, maybe two hundred feet. I'm sure this is the warehouse where you can take the ferry. That's where I want to go. I guess it's a good reason, good enough for me to be here anyway; but what do you care, it's still where I want to go. (*He searches his pockets.*)

Here's a lighter. It's a Zippo. I think it works with some kind of refill, I don't know anything about it, but anyway it works, I brought it on purpose; and some gold cuff-links; and a ring. (*He removes it from his finger.*)

All bullshit. (*He steps forward, puts the objects on the ground and backs up.*)

I don't want to leave my watch just lying around; someone could step on it. It's a Rolex, it runs on some kind of battery I think, what do I know, I don't know anything about it; anyway it's one of the most expensive, and you don't have to wind it.

(*He removes it from his arm.*) I swear it hurts to take this one off. I think it's because I bought it myself, on a whim, one day in a jewelry store in Geneva; not like this ring or the rest, presents, bullshit. That's why it bothers me to leave it on the ground. (*He holds out his hand.*)

Sound of birds taking flight nearby.

Please, be careful; be careful not to step on it. (*He steps forward, puts the watch on the ground, and returns to his place.*)

Now I have nothing left, help me

(CHARLES *grabs his arm.*)

***

CHARLES: (*Quietly*) The others are waiting for you, on the other side, over there. Assholes. Like you'd show up on the river, in a patrol boat in broad daylight. But I knew you'd come from back there, from the darkness, along the walls, like a bastard; I knew it because I'd have done the same if I were you. Maybe you didn't think you'd find someone as clever as you are here; but you're dead wrong if you think we're all assholes. That's why, trust me, you'll get nothing on us, no fuck ups, not a single crime, nothing. Not from me anyway, speaking for myself.

Even before you got out of your car, I spotted it. I heard the engine; I even knew its make, a Jaguar. I'd know it even if it were only the thought of a Jaguar crossing someone else's mind, that's why I'm here.

When I found out the other day that the ferry wasn't stopping here anymore, I told the others: don't be nervous, maybe there's a strike, maybe it's broken down, maybe the boat's too old, maybe whatever. But when the kid came by while I was sleeping and told me: there's no more running water, I thought right away: so they've decided to do something. I knew right away, you don't cut off the water for no reason. Water's the last thing cut off, because fires might spread. When it comes to this, you know they've decided to drive every last rat out from its hole. But you forget that rats are more clever than men. Speaking for myself.

I told the others: careful, they've got their eyes on you, they're watching you, you're under surveillance, they'll prey on your every breath, your slightest move, your secret dream; and if, from over there, from across the river, they suspect the slightest illegality in your breath or dreams, they'll come running and tear it from the silence and darkness of your hole, they'll fatten it up and make it grow, they'll turn it into a crime to show to the entire city, they'll call us scum, and we'll be the deserving assholes.

(*More quietly*) You want us out of here? You have to be more rat than a rat to like it here. There are no more cafes, or clubs, or women; there are no more roads, or electricity, no more boats, no more water. I have a job, a real job, waiting for me in the harbor whenever I want, as a nightclub bouncer. Listen, I don't have any reason to hurt you, not me, look, I don't have any reason not to help you. I don't have a reason to be nervous; I have time and I have patience. Remember, old man, remember whatever happens, I'm on your side.

Don't forget, you're the one who asked me to go over there; and if I help you, it's only because I'm on your side. Insomnia makes people nervous. At night we don't sleep because we used to work, during the day we don't sleep because we don't work anymore. So we never sleep. But I don't need to sleep, I'm not nervous, ever. I am cool and in theory I am on your side.

That's why I was waiting for you here, along these walls, in the darkness, behind the walls, like a bastard; but I can already tell you that you're wasting your time. You won't find anything here. Look around, you won't find anything; check the corners, dig in the ground, pick everybody's brain; nothing's left, not even in the slightest dream, nowhere. There is only wisdom, everywhere.

(*He escorts* KOCH *across the warehouse.*)

("Who are you? He who saw the devil, who are you? I'm trying to say it: I was coming back one night through the big garden with my school bag, I saw a man under the streetlight with his back turned, as I got closer to him, he turned his head, only his head, he had scaly pink skin and blue eyes, I dropped my bag and ran back home. I was trying to say it; who are you? An idea is as slow getting to my head as an ant traveling from my foot to my hair but I'm trying to say it: One night my father woke up just as he wakes up when my brothers are coughing and trembling with fever and I wasn't coughing and I didn't have a fever but he looked at me. That morning he told the women not to comb my hair anymore like they combed my brothers' hair, not to feed me anymore, and that I shouldn't live under the same roof as my brothers. Then, he tore my name away from me and threw it in the river with the garbage. I'm trying to say it: some children are born without color, born for the shadows and hiding places with white hair and white skin and colorless eyes, condemned to run from the shade of one tree to the shade of another and to bury themselves in the sand at mid-day when the sun spares no place on earth. For them destiny beats a drum like a leper rings a bell and everyone goes along; for others, a beast lives in their heart, remains secret and only speaks up when silence reigns; it's the lazy beast that stretches while everyone is sleeping, and nibbles man's ear so he remembers it; but the more I say it the more I conceal it; that's why I won't try anymore, stop asking me who I am." Says Abad.)

***

The pier. A soft white light floats over the river.

(*Enter* CHARLES.)

Foghorn in the distance, muffled.

(*Enter* KOCH.)

Birds taking flight.

KOCH: (*Quietly*) I'm afraid.

CHARLES: (*Quietly*) Why?

KOCH: I'm afraid. I don't know why.

CHARLES: You have a gun?

KOCH: A gun? No. Why?

CHARLES: A cop wouldn't come to a place like this without a gun.

KOCH: I'm not a cop.

CHARLES: Work for the city?

KOCH: No.

CHARLES: Work for yourself?

KOCH: No.

CHARLES: What then?

KOCH: Nothing. Nobody. No one.

CHARLES: If that's true, you should be afraid. (*Very quietly*) Are those Westons?

KOCH: What?

CHARLES: Your shoes.

KOCH: I don't buy my own shoes. (*Even more quietly*) Who is that?

CHARLES: Who?

KOCH: The one, in the shadows, watching me.

CHARLES: (*Even more quietly*) Don't be nervous. Do you have a weapon?

KOCH: I already told you, no.

CHARLES: Nobody would come here without a weapon, without a reason.

KOCH: I have my reasons.

CHARLES: Then you have a weapon.

KOCH: No.

CHARLES: If that's true, then you are crazy old man.

(CHARLES *moves toward* ABAD. ABAD *and* CHARLES *whisper to each other.* CHARLES *returns to* KOCH.)

CHARLES: (*To* KOCH) He wants to know who you're looking for.

KOCH: No one.

CHARLES: Then, why are you here?

KOCH: To die; I am here to die.

CHARLES: (*Quietly*) Who wants you dead?

KOCH: Nobody. Me.

CHARLES: Why?

KOCH: I have a problem, a money problem. I have to account for some money that was entrusted to me, but the money no longer exists. To make a long story short, it's about church money. I don't want to go before the Board of Directors. It's a question of reputation, you might say. My reputation's taking a nosedive. I don't give a damn that my reputation's sinking, that doesn't bother me. I just don't want to watch the plunge.

CHARLES: (*Quietly*) This isn't a good place to skip out of prison.

KOCH: I'm not avoiding prison, who's talking about prison? Can you picture some nuns dragging an honorable man to court, a man they trusted, with complete confidence, with the management of their money? I have neither the will nor the energy to rebuild my character.

CHARLES: (*More quietly*) Why don't you flee the country with the money?

KOCH: What money? I'm telling you I don't know what happened to it. (*After a pause*) I can't remember. Day by day, maybe. Taking a little one day, a little the next day, maybe. I don't recall any big expenses. I have a modest lifestyle. I don't recall any outrageous expenses these last few years. They shouldn't allow someone who is about to retire to become the trustee of charitable funds without anyone to keep an eye on him.

CHARLES: (*After a pause, to* ABAD) He came by car. He's not a cop. He has no weapon. He has no good reason. He's nuts.

(ABAD *whispers in* CHARLES *ear, who then returns to* KOCH.)

CHARLES: He wants to know why you want to settle your dirty business here.

KOCH: I used to know this neighborhood. I was looking for a place that resembles me. I just want you to let me get close to the river, and let me pick up two rocks. I won't make a sound. I don't want to get beat up or hurt. I have nothing left to give.

CHARLES: Did you come alone?

KOCH: Yes. Except for a woman.

CHARLES: A woman?

KOCH: She drives the car. She's probably still over there.

CHARLES: That's it?

KOCH: That's it.

CHARLES: (*Abruptly*) Is there a strike in the harbor?

KOCH: A strike? I don't know. A strike? Why are you talking about a strike? I guess there are always strikes. Besides, I live on the other side of the city, I don't have anything to do with the harbor and I never go outside.

(ABAD *and* CHARLES *whisper together for a long time.*)

CHARLES: (*To* KOCH) He doesn't want to.

KOCH: Why?

CHARLES: He says a body would attract the police.

KOCH: Bullshit. The whole business will be kept quiet. Do you want me to write a note that'll clear your name? You can give it to that woman.

CHARLES: He doesn't want to.

KOCH: Tell him with the two rocks in my pockets, my body will stick to the bottom and no one will see anything.

CHARLES: He says no.

KOCH: Beg him.

CHARLES: No. (*Quietly*) What will you give me, in exchange?

KOCH: I already gave you everything I have. You didn't even bother to pick up the watch.

CHARLES: I don't pick things up.

KOCH: Take the car.

CHARLES: You didn't give me any money.

KOCH: I gave you my credit cards.

CHARLES: No money.

KOCH: But that is money; I don't know of any other kind of money.

CHARLES: In your pockets.

KOCH: I've emptied my pockets. Take my jacket if you like, and shut up about the money. What more do you want? Twenty dollars here, twenty dollars there, alcohol and cigarettes. Bullshit. Bills and coins are a poor man's money, the currency of savages. My credit cards are money, and my Rolex, and my car. It's parked two blocks from here. Don't tell me a car isn't money.

CHARLES: (*To* ABAD) He's not answering the questions. I think he's completely crazy.

(KOCH *approaches the water, picks up two rocks.* CHARLES *goes to him, restrains him by his jacket.*)

CHARLES: (*To* KOCH, *very quietly*) Are you really going to do it?

KOCH: Yes.

CHARLES: Why? You have everything you want, you can go wherever you want. You've got cash I can smell it; the smell stings my eyes. Why would you do that?

KOCH: Let go of me.

CHARLES: The keys?

KOCH: They're probably in the car.

CHARLES: And the woman?

KOCH: She's your problem.

CHARLES: And your shoes?

KOCH: Those I keep. (CHARLES *lets* KOCH *go*.)

(CHARLES *looks at* ABAD, ABAD *looks at* KOCH, KOCH *puts two stones in his pockets.*)

***

The second day, shortly after dawn, as he was resting on his berth, his first mate came to tell him that a foreign sail was entering the bay.
- Melville

The highway. Night. The sound of water against the walls.

(*Enter* FAK, *followed by* CLAIRE.)
(*They stop at the warehouse entrance.*)

FAK: You've come this far, now go in.

CLAIRE: It's way too dark in there for me to go in.

FAK: It's no darker in there than out here.

CLAIRE: Exactly, it's completely dark out here.

FAK: It's not completely dark out here since I can see you.

CLAIRE: Well, I can't see you, so for me it's completely dark.

FAK: If you go in there with me, I'll tell you something about something that I'll tell you only if we both go in there.

CLAIRE: I can't go in there; my brother would kill me.

FAK: Your brother won't know.

CLAIRE: Even if he won't know, I don't want to go in.

FAK: So why did you follow me this far?

CLAIRE: I came this far just to get some fresh air, because I've drunk too much coffee and because it was too hot in my house, not to do anything with you.

FAK: I'm not asking you to do anything, just leave it to me, I'll take you in there and I'll take care of everything.

CLAIRE: It's too dark in there, I'm too young and I'm scared.

FAK: There are holes in the roof and the walls; it's not as dark in there as out here because of the harbor lights coming in from the other side.

CLAIRE: And how am I supposed to know that, and not be scared?

FAK: Just close your eyes, that's how.

CLAIRE: That's stupid; if I close my eyes it's completely dark.

FAK: If you close your eyes, how it is outside, dark or not dark, it's all the same. You could pretend it's bright as day. Your eyes are just closed, and I lead you, and we both go in, and you'll open them when I tell you to, and you'll see it's not even worth it to open them ever.

CLAIRE: If at least there were a streetlight, I could see the door and I could say I'm going in or I'm not going in. But now I can't even see the door and I don't know if I want to or not. I think, I don't want to because I don't see the door, and if I didn't know there was one because I see it every day in the daylight, I wouldn't even know there is one; and if you weren't talking to me, I wouldn't even know if it was you here or somebody else. And either way I'm scared to death.

FAK: You shouldn't be scared for so long and at some point you should stop being a little girl.

CLAIRE: Besides, I know exactly why you want me to go in there and that's why I don't want to; because I know exactly what that's all about.

FAK: If you're so little, you can't know exactly why I want both of us to go in there, and if you knew exactly why we would go in there, then you're not so little after all. Stop talking so much, go in there and that's it.

CLAIRE: Maybe I don't know completely exactly because I'm still a little little, but I'm sure that it's not very very good because my brother would kill me if he saw me here with you right now.

FAK: How do you know it's not very good since you don't know at all how it is?

CLAIRE: Maybe I don't know how it is because I'm little, but it's not because I'm still a little little that you can tell me anything you want and I'll swallow it whole, duh!

FAK: Then tell me please, how could you know how good it is or not since you've never tried it with anyone? And, if you'd tried it and you told me: it isn't good at all, then I would say: too bad, let's not go in. But I know that if you had tried, you wouldn't say: it isn't good at all, but you'd say: it's definitely good, and you'd go in without so much talk. I know you don't know anything; first you have to try it and only afterwards you can say: I know.

CLAIRE: Then, why don't you start telling me here what you said you had to tell me?

FAK: Not here. I'll tell you in there and I'll give you something afterwards.

CLAIRE: What?

FAK: I'll give it to you afterwards.

CLAIRE: Of course, I'm not saying, maybe, one day I won't go in there like if someone very very cute one day tells me: go in there; the problem here is I know who you are, I see you every day, and even if it's dark now, I remember what you're like; so, I hate to say this because it isn't very nice, but you are not so cute that I'd say: all right I'll go in there with this one and forget all the others.

FAK: The truth is, you don't know if a boy is cute or not cute, there's no way you could know about boys.

CLAIRE: Oh please, and why don't I know? That's stupid. I still know how to look at people and say: he's cute, or: he is not cute. It's not up to you to say: I am very very cute. In life, it's up to other people to say whether you're cute or not. Otherwise it would be too easy. Every day I see a ton of people, I'm not completely stupid, I can easily choose and say: I'd go in with this one, I wouldn't with that one.

FAK: You won't always be able to look at boys like a little girl, and right now you don't even know where to look at a boy and how you should judge him; after you've tried some you'll say: what a fool I was to say, this boy is cute and that boy there isn't cute, and now, I know he is.

CLAIRE: If I go in there then, what did you say you'd give me?

FAK: (*Holding out his hand in a fist*) A lighter.

CLAIRE: I don't even smoke.

FAK: It's gold, with some initials. (*He shows it to her.*)

CLAIRE: (*Holding out her hand*) So then all right, I'll take it.

FAK: I'll give it to you if you go in there with me.

CLAIRE: (*Withdrawing her hand*) Then no, I won't take it. When you give something, you give it and that's it, you don't ask for anything else, so there.

FAK: Exactly, I'm not asking for anything.

CLAIRE: What do you mean you're not asking for anything? That's stupid.

FAK: I'm not asking you to say: yes, I'll go in there with you, I'm asking you not to say: no, I won't go; so I'm asking you not to do something; I'm not asking you to do something; whereas if you don't go, you refuse, so you are doing something, I haven't asked you to do that, just the opposite.

CLAIRE: My brother will kill me.

FAK: Nobody will know.

CLAIRE: There is a lady, behind you, watching us.

(FAK *turns around.* MONIQUE *is there.*)

***

MONIQUE: Did you hear a splash? I'm sure I heard the sound of a man falling into the water. (*She brusquely approaches* FAK) It's his, Maurice, his lighter, what have you done with him?

We hear a body fall into the water on the other side of the warehouse.

Jesus Christ! I knew it. (*She rushes to* CLAIRE.) Be a nice little girl, show me the way, I've got to get him out of there. The water must be ice cold, and dirty, full of oil and he doesn't know how to swim. I can't see a thing, I'm lost, show me the way. (FAK *laughs*) Here's some money, I'm giving you some money and I'll give you more later. (FAK *laughs*) Little brat. I won't give you anything at all. (*She heads in one direction.*)

CLAIRE: It's not that way, not that way at all.

MONIQUE: You want me to beg, that's disgusting. (*She heads in another direction.*)

CLAIRE: It's not that way either, not at all.

MONIQUE: Why are you being so mean? What have I done to you? Why are you so stupid? Show me where to start, just the direction, at least give me a hint.

CLAIRE: Take my shoe. (*She holds her shoe out to* MONIQUE.)

MONIQUE: I don't give a shit about your shoe.

CLAIRE: Then I'm not showing you the way.

MONIQUE: Give it to me then, give me your shoe. (*She takes it.*) What should I do with it, Christ! Hurry up. I don't have all day.

CLAIRE: If you're in such a hurry, I can't take you. I can't run with only one shoe.

MONIQUE: Jesus Christ! (*She rushes to* FAK) Help me, sir. (CLAIRE *laughs.*) I won't say a word about the car. I know you took the keys, but I won't say anything. We'll walk back. I'll manage. Please take me to him so I can get him out. (FAK *holds out his hand.*) I knew it; you seem like an incredibly nice guy; you'll be rewarded for your help. (*Just when she's about to enter the warehouse where* FAK *is leading her*) It's way too dark in there. I don't want to go in there. There must be another way.

FAK: There are holes in the roof, and the harbor lights coming in from the other side; there is no other way.

MONIQUE: Oh please, come on, you think I'm an idiot?

Sound of body falling into the water a second time.

This time it's too late: He's lost. (*To* FAK) Stupid fool, with that face you won't get a mile in that car without being stopped by the police; you'd better give me those keys right away, before I make a scene. (*She begins to cry.*) Fine, let him die, let him drown, let his stomach bloat, let him be gobbled up by the fish, let him turn to seaweed, oyster, I don't care. I'm really sick of this bullshit.

(*Enter* KOCH, *soaking wet, carried by* CHARLES.)

MONIQUE: Jesus Christ! (*To* CLAIRE) Don't sit there like a statue, you little brat; can't you see he's soaking wet? Find some towels. (*To* FAK) Give me those keys, hurry up; I have no intention of rotting in this hole until dawn. (*To* CHARLES) You, put him down.

CHARLES: (*To* MONIQUE) He broke his ankle.

MONIQUE: (*To* CHARLES) Idiot. Give him to me. (*To* CLAIRE) Well?

CLAIRE: (*To* MONIQUE) I don't know you; I'm not your maid.

CHARLES: (*To* CLAIRE) Claire, hurry up.

MONIQUE: (*To* CLAIRE) And also a shirt for some bandages.

CHARLES: (*To* CLAIRE) What happened to your shoe?

MONIQUE: (*To* CLAIRE) Let's go, hurry up.

CLAIRE: Look. (*She laughs, points to the sky, dawn breaks suddenly.*)

(KOCH *faints in* MONIQUE's *arms.*)
(CHARLES *approaches* FAK, *but bumps into* CLAIRE *who pulls him along the warehouse.*)

***

By the warehouse, pink light of dawn.

(FAK *watches* CLAIRE *and* CHARLES *from a distance, pretending not to.*)

CLAIRE: (*Holding* CHARLES *by his arms.*) Are you really going to take off with the car without telling us, without saying good-bye, and leaving mother, father and everyone without saying good-bye?

CHARLES: Leave me alone. I don't have time to talk to you. (*He looks at* FAK)

CLAIRE: No time, no time. You don't have shit to do and you say: no time.

CHARLES: I'm very busy. I can't talk to you.

CLAIRE: Then I'm running to tell mom that you're taking off with the car and there'll be a terrible scene.

CHARLES: I haven't said: I'm leaving with that car; I haven't said I'm leaving; I haven't said anything at all and you're just a kid.

CLAIRE: I'm already not a kid anymore. I started drinking coffee yesterday morning and I drank until nightfall. I've never gone a night without sleeping. How do you manage to never sleep, day or night, without even trying?

CHARLES: During the day, the light keeps me up and at night, since it's dark, you have to keep your eyes wide open to see what's going on, and you can't sleep with your eyes wide open.

CLAIRE: My eyes are always closing. I want to know your secret. Take me with you, Charlie. I don't want to stay here by myself, I don't want to take care of mama by myself; why do girls have to do chores while boys don't do shit and run away in cars snickering together? When you leave, I want to go with you.

CHARLES: Who's talking about leaving? I don't have a car.

CLAIRE: (*Pointing to* FAK) And that one with the keys who's waiting for you? I know your secrets.

CHARLES: He's not waiting for me. What I have isn't his and what he has isn't mine. You don't know anything.

CLAIRE: Yeah, yeah, I know you all; you're like dogs; you bark and you fight but you always end up licking each other's ass.

CHARLES: Hurry up Claire. Go home. I can't talk to you. I'm too busy.

CLAIRE: You, busy? You don't even work anymore. Mama says poverty was down the hall and now, it's knocking at the door and soon it'll be on the kitchen table. The girls were telling me that poverty and its hardship makes girls get fat, and I don't want to get fat; so I've decided not to sleep until I get peace of mind.

CHARLES: You don't have to worry, you're skinny, and you don't have any hardship yet.

CLAIRE: If you left, how would I defend myself all alone?

CHARLES: Everyone has to learn how to defend themselves on their own.

CLAIRE: You teach me; a brother should teach his sister.

CHARLES: I don't have time to teach you.

CLAIRE: Then you really are going to take off with the car. I'm running now to tell mom you're taking off; I'm going to make a scene, I want a scene, you boys won't get away without a scene, or else I want to go with you. You make me angry, boys who snicker together make me angry, everything makes me angry, that stupid car makes me angry! I'm going to drink coffee until I die. Does it take very, very long to learn how to defend yourself on your own?

CHARLES: Pretty long, yeah. Real, real long.

CLAIRE: So then start teaching me, there's just enough time.

CHARLES: I'm pretty good at defending myself, but not at teaching someone else.

CLAIRE: I don't want us to say good-bye.

CHARLES: It's not such a big deal. One day, I won't be here; you'll remember the last place you saw me, you'll go there to find me, and I'll be gone and that'll be that.

CLAIRE: I don't want to say good-bye.

CHARLES: Hurry up and get the towels.

(CLAIRE *lets go of* CHARLES.)
(CHARLES *goes to* FAK.)
(CLAIRE *watches them from a distance, pretending not to.*)

***

CHARLES: I'll kill her.

FAK: Why would you kill her?

CHARLES: Because she followed you.

FAK: She didn't follow me, I followed her.

CHARLES: I'll kill her anyway. What the hell's a girl her age doing in the street?

FAK: It's because she had too much coffee.

CHARLES: She's not supposed to drink coffee at her age.

FAK: She's not too young to drink coffee. You're her brother, that's why you can't see she's not that young, not at all, not for coffee anyway.

CHARLES: Exactly, I know very well how old she is, which is why I say she shouldn't go out at night, she's no longer young enough for that, and I'll kill her because she followed you.

FAK: I'm the one who followed her, I swear.

CHARLES: So then I'll kill her for giving you the idea to do what you did.

FAK: I haven't done anything.

CHARLES: You followed her.

FAK: When it's pitch black, it's impossible to know who is following who and you end up face to face, without knowing why or who's in front of you.

CHARLES: You had the idea to get her to go in.

FAK: I didn't have any ideas, I swear. I only spoke to her because at night, we found ourselves face to face, by accident. I had to say something so I wouldn't look stupid.

CHARLES: Did you put your hands on her?

FAK: I didn't put anything; maybe just a little, but still, I'm not sure because I couldn't see anything.

CHARLES: Where were your hands?

FAK: Maybe here, nowhere else anyway. I could see enough to know where to put them.

CHARLES: I don't want your hands on her anywhere. I don't want you getting any ideas about trying to get her to go in there at night, without you telling me what idea you're having, so I can tell you whether you can keep having the idea or not. She's way too young to have any ideas herself, or to know who not to trust and to know what you're up to the way I know what you're up to, as always, creeping like a little snake and saying one thing with another thing in your head. I know how you work; but afterwards it will be too late and I'll have to console her. I don't want to have to console her, I'd rather kill her beforehand if I ever suspect that you might have the slightest idea without asking me right away if you can have it and keep it.

FAK: I swear to you I'd never have an idea without asking you if I can keep it. Right now, I've got other things on my mind.

CHARLES: You swear you'd ask me?

FAK: Of course I swear.

CHARLES: What are you willing to swear on?

FAK: On whatever you want me to swear on, I swear.

CHARLES: I don't see what it could be; I don't know what you could swear on that would matter to me, and what I could make you swear on that matters to you.

FAK: When you figure it out, you let me know.

CHARLES: Okay, for example, let's swear, on the keys to the Jaguar you have in your pocket.

FAK: I swear on them. (*He puts his hand in his pocket*)

CHARLES: I don't know what you swore on.

FAK: You know there are keys in my pockets, you must know what I swore on and that it's something that matters to both of us.

CHARLES: Take them out of your pocket anyway, don't try anything.

FAK: I'm not trying anything. But, I'm not taking them out, and that's that.

CHARLES: Fifty-fifty then.

FAK: Fifty what? I'm not asking you for anything.

CHARLES: You followed her, you put your hand on her, you got ideas without asking me first: I'll kill her.

FAK: You're her brother, she's just a kid, you should kill her; that way she won't grow every which way. I don't care, I'm not her brother.

CHARLES: Don't try to make me forget what we're talking about. I know how you operate.

FAK: You know nothing about how I operate. What we are talking about is, if I could, if it came to me, if I could keep the idea to put my hand wherever I want and keep it there, and the idea to take whoever, wherever, whenever I want, without having to tell anyone or ask anyone anything.

CHARLES: I think you could. (*He holds out his hand.*)

FAK: And I could hold on to the idea, for instance, to get her to go in there, even if she doesn't know what it means, even if she's a thousand times too young or a thousand times too old, even if she has older brothers, to get her to go in there when I'd want to without someone killing her and without someone consoling her and without anything at all.

CHARLES: If you have the idea, you can keep it. That's all I say. So we're even, nobody gets killed.

FAK: You swear?

CHARLES: I swear.

FAK: On what?

CHARLES: On the same thing you swore on.

(FAK *gives him the keys.*)
(CECILE *appears, the sun rises in the sky with great speed*)
(*When* CHARLES *sees her, he closes his eyes.*)
(FAK *and* CLAIRE *look at one another and exit each to one side.*)

***

At the base of the white wall bathed in sunlight.

(CECILE, *after approaching* CHARLES)

CECILE: So, Carlos, tell me. Tell me how you're planning to milk him for all he's worth, make him cough it up, pluck this pigeon, bleed this old peacock to the last drop before he, through betrayals and deals, gets his car running again and takes off with the hen and all our hopes and the whole pie without leaving us a piece, leaving us in the dark and dark dirt poor without water without money, just good enough to walk on all fours and lick the dog piss off the sidewalk and drink rainwater from the dumpsters and die under a downpour of sewage while you, Carlos, larva rotting in the sun, you sleep while you should already be clawing at him like a bat in his hair.

CHARLES: Don't call me Carlos and give me some shade.

CECILE: Stop sleeping. Answer me first.

CHARLES: I'm not sleeping.

CECILE: You're always sleeping when I ask you questions.

CHARLES: No, I'm thinking.

CECILE: It's always the same thing; whenever there's something to do, either you go back to sleep or you're already sleeping, whenever I look at you, your eyes are shut and I've forgotten their color. When I look at you, I ask myself if this is really my son I'm trying to talk to, is he this larva rotting in the sun that I brought over one day from our country to this country with the hope of making him a first-class human being, looking at you today, there's nothing left of the hopes which made me stand so tall in the boat that brought us here, nothing but this ignorant larva, incapable and good for nothing, pale like the people here, dressed like the people here, spoiled by the sun and the ways and the crocodile laziness of the people here, disdaining school, turning against honor, forced to work at night, at some unspeakable job, a job with no pay check and no promotion or honor, and you even let that slip away and now you let yourself go like a dead larva in a puddle, and the whole time our piece of the pie is over there drying off and you're letting it get away, without showing us the proper gratitude, that is rightfully ours since you are the one who fished him out of the water.

CHARLES: I'm not the one who got him out of the water.

CECILE: Yes you are, yes you are. I saw it all from my window. He must pay for stumbling into this hole, Carlos, he will have to pay.

CHARLES: I don't want you to call me Carlos.

CECILE: It's your name.

CHARLES: My name is Charles.

CECILE: Not before God, not before God and not before me.

CHARLES: You keep me from thinking.

CECILE: Quit thinking and answer me.

CHARLES: Either we talk, or we think. We can't do both.

CECILE: Who are you thinking for? For yourself or for all of us?

CHARLES: I think, in general.

CECILE: We are too miserable and not rich enough to think.

CHARLES: You have to think to make a plan.

CECILE: We don't need a plan.

CHARLES: I need a plan to do something.

CECILE: You're not making any plans, you're sleeping.

CHARLES: I'm not sleeping, I'm thinking.

CECILE: All right, tell me what is the conclusion of all that thinking.

CHARLES: Give me some time.

CECILE: We're too old to take time; if you're not going to do anything, I'll take care of it myself and make him cough it up.

CHARLES: Don't do anything, stay out of it, it's none of your business. You're way too old and sick for making deals.

CECILE: He came for all of us, not just for you. Is that it? A car arrives in the middle of the night, everyone goes out to make deals and leaves me behind just because I'm too old and sick? I'll make deals anyway since you're not doing anything.

CHARLES: If you keep talking, I can't think; if I can't think, I won't have a plan; if I don't have a plan, then I won't be able to do anything, so get off my back.

CECILE: No, Carlos, don't sleep. Don't sleep Carlos.

CHARLES: Charles, damn it!

CECILE: Don't sleep.

CHARLES: I've got the sun in my face.

(*She moves and gives him some shade.*)

CECILE: I want to be in your plan, right in the middle of your plan, to devour my piece of the pie with you. It's only fair I devour it before I die. I don't want your plan to be only for you, for you to leave us standing here in this shit among savages I still don't understand, not their habits, not their ways, not their religion, without water, without money, without light, with a girl on my hands I'll never know who to give to since I don't know anyone here, and this old warrior husband who's never done dying, and myself to take care of, so old, so sick, with a sickness from here, cruel, cunning, with no name and no patron saint to invoke, when you were the only one I could count on to name my disease so I wouldn't die of it the way I will die, without ever having known a single moment free from suffering, free from poverty, like a fly trapped in a closet who dies at the end of the day before the closet has even been opened a crack.

CHARLES: You're not that sick, or that old, you just pretend so you can bitch and moan and keep me from thinking.

CECILE: Yes, I like to bitch and moan, and I will go on bitching and moaning at the foot of this crocodile you fished out of the water, who's drying out over there and who, if you keep on dozing like a hippopotamus, is going to crawl out of here without giving us our due; but if you won't make a move, I'll slash his tires myself with a kitchen knife and I'll sink my teeth in his thigh and make him shed tears until he's completely dry, Carlos, answer me.

CHARLES: I don't want to hear that name.

CECILE: And I will never call you anything else.

CHARLES: Then I will never answer you.

CECILE: It's a crime to change the name by which God knows us; whatever is on your account will be transferred to someone else's account, and God knows what will be put on yours, Carlos.

CHARLES: I can't hear you.

CECILE: But since we're alone, since no one can hear us, since no one, not even with good eyes, can see my old lips moving, I can call you whatever I want.

CHARLES: No, I don't want you to.

CECILE: Well I want to, I can't call you anything else.

CHARLES: The sun's in my eyes.

(*She moves and gives him some shade.*)

CECILE: (*Quietly*) In secret, Carlos, in the bottom of your heart, don't you ever think about returning to our country to live your life over there? Don't you ever secretly dream of the country we are from, where everything would be easier for you, where you wouldn't be a foreigner, where they speak your language, and where you would be honored? Tell me Carlos, secretly, do you ever dream of our country where the streets are so clean, where it's so cool while here we are sweating, and warm while we are freezing, where people are Christian and we are respected? Tell me, secretly, how many times have you already dreamed, Carlos, of the landscape of our country, the houses of our country, the water, the storms, the springs over there. At least tell me this.

CHARLES: Don't call me Carlos, I won't answer.

CECILE: Answer me. Answer me. I won't call you at all.

CHARLES: I never think about it.

CECILE: But in dreams. Do you dream about it?

CHARLES: No, I never dream about it.

CECILE: What do you dream about then?

CHARLES: I don't dream.

CECILE: Don't sleep, don't sleep.

CHARLES: I'm not sleeping.

CECILE: Fine. I don't want you to go back there to live your life. I don't want you to think about it; I don't even want you to dream about it, Carlos, not even the slightest dream, not even in secret, about the spring time there, the rivers, the storms, the water, the white streets. I don't want you to dream of our country where life would be easy, where the people are Christian and where we are respected. I want you to stay here, with us, stuck in this shit here.

CHARLES: Give me some shade.

CECILE: I have no more shade. (*She cries.*)

CHARLES: (*Opening his eyes*) I have things to do.

(*He exits.*)

***

Night blew on him, blew softly. . .
- Faulkner

(ABAD, *soaking wet in the sun, on the pier.*)
(CHARLES *approaches him.*)

CHARLES: Fak tells me you want to do business alone now. You have the right to keep secrets; even a brother has the right to keep secrets from his own brother; but a brother who keeps too many secrets from his brother, he isn't a brother, he's a stranger, and if he's not a stranger, then he's a traitor. When we worked together, we always went fifty-fifty, right? And since you don't have a family to feed, you must have put aside a shit load of cash; you know how to stash it away, so I know you have a shit load of cash. It's true, you can do business alone. Fak says you have the right, Fak is always right, and you're also right. If that's how it is, then you just tell me good-bye, you go your way and I go mine. But I won't leave first, get that through your thick head. You're the one who'll say good-bye first, Negro, not me.

    Fak says there aren't enough full-time workers coming through here anymore and now they all live in the harbor; Fak says a company can't keep a ferry line going if there aren't enough people using it. He must be right, that's business. Anyway, Negro there will never be another ferry here again, that's for sure, and what's more, you're better off doing business alone. Fak says you're right; he's right: you're always right. That must be because you don't say very much and you hold your cards close; so, of course, you're not wrong very often. Anyway, I wouldn't go out on my own without you, I'll never keep any secrets from you, Negro, I'll never be a traitor.

    For us, Negro, it's over, the way we used to operate. Our blood is too rotten, it's time to change the way we operate while we still can. Look at everyone else: all of them, they've all left; they're all making cash somewhere else, in other ways. You have to get out while there's still time. We don't need to do the same thing as everybody else, we can do it our own way, on the down low. We've got to keep doing bizness together. Besides, I'm the only one who gets you, Negro, that's why it's good for you that we keep doing bizness together. And you'll never be able to do anything with your cash, nothing Negro, because you need me to do the talking. I, on the other hand, know what to do with your cash, that's why you'd better give it to me right away. Your money shouldn't rot with you.

    Look how I'm dressed, look at my shoes; she'll see right away I'm a loser. Rich people can see money in the other person's pocket, they see right through the fabric, they see empty pockets before they even see you. I don't want to look like a loser, Negro, that I really don't want.

I want to go after the woman first. You know, Negro, they say, nothing can stop a Jaguar, not even the brakes. Once we get the woman, we get the car, Negro, but not the way we used to operate, our blood is too rotten for that, and we wouldn't get very far. The future, it's all about bizness and finesse; and for that, leave it up to me, be patient, relax. Then, we won't need to put on the brakes anymore, I swear.

Listen, I can't go see her without any cash in my pockets. Your cash, I just want to have it in my pocket, I just need it to talk to her, and after that, I'll give it back to you. They need to show us respect.

Anyway, Negro, you know what's in your best interest; Fak says you never lose your way, even when it looks like it, and he's right about that. You knew perfectly well, from the first day, either you save yourself with me, or we both go down. (*He snickers.*) We're brothers, Negro, we're brothers by blood, we're brothers by cash, we're brothers by itch; lucky for you I'm not a beggar with lice, Negro, because you'd be the first one to have to scratch it. To tell you the truth, you don't really have a choice.

When I was a kid, I always had lice on my head, under my arms, on each and every hair, a whole colony of black lice. My old lady slathered me in motor oil but as soon as we thought they were all gone, they would tiptoe right back and I'd start itching all over again. So then my old lady would scrub my nails and say: there must be one hiding under there. Then she'd make me drink broom and sweet woodruff tea to clean the blood that carted the eggs around; but there was always one that managed to hide, and we could never figure out where. When it comes to the last louse, there's nothing you can do, you just have to give up. (*He snickers.*) In the end, it's a lot easier to get used to lice than to get rid of them.

You know, there's not much I could do with your cash on my own. (*He snickers.*) Not very much, you don't need to worry. (He snickers.) You know that, Negro, but maybe you don't know that I know it too. Maybe I forgot it a while ago, maybe I forget it this second. But now I know it, and, Negro, don't forget I told you that.

We should have been born as different people. To be born rich and stupid, to be born the stupid kid of a banker or a yacht owner, it's the only dream worth having, Negro; besides that, nothing else is worth dreaming of dreaming about. That's why we don't dream about anything, Negro, not your fault, not mine; we were born on the wrong side of the tracks, that's all. (*He picks up the money that* ABAD *put in front of him.*)

That's why I love you Negro. (*He snickers.*) That's why I love you. (*He kisses the money.*) Don't forget I told you that.

(CHARLES *exits.*)

***

The highway. Siesta time.

(KOCH *is lying down, soaking wet in the sun, eyes closed*.)

(MONIQUE *and* CHARLES *speak quietly*.)

MONIQUE: Please, let's be civilized and don't raise your voice, let's speak politely, we don't need to frighten each other. Besides, I don't even have the strength to be scared. If only people would negotiate nicely, without vulgarity, and without raising their voices, everything would be so much less exhausting. Don't you have a comb, at least, a broken comb, even with some teeth missing? The only thing I cannot bear is not having a comb through my hair after a sleepless night. No, I don't want to see him thrash around again; let him sleep off his nonsense, I'll wake him up when the car's running again. As for me, Jesus Christ! I would like to know; fix it; I'm willing to pay whatever you ask.

   You look so shy, Christ! The light makes everything look so kind and intimidating. I couldn't bear to look at myself. My hair is so dry, it must be sticking out all over the place. Your shyness is contagious, I feel it. In a minute I'll be running to hide over there from blushing, and that's no way to carry on business. I am so utterly exhausted and subject to fainting spells, Christ! Don't look at me that way, I must look like a witch; aren't you going to find me a small piece of a dirty old comb somewhere?

CHARLES: I want to talk bizness. I don't give nothing for nothing; so, I want to talk to him, not you. I don't know how to talk to women anymore. You know with that mop on your head you look like a broom. I'll tell my sister to help you comb it while I talk bizness with him.

MONIQUE: Really! With him! With him, Hooray! He's there, slumped over, all sick, with sand and shells still in his ears and down his throat, but you want to talk with him. You really are amazing. Go ahead, try, ask him what a car runs on; talk to him about a distributor cap if you want to see him pass out. Good luck! He's only interested in himself. As for your sister, I know how she is; I'm still waiting for the towels she went looking for. But, I'm not hoping for towels anymore, no shirts, no combs, no help from anyone, I'm not hoping for anything.

CHARLES: You're not going to faint, are you?

MONIQUE: Good thing you're so nice, at least; I'm not feeling very well. Still there's no reason we should camp out here until kingdom come. We must come up with some kind of an arrangement. But I don't have any money left. Zero.

CHARLES: I've got money, I don't want your money.

MONIQUE: Very good. I could tell right away you weren't a low-life. I'm so sick of low-lives. I want to leave, I want to go back, I want this car to start, I don't want to show up in the city with this mop on my head; help me. Jesus!

(*She faints.* CHARLES *holds her up.*)

CHARLES: I said I was going to help you. It's not dark yet. Don't be in such a hurry. (*After a pause, quietly*) Is it an SJX, the coupe?

MONIQUE: It's a four-door. The Vanden Plas.

CHARLES: Five point three liters.

MONIQUE: Yes. Twelve cylinders.

CHARLES: Twelve cylinders. Is it true there's a brake problem?

MONIQUE: Bullshit. Four anti-lock, double circuit, servo-assisted on deceleration.

CHARLES: It's weird, a woman who knows car.

MONIQUE: Do you have any family?

CHARLES: My sister.

MONIQUE: You love her?

CHARLES: She's sharp. She'll learn fast. She'll make something of herself if she puts her mind to it.

MONIQUE: My brothers and sisters are the only ones I ever get along with. One should never leave one's brothers and sisters. Everything else is bullshit. Why leave the people you get along with best and who don't expect anything from you?

CHARLES: (*Pointing at* KOCH.) Doesn't he know how to drive?

MONIQUE: Not even. He doesn't know how to do anything. He's not sharp. He doesn't learn fast. (*Pause*.) Don't look at me.

CHARLES: Someone dressed like a bum is like a luxury car with no engine, left in a corner. (*Pause*) I can only speak for myself.

MONIQUE: You know with your shy puppy-dog look you're making me nervous.

CHARLES: (*After a pause*) I'm too old. I don't know how to talk to women anymore.

MONIQUE: (*Brusquely*) Come. Come with us. (*She holds out her hand*.) I don't want to talk to him. You'll keep me from talking. Come with us. (CHARLES *holds out the keys*.) Yes, it'll be much better that way. (*She takes the keys, keeping her hand outstretched*.) Hurry up, I feel night is about to fall, I'm scared again.

CHARLES: Wake him up. You've got the keys.

MONIQUE: Keys, keys, keys, what do you want me to do with keys? Do you think I need keys to start a car? A little girl could start a car without keys; do you think I'm an idiot? (*Quietly*) The distributor cap. And you forced the hood; it's all scratched up.

CHARLES: Who?

MONIQUE: Who? You are asking me: who? Jesus Christ! You, I guess.

CHARLES: I knew I should never talk business with a woman. (*He snickers*) Now I remember. (*Quietly*) If you want to get out of here, you'll have to carry him. It's eight miles all the way around.

MONIQUE: Get lost; be civil when you speak to me.

CHARLES: If you leave right away, you might get there by nightfall.

("Because I said, balls or no balls, frozen off or not, we'll meet again. Captain, you led us from a warm country to a freezing country without leaving us time to put on our boots and our woolen trousers, hurrying us, giving us just enough time to hop from the house to the barracks, from the barracks to the docks and from the docks to the boat, like fleas wearing sandals, and how will we replace the sandals, ruined by snow and ice, and the feet that were inside? He snorted and said: shut up, corporal, just walk and shut the hell up; the soldier leaned into my ear: corporal! I said to him: shut up, soldier, and walk; then I had respect for rank.

Captain, captain, despite the respect I still have for rank, why don't you tell the ranking officers that the men, poor men, have frozen off all their feet in their torn sandals, tell them we can't go on, the fog is setting in, tell them we should go back to the boat and wait for boots, or else we sit here in the snow in our canvas pants and freeze our balls off, captain, that's what's in store for us, we're getting further from the boat, I don't see them anymore, I don't see my men anymore, I don't even see you anymore; the captain said: corporal, shut up and walk; the soldier had grabbed my arm: corporal! I told him: Shut up. Then, I couldn't see the captain anymore, lost in the fog, I couldn't see the soldier anymore, I just saw the cap sinking in the ice, couldn't see anyone, couldn't hear, only the fog and the snow and the ice, and I sat down to wait for orders, wearing my very light canvas pants, the kind we wear in temperate countries. That's how you all got out of it, I said, balls or no balls, we'll meet again." Says Rodolfe.)

***

The warehouse crisscrossed by golden rays.

(CECILE, *deeply preoccupied and solitary, slowly crosses the warehouse.*)
(*Once in front of* ABAD, *she stops, barely looks at him, takes a handkerchief from her pocket and holds it out to him.*)

CECILE: I want to smoke a cigarette. I'm a sick old woman, I definitely shouldn't smoke because of my cough, my husband definitely doesn't want me to smoke, he thinks it looks like a whore; I wanted to bring you towels to dry you off, some cigarettes to drug you and my sweet talk to corrupt you, but I'm a very old woman with no memory, I have only an old handkerchief that's not very clean and the desire to smoke, you're going to catch a first-class case of pneumonia if you don't dry yourself off. (ABAD *takes the handkerchief.*) I get along well with savages, I'm an old savage myself, my husband says I'll always be a savage even if I'm a whore, you should be able to laugh when you feel like laughing, I don't have a light either. (ABAD *gives her a lit cigarette.*) It's an upside-down world but God, thanks to him, will know pure animals from impure animals, we'll never sleep on the same bunk, thank God, you'll never board the same ship as us, just dry yourself off. (*She coughs.*) Me, a whore! (*She sits.*) Just between you and me, I only want to smoke a cigarette, I want to breathe a little, just between savages. (*They smoke.*)

I have to hide until dark, when night begins to fall I'll meet this distinguished gentleman with my sweet talk, if I start too early I'm finished, my sweet talk only works during the first hours of twilight. I'm so tired that as soon as I have the tiniest idea I have to sit down to catch my breath. But what do you care? Anyway, he didn't see anything, he's too old, he's six hundred years old and his eyes were full of water, so, I'll do the sweet talk of the sick old woman whose son pulled him out of the water and I'll get the stash, I'll make out a list just like at my wedding, the shop is first-class, I saw the car very very close up in the sun, that's why I have to hide. A savage, in this country, has to know how to keep a low profile; you're low profile, thank God, if I hadn't heard the drops of water dripping off your head I would've practically bumped into you; what are you waiting to dry off for? For him to get pneumonia? What do you care? Anyway, you'll get nothing, thank you very much. This distinguished gentleman will know how to tell the difference, you and I will never float on the same piece of wood; my husband says you have to laugh when you feel like laughing. (*She coughs.*) Cigarros Winston, cigarros de maricon. (*She tosses the cigarette away.*) Don't let my clean handkerchief fall in that shit. (*She picks up the handkerchief.*)

It's very dirty here. (*She looks around.*) It's disgusting. I'm embarrassed for you, I've never seen such disgustingness. In my country we would be ashamed to imagine such a place. Even the rats in my country would refuse to copulate with the rats here. But my son has never been completely normal. Too bad, I'll get by without you; everyone knows savages only bicker among themselves instead of helping one another. (*She stands up, moves away from* ABAD.) He told me there was a place to get water here, a faucet. I haven't seen anything. At least, he could have painted some landscapes of his country on the walls. You could have painted some landscapes of your country on the walls. I don't know your country, or your religion, or your mother's name, nothing; I don't know anything about my son, and my husband says I don't know how to paint. I don't even remember my country. I'm a whore in perfect health, good for slashing tires with a kitchen knife and waiting for twilight. (*She laughs.*) Me, sick! I can hear him panting, back there, he must've caught a first-class case of pneumonia in that icy water, may you die of an icy pneumonia yourself since you don't want to help me; I have to speak to him before he dies, what are these days that last for hours and hours? If I go out too early, I'll be finished. (*She turns her back to* ABAD, *looks at the ceiling, paces back and forth.*) Set, go down, crash down, aren't you tired yet of roasting us like larvae, aren't you sick of bothering me yet? Wouldn't you like to be nice please, and do your dive and give me the space?

(*Abruptly returns running toward* ABAD) And you, tell those drops of water to stop running down your thick skull immediately, to stop crackling on the ground, the noise tires me, you have no right to make this noise, no authorization, nothing, you don't have the right to exist at all.

What price did you pay to live in peace in this country? Why did you leave your home? Did you murder your mother? Were you involved in politics? A man doesn't leave his country without the shame of his mother's name, without a crime. You bring us bad luck sir, with the stink of your crimes, of your shame, of your silence, of everything you're hiding. They came here with you, with no father, no mother, no race, no belly button, no language, no name, no god, no visa and the bad times came one after another; because of you misfortune entered our home, it climbed our stairs, it knocked down our doors and so began the time of poverty, the beginning of no money, the beginning of darkness when we need light and suns that refuse to set; the beginning of boats that don't stop, the abandoning of houses by honorable people, the beginning of chaos, of insults, of stabbings, of the fear of night, of the fear of day, of the fear glued to our shoulders, the mixing up of day and night; the beginning of diseases pricked in our blood by flies that hide in your hair. Before, the sun was a sun and it obeyed the snap of a finger, and the night the time to sleep; doors were locked, windows had panes and faucets had running water, but you drank from our faucets to the last drop of water and you didn't leave any for anyone else. Before, everything was good here; there was no pain in the legs, no pain in the back, in the neck, in the eyes, no fever kept us from sleeping, no stomach ache, no chest pain. Then our bodies were walking tall, shoulders high and backs strong. But your shame slowly hunched our shoulders and lowered our heads, and that was the beginning of our misfortune. I don't want to see you anymore, I don't want to see anything. (*Turning toward the ceiling*) Set!

The golden rays flicker faintly and lose their brilliance.
(CECILE *exits*.)

***

Running along the warehouse still faintly lit by the sun.

CLAIRE: I don't have time.

FAK: Me neither.

CLAIRE: I don't want you to talk to me.

FAK: I can't talk to you since I don't have time.

CLAIRE: I don't want you to look at me, even very fast.

FAK: I don't have to look at you anymore. Since, I've already seen you easy, everything, all of it, without any clothes on.

CLAIRE: You haven't seen anything without clothes on, what are you talking about?

FAK: Yes I have, yes I have. I saw it all this morning.

CLAIRE: And tell me please how you could have seen it all, so easily, give me a break.

FAK: When you washed it all off in the river this morning, everything, I saw it.

CLAIRE: I would never wash it off in the river, what are you talking about? The water is way too filthy, we have a house, there's the faucet and clean water inside.

FAK: There's no more water inside and this morning your mother made you wash in the river and she was looking around to make sure no one was watching while you were washing it all off, but I was up there on the roof and I saw everything, like I see you now with your clothes on.

CLAIRE: I don't see what difference it would make anyway.

FAK: The difference is, now you'd better want it with me to get even and to see all mine too or else you really look like an idiot.

CLAIRE: I don't see the difference since I saw you also very easily when you were washing it off this morning in the river, so there, we're already even and now you have to find another trick.

FAK: You didn't see anything at all since I didn't wash it off or anything else, not in the river, not in the house not in any kind of water dirty or clean, never.

CLAIRE: And you'd want me to want it with you when you yourself say that you don't wash it off at all, anywhere, ever? Give me a break. Maybe, I would maybe want it with someone who washes himself off every day and everywhere and without fail, but since you tell me yourself that without fail you never wash yourself off, I don't see how I could want it, since I'm completely clean always and everywhere.

FAK: Me too, you can see, I'm completely clean always and everywhere.

CLAIRE: How can you be clean? I'm not falling for that. You just said yourself that you never wash off, I'm not the one who said it, am I?

FAK: Exactly, people who never wash off from the time they are very young are always clean, because grime isn't interested in them and slides right off. While people who are always rinsing themselves and spend a lot of time at it, grime chases them, the more they wash the more it clings; and later, when you are much older, you'll have to wash more and more often, and later, when you're a very old man, you'll always be washing off and you'll always be dirty, while I'm clean until the end of time.

CLAIRE: Anyway, even if we're not even, I'd never want it because I know very precisely that my brother said you could, whether I want it or not; so for me, whether you can or can't, I'd never want it.

FAK: I don't see what difference it makes to you whether I can or can't since what I want now is for you to want it too.

CLAIRE: And tell me please, why you need for me to want it too since you already can?

FAK: Because it's much better when everyone wants it and you'll see yourself how much better it is.

CLAIRE: Well get this, even if I knew it'd be much better if I wanted it, I still wouldn't want it with a boy because boys always want to trade something for something else and you never give anything, so I don't want anything at all.

FAK: I'm not trading anything; you give or you don't give, I take or I don't take, I give or I don't give.

CLAIRE: Oh please, and how is it you're not trading? I even saw you with my brother this morning, trading the car keys so he could run away, and I know very precisely what for.

FAK: I haven't traded anything at all since I didn't give him anything that would help him run away and it's still in my pocket.

CLAIRE: What?

FAK: The distributor cap.

CLAIRE: (*Holding out her hand.*) So give it to me.

FAK: Here. (*He gives it to her.*)

CLAIRE: (*After a pause*) I'm very unhappy.

FAK: If you were very unhappy, you wouldn't always say no. Someone who's very unhappy says yes and someone who says no is still always a little bit happy.

CLAIRE: But I'm not even a little bit happy anymore.

FAK: If that's true, you have to say yes.

CLAIRE: Yes.

FAK: When exactly?

CLAIRE: When it gets very dark, maybe then, I'd say yes.

FAK: When it gets dark, you'll want it, really?

CLAIRE: Completely dark, yes, then, I'll want it, really.

FAK: I'll wait for you. (*He exits*.)

CLAIRE: Yes. Yes. Yes. (*She exits*.)

***

On the pier. Abad is curled up at the water's edge.
CHARLES *squats at his side. The sun, low, is reflected by the river.*

CHARLES: So long, Negro; I'm looking for Fak and, when I find him, I'm outta here with the car, on my own. Don't try anything stupid before I go, don't think too much. Don't get worked up, don't make a move until I'm gone. That's all I'm asking and you owe me that much.

    I've taught you everything I know, Negro, I gave you everything I had. When you first came here, you were hiding, I didn't ask any questions. But what you give one day, you always have the right to take back the next; the only person you give something to for good is yourself; to anybody else, you lend, and someday he'll have to give it back. Today it's your turn to give back, Negro. So, until the Jaguar takes off again, and I will be in it, Negro, believe me, don't make a move, relax, don't do anything stupid, don't try to understand.

    Maybe the night ferry will come back and you could start working again, even by yourself; as for me, I'm switching sides, I'm heading off for the harbor; first I'll be a bouncer in a club, I'll make a lot of cash and you'll never see me again. It's as simple as that my friend: we each go our own way.

    Maybe we've worked together until now, Negro, and it was good; but now we can't work like before; so maybe it's time we do business on our own. Maybe we were like brothers, but now it's time we split.

    Besides, you never get what I tell you, and I don't get whatever you're thinking; you always do things that I think you don't really feel like doing, and afterwards you make do; that's how I think you work; but you won't always be able to change your mind, Negro. To tell you the truth, I just don't get you. And you don't even get yourself. Just forget about it. Don't move, stay cool.

    On the other side, over there, it's the highs; here, it's the lows; right here, we are the low of the lows, we can't get any lower, and there's not much hope of climbing up even a little. Anyway, no matter how high we climb, we'll never be anything other than the high of the lows. That's why I'd rather switch sides, Negro, I'd rather go over there; I'd rather be over there the low of the highs than here, the high of the lows. You don't get it.

    I never worked, Negro, never; I don't even know how; slave's work, honest work, I know nothing about it, I've never had a boss, never served, never obeyed. And yet, that's what I'm going to do now, I'm switching sides. You don't get it.

The fact is you don't really have a choice, Negro. It will take too long for you to get to the other side. Maybe the ferry will stop like it used to and you'll go on working by yourself, and everything will be the same as before; or maybe not, I don't give a damn. Anyway you have Fak; so you'll be OK. Either way, I don't give a damn.

It was bound to blow up in your face one day or another anyhow, Negro. You were on reprieve because of me, but one day or another it was bound to blow up. When they cut off the water, I knew right away it would blow up in your face, my friend.

There'll be no place for you to take cover, Negro, your blood is too rotten, and here, they won't even bother to try to understand someone who doesn't speak. You'll have to pay. So you'll pay, Negro, it's OK; I can't pay for you and there's no reason I should pay along with you. I'm clearing out.

We are so old, Negro, so old already, and we are far behind my friend. Together, we wasted too much time. We've got to try to catch up separately. Look at the fifteen-year old kid today, he does at fifteen what we were doing at twenty-five, and he's already got more cash than us. When we were working with bare fists, the fifteen-year-old shit heads were using brass knuckles, when we discovered brass knuckles, they already had knives, and by the time we settle into knives, they already had guns. They all left, one after another, and when they come back, they'll be kings, and we'll be their slaves. So, I'd rather clear out. The future, my friend is honest work. In the end, honesty is all right. In the end, I like it all right. Either way, that's where the money is.

You're too stupid, Negro; I can't really figure out what you really like, but what I know is you're stupid. I don't think you like anything; you're not even hungry. I'll always be hungry, always, even when my cash runs out, I'll still be hungry. He who stops being hungry is already dead. I'm dying of hunger and you, you're already dead, so we don't match.

Have you ever smelled cash, Negro? I smelled it not long ago, when I heard the sound of the car. I smell money even before it's here, before it's in the pocket, even before it's in the bank. I can smell the bills even before they're printed. I like it. It's what I like best in the world.

If you'd wanted to, Negro, if you had wanted to, my friend, we would've worked with a weapon and we'd be kings. But you're too stupid.

A gun, Negro, doesn't ask for any favors, or that you wake up in the morning, or come on time, you respect it or call it sir, or polish its boots; it doesn't force you to work, or sweat, or obey, or get tired; it doesn't make you do anything and it gives you everything you want. It is the only boss I ever want to have. He who is not armed these days is a slave, Negro. You are a slave; and also you're too stupid, I don't want to see your face anymore.

Don't forget, Negro, don't forget to stay cool until I talk to Fak, until I'm gone, and don't think too much, Negro, so you don't fuck up. Don't forget it's your turn, Negro. I'm clearing out. Good-bye.

(*He exits.*)

***

It's not yet death. Death itself is never painful.
- London

The highway. Early evening before sunset.

(KOCH *in* MONIQUE's *arms*.)

KOCH: It hurts.

MONIQUE: I know.

KOCH: I want to go back.

MONIQUE: I know.

KOCH: Do you remember where the car is?

MONIQUE: Of course.

KOCH: I want to go back, Monique, I've had enough of this nonsense.

MONIQUE: I know. I know. I know.

KOCH: It hurts.

MONIQUE: Jesus Christ! Maurice. Why are you pestering me? What did I do to you? (*After a pause*) What have I done that's so terrible to deserve this?

(CLAIRE *enters*.)

CLAIRE: (*Quietly*) Get out, move, get out right now and be quiet. I don't want to see you here anymore. (*She holds out the distributor cap.*) Take it, hurry up, I'm not asking for anything in exchange. I'm warning you, it will be dark soon if you don't hurry up.

KOCH: What is it?

MONIQUE: (*To* KOCH) Mechanics, nothing. (*To* CLAIRE) And the towels?

KOCH: I want to go back. Carry me.

MONIQUE: (*To* CLAIRE) And the shirts for a bandage?

KOCH: It hurts.

CLAIRE: (*To* MONIQUE) And what else, what else? You have the car, get out.

MONIQUE: Jesus Christ! Maybe you think I like being in this hole.

KOCH: I want to go back, I want to go back.

MONIQUE: I know.

KOCH: Did you lose the keys?

MONIQUE: The keys, Jesus Christ! Of course I didn't lose them.

KOCH: So what?

CLAIRE: Maybe you don't know how to put that in; maybe I should get a boy?

KOCH: What is it?

MONIQUE: The distributor cap.

KOCH: Stop nagging me. I want to go back.

MONIQUE: You want to, do you? Hooray, you want to? That's just wonderful; but we can't, and get this through your head, it's all your fault. (*To* CLAIRE) Little brat. The tires. Little brat. Someone slashed the tires, all four tires. You did it, I'm sure. I'll remember that. A cop will show up sooner or later, don't you think? A cop on a bike or a horse? A big fat cop's got to come around sooner or later, right? In the meantime, go look for those fucking towels, little brat, go look for that fucking shirt so I can tear it up.

CLAIRE: And what else, what else?

MONIQUE: Hurry up, I told you to hurry up.

(CLAIRE *exits, bumps into* CECILE *who enters dragging* RODOLFE *behind her.*)

MONIQUE: (*To* KOCH) What good was all this bluffing other than to create all this trouble for nothing? If you would say things right away, without lying, instead of all this bluffing, we wouldn't be stuck here with your ankle. Christ! And these people watching us, I feel it; we don't even know what they want from us. Meanwhile, I could be happy with my family where we love each other peacefully; you don't know what a family is, brothers, sisters; and I'm here on one of your whims.

KOCH: I'm freezing to death. Even my underwear is soaking wet.

MONIQUE: I'm waiting for the towels someone went to get.

CLAIRE: (*To* CECILE) It's because I drank too much coffee, mama, so much coffee I don't know any more if it's day or night or something else, so I'm going to get a towel for that guy over there who's all wet.

CECILE: No towels for anyone. What did you do with your shoe?

CLAIRE: I lent it to someone so I know whether I'm asleep or not.

CECILE: A proper young girl is at home asleep at this hour; get out.

CLAIRE: I'll go off and sleep when they're gone.

CECILE: They're not going anywhere, they'll pay first.

CLAIRE: But I can't sleep, mama.

CECILE: Stand vigil over the faucet until the water runs.

CLAIRE: I haven't had so much coffee that I need to stand vigil alone over the faucet, mama.

CECILE: Idiot. You don't think you'll have to catch up on this sleep? You haven't saved a minute with all that coffee you drank on the sly, idiot. Get moving.

CLAIRE: (*Crying*) I don't want to stay alone at home tonight.

CECILE: Off with you. (CLAIRE *exits. To* RODOLFE) Mira, Rodolfo, mira. (*They look at* MONIQUE *and* KOCH.)

KOCH: (*To* MONIQUE) Don't torture me; I have a broken foot, I'm beginning to catch pneumonia and you're talking to me about money, the only thing you know how to talk about is money.

MONIQUE: I was sure of it. I knew it.

KOCH: You don't know anything. I don't want to talk about money.

MONIQUE: (*Quietly*) What have you done with it? Jesus Christ, Maurice!

KOCH: I forget.

MONIQUE: Forget what?

KOCH: Everything.

MONIQUE: You're trying to get away with it.

KOCH: I swear, I don't know.

MONIQUE: Don't lie, don't lie.

KOCH: I forget, I swear.

MONIQUE: Do you think I'm an idiot? You can't spend seven million on cigars.

KOCH: I don't buy cigars anymore. I forget.

MONIQUE: What will become of you, Jesus!

KOCH: I want to dry off.

MONIQUE: And me?

KOCH: Go without me to the Board of Directors. Say that I'm sick. Say I've run away. Say whatever. Put it all on me.

MONIQUE: Never.

CECILE: (*To* RODOLFE) Look, Rodolfe, look. Can you see well enough to see or do I have to explain how it is?

MONIQUE: (*To* KOCH) Don't you understand, Maurice, how much I could understand everything, forgive everything? How much, Maurice, I love you, enough, enough to help you, if only, Christ! You wouldn't lie to me.

KOCH: I don't want your help. I don't need your forgiveness, you don't understand anything at all and I never lie.

MONIQUE: Yes, you lie, you lie, and I understand everything. (*She cries.*)

CECILE: (*To* RODOLFE) Come on, Rodolfe, now is the time.

(CECILE *and* RODOLFE *move toward* MONIQUE *and* KOCH.)

KOCH: (*Suddenly irritated*) Why, why must you keep nagging me about this money? Why can't everyone just leave me alone about this money? Why is it always up to me to take care of everyone else's money?

MONIQUE: Here comes someone, here are some old people, we are saved.

KOCH: If everyone would just learn how to take care of their own money and leave me the fuck alone! I'm not doing anything wrong, I have nothing to do with money; they shouldn't have dropped the money in my lap.

MONIQUE: (*Quietly*) Quiet down, Maurice, we'll talk about that later, quiet down, someone's coming.

KOCH: Wasn't I old enough to be left in peace? Hadn't I reached retirement age? The age where an innocent ordinary man finishes out his days in peace with his savings and isn't bothered with someone else's money? Besides, it's your fault too if I agreed to take care of this money again; and now, yes, you'll act like all the others, you'll be the first one to say: where did the money go? What did you do with it? It must have been spent on something? Looking for mysteries where there are none.

MONIQUE: Quiet down, behave yourself, let's make a good impression, they are very old, Maurice.

KOCH: How many years of peace have I had in my life? How many years of being left the fuck alone and out of other people's business? Six? Eight? At what age do we learn to count? I should never have learned how to count, damn it! People trust me with money just so they can corner me and now they're waiting in that corner for me to settle the accounts. Well, I'm not going, and that's that.

MONIQUE: Maurice, I beg you, they can hear you. Shush: they're going to say something.

CECILE: (*To* KOCH) I come to offer you our help, sir.

MONIQUE: (*To* KOCH) I knew it.

KOCH: Nonsense. I don't want any help.

MONIQUE: (*To* CECILE) Thank you, thank you. Christ! Do you have a phone?

CECILE: (*To* KOCH) Because I saw right away, sir, you were a distinguished man; I know how to recognize distinguished people, in whatever state they may find themselves; that is why I have asked someone to find clean towels and to bring them for you; and if you've come to this far-away land, I don't believe in chance but in the hand of God, and God brings the exiles together even in darkness so they may help one another.

MONIQUE: Do you have a phone?

CECILE: (*To* KOCH) Yes, I saw right away, sir, that you recognize your own kind, just as we recognized you. We live here like poor dogs forgotten in the dark, this man half-destroyed by the war, my son who carried you when you fell, and an entire family waiting for visa papers that climb the never ending ladder to the top; but the top in a big city is hard to reach, unless a highly positioned distinguished man gives a leg up. That's why I'm so glad my son was there the moment you needed help and you could appreciate us for our true worth.

MONIQUE: A phone, for Christ's sake! You can see he can't walk.

CECILE: (*To* KOCH) Because to see us like this, anyone would take us for stray dogs; but we see ourselves for who we are and it is our consolation. In fact, back home, we are distinguished people, and if we return tomorrow, the top family of Lomas Altas would kiss our hands as we descend from the ship; they kissed our hands, sir, when we boarded the ship at the end of the war, with this poor man left half-retarded and who nearly couldn't walk, and this failed war, and money that wasn't worth a thing. We found ourselves in the port, because I wanted my child to become a first-class human being and since, over there, money wasn't worth anything, what was the use of being a distinguished person, sir? At the port, ten ships were about to leave toward ten unknown destinations, we didn't know which one to take, the child was pulling my left hand, we followed him and here we are, in the dark, while over there in our absence, the best families go on honoring the heroism of this man, sir, who lost half his feet and nearly all his strength and practically his whole head in a forgotten war, and who's losing his sight today. But here, no one honors this war, no one honors this man, and here we are reduced to stray dogs, with semi-visas, in the dark.

MONIQUE: (*To* KOCH) What war is she talking about? We haven't had a war in ages, have we?

CECILE: (*To* MONIQUE) Exactly, someone had to have it, ma'am.

MONIQUE: This is not one of our wars, is it?

CECILE: (*To* MONIQUE) The heroism is all yours, ma'am. (*To* KOCH) Among distinguished people, shouldn't we lend a hand, sir?

KOCH: (*To* CECILE) Of course, but I don't know anything about wars.

MONIQUE: (*Quietly, to* KOCH) I find this woman's antics disgusting.

KOCH: (*Quietly, to* MONIQUE) Well, I like them.

MONIQUE: You like them, hooray. So then ask them who's going to help us here, ask.

CECILE: (*To* MONIQUE) We will. We're the only ones here. (*To* KOCH) You can count on us, sir.

MONIQUE: (*To* KOCH) Count on them, count on them. They won't even bring towels. It's going to get dark, Jesus!

KOCH: (*Abruptly, to* CECILE) Help me find my watch, please. I lost it in the warehouse there. It means a lot to me.

MONIQUE: Your watch, Christ!

CECILE: (*To* RODOLFE) Rodolfo, adelantate y asusta al negro.

(RODOLFE *moves away toward the warehouse.*)

MONIQUE: Maurice, you are not going back there? We still have our legs, Maurice, we still have mine. I'll carry you.

CECILE: (*To* RODOLFE) Apurate, machorron, apurate!

(RODOLFE *disappears.*)

KOCH: (*To* MONIQUE, *trying to stand*) So, help me.

MONIQUE: Never.

CECILE: (*To* KOCH) Lean on me, sir. I'll guide you.

(KOCH *and* CECILE *move away.*)

MONIQUE: I'll go alone, alone; I'm so tired of you and your bullshit.

(*She turns around;* FAK *is behind her.*)
MONIQUE: Jesus Christ!

***

The warehouse entrance, outside. The sky reddens; the wind begins to blow forcefully.

(RODOLFE *moves forward, knocked around by gusts of wind.*)
(*A strong burst makes him bump into* CHARLES, *who is hidden near the door.*)

CHARLES: (*Grabbing his arm*) You're spying on me.

RODOLFE: Let go of me, let me go.

CHARLES: What is it? All morning I catch you hiding behind me in the shadows every time I turn around, I crash into you in front of me hiding in the shadows every time I move forward. Speak, now you have me in front of you.

RODOLFE: I'm not the one who wants to talk to you. It's your mother.

CHARLES: So why are you spying on me? Why are you hiding from me?

RODOLFE: I'm not spying on you, I'm hiding in the shadows, I'm not hiding from you, I'm just hiding, because I'm useless and ugly and a very bad father, and fortunately there are still corners where very bad fathers can hide. Let me go.

CHARLES: I'm not touching you, you old fool; you're the one digging your nails into my arm.

RODOLFE: No, you're the one, it's you, and you raise your hand against me; don't raise your hand against your father.

CHARLES: I'm not raising my hand against you, you old fool, you're the one shaking head to toe.

RODOLFE: Let me go.

CHARLES: And where do you want to go?

RODOLFE: Leave me alone. There's your mother; talk to your mother. Leave me alone.

CHARLES: Where do you have to go? What else do you have to do? Why are you getting mixed up in the business of life, old fool?

RODOLFE: Nothing, I have nothing to do; I'm just hanging around; you have to go somewhere when you walk, don't you? And it's your mother who told me to walk and to hurry up. I'm hurrying, that's all. But I swear I don't get mixed up in the business of life, I don't get mixed up in any kind of business, I'm not the one who's mixed up in whatever it is. Don't hit me, don't hit your father.

CHARLES: I'm not touching you.

RODOLFE: Let me go.

CHARLES: I'm not touching you, you old fool. The wind is making you lose your balance and the first frost of winter is making you shake from head to toe.

RODOLFE: There's your mother, there's your mother. Here's your good mother, she wants to speak to you.

(*He disappears into the warehouse.*)

***

Inside the warehouse, in the red light of sunset.
Roar of the river in the distance.

(RODOLFE *stops in the middle*.)

RODOLFE: I'm too old, too fucked up, I have too much trouble moving around. It's up to you to move. If you have any respect left for the elderly, come closer so I can see you; even if you don't have any respect for the elderly, come anyway, it's in your best interest; and if you don't care about what's best for you, just come because I say so. (ABAD *moves toward* RODOLFE.)

    Maybe my eyes are too wrecked to see your mug, but I don't need to see it, Negro, to know right away you're not legit; you don't make enough noise when you walk to be legit, and get this, we don't like that here, guys who aren't straight. They're fucked. That fatso, over there, he's crossing to the other side, he'll tell them: I heard people over there on the other side, who walk without making a sound; and you'll be fucked. And if he's not the one turning you in, it'll be this rabid puppy who wants to save his skin; and if not him, it'll be this bitch, my old lady; and if not her, me, I'll turn you in, Negro, old and wrecked as I am, because there are too many of us on the earth and not enough room, anyway, you're the only one who'll get fucked up, it's going to be one hell of a shock, because you got nothing to soften the blow, Negro, no past, no family, no war, no old age, no savings anywhere, you're better off not respecting the elderly either, otherwise you're no better than garbage. In the meantime, come and help me, Negro.

    (*Searching through his clothes*.) These dogs think I'm so wrecked by the war I can barely walk; they think this war has frozen me up; my feet, my legs, my brain; but if I have so much trouble walking, it has nothing to do with the war. It's this thing that weighs 15 pounds and is 2 and half feet long; and that I've carried on me day and night since the defeat. Help me get rid of it, now, I'm tired of being old. (He takes a sub-machine gun out from under his clothes.)

    It's a AK-47, Soviet-made; it's not really modern, but I swear it will blow your head off. I don't see why we need high-tech material when all we want is to blow heads off, and this thing fires 650 rounds per minute and up to 900 feet, so that makes 650 heads blown off a minute, if you do well that's not so bad. Taking it aside and stashing it wasn't hard, it's always easier to dupe officers after defeat than after victory, but now I'm sick of it, it's too heavy. (*He sits, puts the weapon on his lap.*)

Now I can see you a little better, but I don't need to see more now to know you're not straight, Negro. Just look at your legs; you can see right away those legs are too used to running; we don't like that here, people who run too fast. Come here. (ABAD *moves closer.*) Have you fathered a child yet? (ABAD *shakes his head.*) Not one? No little one? Not even one you wouldn't know about, a little thing lying around somewhere? (ABAD *shakes his head.*) Then, have you at least had a little girl, at least? (ABAD *shakes his head.*) Not even that? (RODOLFE *spits on the ground.*) Come here. Let me tell you how it works. (*He demonstrates with the weapon.*) You put the cartridge in this way, no other way or else it might blow up in your face; this is the fire selection; this position's for a burst; this position is shot by shot; it depends how many heads you've got to blow off and the accuracy of the shot; in theory, one shot is enough. (*He holds out the weapon.*) A man without a son dies like a dog, nothing is left of him, anywhere, it's like he never existed. Even if his son is a bastard, that doesn't matter. Your life is worth less than a chicken's life, Negro, you didn't deserve it; it's like you never existed.

(ABAD *takes the weapon.*) Now, I can see your face. At least you've earned your death, that's for sure. Come closer. (ABAD *leans in.*) If you've killed only one man, you are even with your fucking death, but your death won't leave a trace, nothing, as though you hadn't even died. You must kill two men to earn it; with two men killed you automatically leave a trace of yourself, something more, whatever happens; no one will ever be able to kill you twice.

(*He stands, moves toward the exit, and comes back.*) I'm warning you, if you don't use this thing to kill the fatso, Negro, I'll walk over to the other side, now that I walk as good as a kid, and I'll tell them, over there: I saw someone on the other side who's got a Ak-47, like you have one now; and they won't like that; I'll tell them: go, a bunch of you, surround the area because he runs fast, and he doesn't make a sound when he walks. And you'll be fucked.

Blow the fatso's head off, son, and let him feel the shot coming; a shot here, a shot there, take your time, make him shit his pants; do that for me, son, I'm asking you because I can't do it myself. (*He cries.*) My hands have had it, my brain is wrecked, my goddamn handshakes, look at that, son, look; I'd never be able to do it, I'll miss him for sure, and his goddamn fathead won't blow off. You can do it, son. Take pity on me, take pity on an old man who froze everything up, an old man all alone; don't let him get away with it, kill him.

(*He continues crying.*)
(*Night falls so that* ABAD *disappears.*)
(RODOLFE *moves away toward the exit.*)
(*On his way out, he bumps into* CHARLES *who's on the lookout, inside, near the door leading to the highway.*)

***

The night is pitch-black.
The wind, gusting through the door, rustles RODOLFE's *and* CHARLES' *hair and clothing.*

RODOLFE: (*Looking out the door, smiling*) Look, kid, look. (*He grabs* CHARLES' *arm.*) Look at your mother, how she shows her legs, in the middle of the night, in the cold, how she uncovers her legs: not one vein, not one bruise, not a shiver, not the slightest sign of the tiniest goose bump. She holds that fat squishy wobbling mound without trembling. Look, kid, look, how beautiful her legs are; despite the cold night, look at the legs of that savage, holding that pink and scaly mound, moist and dirty, look. With a mother like that, how could you expect me to be a good father? Look, how beautiful and strong: look at the savage approaching.

(CECILE *enters, holding* KOCH.)

CECILE: (*Rushing to* CHARLES) It's him, it's you, Charles, my Charlie! (*She kisses his cheek.*)

***

Around seven thirty, the pitch-black night turned to a ghastly gray around us and we could tell that the sun had risen.
- Conrad

The warehouse plunged in darkness, except for rays of moonlight filtering through the holes in the roof.

KOCH: (*To* CECILE) What are you talking about? He's not the one who got me out of the water.

CECILE: Yes he is, of course it was him.

KOCH: He's not even wet.

CECILE: He dried off, that's all. (*To* CHARLES) Say something larva, tell him that your sister brought you some towels; move it good-for-nothing. Why aren't you even wet?

KOCH: I want my watch.

CECILE: (*To* CHARLES) Look for the gentleman's watch, find the watch. Help the gentleman walk, you see he has a broken foot. Move it, good-for-nothing. (*Quietly*) Try not to find it, larva. (*To* RODOLFE) Que hiciste del negro, machorron? Lo siento por los parajes.

KOCH: I put it there.

CECILE: I'm telling you that he dried off; it's nothing unusual. He's waterproof, that's all; he's a good-for-nothing. But I still saw it all from my window. (*Quietly*) The bastard doesn't want to pay; but he'll pay. (*To* RODOLFE) Y el negro machorron?

(KOCH, *supported by* CHARLES, *bumps into* FAK *who is leading* MONIQUE *by the hand.*)

MONIQUE: (*To* KOCH) This gentleman was kind enough to lead me here. I've finally found someone kind; this gentleman is incredibly good. Come on, I'm going to help you, I can see perfectly. (*She takes* KOCH *from* CHARLES' *arms.*) Is this where you put it? Jesus Christ! What a pigsty!

CHARLES: (*To* RODOLFE, *quietly*) What did he tell you, did he tell you something?

RODOLFE: (*To* CECILE) Cecile, Cecile, tell him to leave me the fuck alone.

CHARLES: (*To* RODOLFE) I'm the only one who understands him, I'm the only one who has the right to speak to him, I forbid you to speak to him, I forbid you to go near him, god damnit. (*Even quieter*) He's after me, you stupid old man, he's against me. Where is he? Tell me where he is, so I can talk to him before he gets all worked up.

RODOLFE: (*To* CECILE) Tell him, Cecile, tell him que me deje en paz. (*He cries.*)

CECILE: (*To* CHARLES) Don't swear; go help the fatso, don't you see the others are taking care of him while you're here basking in the sun?

CHARLES: (*To* CECILE) Why do you let this stupid old man meddle in my plans?

CECILE: Shut up. Don't talk about your father like that. Where's your sister? Leave us alone. Where is my little Claire? (*She cries.*)

KOCH: (*To* MONIQUE) You haven't lost the car keys, I hope?

MONIQUE: The car? Don't make me laugh. We'll have to walk back and in this condition, Christ! Look at us.

KOCH: But the keys, I'm asking you, the keys?

MONIQUE: I have them, I have them, what does it matter?

KOCH: What does it matter? It's my car, right? And we could trade it for something.

MONIQUE: Your car, oh really, that's just great. Your car, Jesus Christ!

RODOLFE: (*To* CECILE) No llores, cabecita negra, o voy a acabar llorando contigo.

CECILE: (*To* RODOLFE) Ven, acercate. (*They sit side by side.*) No me abandones machorron.

MONIQUE: (*To* KOCH) Your car, your watch, your whims, your bullshit, and my legs to take you back to town.

KOCH: (*To* CHARLES) So, you help me; you must remember where I put it. (KOCH *moves from* MONIQUE's *arms to* CHARLES'.)

CECILE: (*To* RODOLFE) You, Rodolfe, who taught me everything, who pulled me from the swamp where I was festering to raise me up to shitty Lomas Altas and pulled me from the shit of Lomas Altas to drag me in the shit here, old, sick, no strength, no ideas. Why, when we are so old, is misfortune still allowed to stomp and dance all over us and stick our faces in every new pile of shit as if there hadn't been enough time to do it when we were still strong?

RODOLFE: Stop bitching. Hide your legs, slut. (*He pulls on* CECILE's *skirt*.)

CECILE: I'm not bitching, I'm resting. Where's my daughter?

MONIQUE: (*To* FAK) Tell me here what you had to tell me.

FAK: Not here. There are too many people. I said, I'll tell you up there.

MONIQUE: When I find the watch, I'll go up there.

FAK: When we find it, then?

MONIQUE: When we find it, yes; but he's going to have a fit if we don't find it for him.

FAK: So here. Here it is. (*He holds out the watch in his hand*.) You found it.

MONIQUE: Give it to me, don't say anything, I want to surprise him.

FAK: When you go up there with me I'll give it to you.

MONIQUE: Give it to me first, we'll see about after.

FAK: You have to go up there with me first, since I brought you this far.

MONIQUE: I'll give you money, take the jaguar for a spin, I'll give you something else, don't be so disgusting, Jesus Christ!

KOCH: (*To* CHARLES) Nonsense. Your ignorance, your style, it's all nonsense. If I had time I'd send you for training at the stock exchange, you'd lose your taste for nonsense. You'd stop loving something that doesn't exist. Money doesn't exist, my poor friend, at least you'd learn that, you don't put money in your pockets, money as you know it, is nonsense. Business exists, that's it, but you don't know a thing about business. See, I wouldn't even want you as a chauffeur. I think you would empty my pockets. Money, the way you like it, is scrap you throw to the dogs in the backyard. Your appetite for money makes me sick. You are just stupid, my poor friend.

    Take your thug job, yes, that's very nice; take back these trinkets, that I scattered on the ground; amuse yourself with it all. I'd rather go back. Let me go. (*He detaches himself from* CHARLES *and stumbles*.) Monique!

CECILE: (*From far away, to* MONIQUE) What are you doing with my daughter's shoe?

MONIQUE: Your daughter? What shoe? Jesus Christ! (*To* FAK) Who is this clown, slouching in the garbage?

CECILE: (*Rushing to* MONIQUE) Thief, bimbo!

(*She grabs the shoe from* MONIQUE*'s hand and moves away.*)
(FAK *has approached* CLAIRE *who entered discreetly.*)

MONIQUE: Brutes, bums, perverts, scum, human waste. I'm so sick of all these lunatic dirt bags; I'd rather live with rats and dogs, Jesus Christ! All these people disgust me. I'm going to live locked in by four concrete doors, I'm going to barricade myself in as soon as I get back home, I'll have food delivered through a tunnel so I don't have to see or smell the stench of human feces; I want concrete poured from my hair to my feet with a hole only for my mouth and my nose, Maurice, I want to go back. (MONIQUE *and* MAURICE *fall into each other's arms.*)

CLAIRE: (*To* FAK) I've already told you a thousand times that I don't even smoke.

FAK: It'll help you to see the ground. (CLAIRE *takes the lighter that* FAK *is holding out*.)

CLAIRE: What does it mean, what's written on it?

CECILE: (*Rushing to* CLAIRE) What are you doing here?

CLAIRE: I'm looking for the watch.

CECILE: Get out, right now.

CLAIRE: I don't see why I can't look for the watch when everyone else is looking for it.

CECILE: There's nothing for you to look for here, go home, sleep, go to bed, get lost in your mattress, disappear into the bedframe.

CLAIRE: I can't, it's the coffee. I want to stay.

CECILE: No way. And put on your shoe, idiot.

CLAIRE: No, I don't want to put on my shoe. I want to know.

CECILE: There's nothing for you to know, idiot, who asked you to know anything? Put on your shoe.

CLAIRE: No, I don't want to. I don't want to.

CECILE: Well, you have to. (*She forces her to put on her shoe*.) And now scram!

CLAIRE: I don't want to scram.

CECILE: Scram. Idiot.

CLAIRE: I'll come back.

CECILE: Just try it. (CLAIRE *exits. To* FAK) Hey you, stop eyeing the little slut.

KOCH: (*To* MONIQUE) I slipped. I wonder on what muck. Do you see something?

MONIQUE: No, I don't see anything.

KOCH: Do you hear?

MONIQUE: No.

KOCH: You don't hear that racket out there?

MONIQUE: It's the dogs, in the dumpsters.

KOCH: Look, Monique, look at my foot.

MONIQUE: It's swollen. (*She bursts into sobs.*) Everyone insults me, all these people I don't know.

KOCH: Hold onto my arm, Monique. We'll try to get out of here quietly.

MONIQUE: I'll say we put the money to work, I'll show some investment plans. In two hours, Maurice, I could prepare that. It'll buy us some time. I can easily make the Board of Directors swallow that. You know I can make anyone swallow anything.

KOCH: Yes, I know.

MONIQUE: Only you will have to tell me where the money went. Not now, not right away, but you'll have to, Maurice.

KOCH: Yes, I will have to tell you, I know. (*He suddenly begins to cry.*)

MONIQUE: Come on, Maurice, quietly. No one is watching us.

KOCH: It hurts. I can't walk.

MONIQUE: We're almost there, we're at the door. Lean on me.

CECILE: (*Toward the door*) I can still hear your little footsteps, you little slut, you'd better get on your mattress before I come after you.

RODOLFE: (*Yelling*) Se largan, se largan!

CECILE: (*To* CHARLES) Carlos, stop him!

MONIQUE: Jesus Christ!

(ABAD *appears, holding the sub-machine gun.*)

KOCH: (*Pointing out* ABAD) It's him, look, Monique; he's soaking wet like me.

CECILE: (*To* KOCH) Don't go near that one, he bites.

RODOLFE: (*To* CECILE) Callate, cabecita negra, callate.

CECILE: (*To* KOCH) Don't go any closer, sir, he's not of our race, sir, he's not of a race that accepts gratitude.

KOCH: Gratitude? Gratitude for what? I don't want to thank anyone, get it, I'll give you fucking hell.

MONIQUE: Don't bluff, Maurice, Jesus Christ! (*To* ABAD) Here, here are the keys, take the keys.

KOCH: No, give me those keys.

MONIQUE: Never.

CECILE: (*Moving in front of* KOCH) He won't touch you. (*She leans on* KOCH.) Let's stick together, sir, it's too dangerous. Hold my hand. God himself led you here by the hand so we could unite against the dogs and savages. Let's not drown among savages, let's not be mistaken for the dogs we live with; give me your hand.

(*Pointing out* CHARLES) Look at this child's feet. The pope kissed them one Holy Thursday, washed and kissed, out of ten children feet chosen of Lomas Altas. God can't first choose and then forget. We will protect you, we will feed you, we'll heal your foot, and we'll serve you like slaves. But if the pope kissed this child's feet, you could kiss his mother's hand. (*She holds out her hand to him.*)

KOCH: (*To* CECILE) Shut up.

MONIQUE: Jesus Christ! He's going to kill us all.

CECILE: No, not him, not him; he hasn't kissed my hand yet.

(ABAD *approaches* CHARLES *and hands him the sub-machine gun.* CHARLES *takes it for a while, plays with the fire selection.*)

KOCH: (*Getting away from the two women*) Nonsense.

(CHARLES *snickers, drops the weapon on the ground.*)

Ship's horn nearby on the river.

(*Casually, hands in pockets, taking his time,* CHARLES *exits.*)

KOCH: (*After picking up the weapon, to* ABAD, *leaning on him.*) Not in front of them, not in front of these people.

(*Together they head toward the pier.*)

MONIQUE: (*Watching* KOCH *disappear*) I'm getting the police.

CECILE: The police, right, only the police can do something.

MONIQUE: (*To* CECILE) Do you have a phone?

CECILE: No. But if you walk. . .(*She leans lightly on* MONIQUE.)

MONIQUE: What is that noise?

CECILE: Dogs. All day long they beg, they lick men's shoes, they whine at their feet, and at night they avenge themselves for a day of begging and contempt by chasing the silence off the streets.

MONIQUE: Maurice, his watch. (FAK *has gone.*)

CECILE: Let them die. (*She falls down.* RODOLFE *laughs and exits.*)

MONIQUE: Maurice! Jesus Christ!

CLAIRE: (*Appearing near the door; quietly*) Come on, it's almost daybreak; you'll be able to leave.

(*They carry out* CECILE's *body.*)

Very softly, the warehouse is lit by the day's first light.

***

On the pier.

(*A very strong wind, a hailstorm is knocking* KOCH *and* ABAD *around as they hold on wherever they can. The sub-machine gun is passed from hand to hand.* KOCH *yells over the uproar.*)

KOCH: Hurry up, hurry up, you're like a man who's too slow to know what he's doing. Anyway, you've got nothing to lose if you let me do it myself. I'm not holding on to you, I'm holding onto this weapon. How does this work? I don't know if I can figure out how to use it. Of course I could, I'd be able to if I really wanted to. Show me how and what I have to press, which button. Calm down, I'm just trying to figure it out, I'm not going to press anything. You hold it, if you're afraid.

Hurry up, hurry up. This wind is killing me. Believe me, if I go back with that woman, we'll go right to the police, all civilized people like us would do that; she'll want to, she'll want to get revenge, she always wanted to advance her status, she's scum. I hate her. She'll blame you and I'll go along with it. That's why you're better off letting me do it myself. I will rid myself of her, I'll rid myself of you, and then I swear, she'll have no reason to hurt you.

Take this machine, it's too heavy. I can't manage this thing myself, you have nothing to lose by doing it yourself. I hurt you, I didn't mean to, because, because I'm a civilized man, and you're not. That's all; the two of us don't match up. Do it yourself. Do it. You'll get revenge, and I'll be relieved.

What path do your thoughts travel to take so long? Where are they now? Your belt? Your chest? Pick up the pace.

She's scum, and I hate her. You hate me. We should each live on our own side, eyes turned into our own territory. We should ban encounters. We should tear curiosity out of people's heads. We should hate each other thoroughly, not like a man hates a woman living with him, like you are supposed to, not like a low-life hates a man of the world, but like bare skin hates battery acid.

Please let's not waste time staring at each other. I'm cold, my foot hurts, and I hurt all over. I can't take it anymore. (*He holds out the butt of the gun to* ABAD.) Can't you see I'm sick? Help me.

(ABAD *puts his hand on the sub-machine gun.*)

Dawn is over, birds taking flight, the wind calms.

***

In the warehouse, daybreak.

(FAK *with* CLAIRE *in tow.*)

CLAIRE: Actually, it's not that dark, I said I'd go in when it's completely dark.

FAK: It is completely dark, can't get any darker.

CLAIRE: It's not that dark since I can see you.

FAK: You can see me because you're used to the darkness.

CLAIRE: Hurry up, my mom's sick, I have to take care of her.

FAK: I am hurrying up, you're the one slowing down. I'm dragging you.

CLAIRE: It's just that I don't know how and I'm a little scared because it's not completely dark.

FAK: Close your eyes, I'm guiding you, you just have to follow me, I know the way by heart.

(*They cross the warehouse,* CLAIRE *stumbles.*)

CLAIRE: Why don't you look where I'm stepping?

FAK: Because you have to look where you're stepping and I have to look somewhere else.

CLAIRE: Why do you have to look somewhere else when you're with me?

FAK: Because when you're doing something, you've got to think about your next move or else it goes too fast.
CLAIRE: You told me it would feel really good to go with you, inside here.

FAK: Yes.

CLAIRE: So good, you told me, I'd always want to go in here with you.

FAK: Yes.

CLAIRE: But, I don't feel anything good right now.

FAK: You already did.

CLAIRE: When?

FAK: Before.

CLAIRE: When, precisely?

FAK: When I was asking you to go in there with me.

CLAIRE: That's it?

FAK: Yes.

CLAIRE: What do I do now?

FAK: Nothing.

CLAIRE: How long do I do nothing for?

FAK: Not long.

CLAIRE: I'm scared.

FAK: It'll stop.

CLAIRE: I'm still scared.

FAK: It's normal.

(*Hail of gunfire on the pier;* FAK *takes* CLAIRE; MONIQUE *screams on the highway;* FAK *lets go of* CLAIRE.)

FAK: That's it. I have to go.

CLAIRE: You brought me here you can't just leave me here alone in the middle now.

FAK: I've got more important things to do.

CLAIRE: What about me? What happens to me, stuck in the middle?

FAK: What do I know? Whatever you want. Nothing.

CLAIRE: (*Grabbing onto* FAK) Don't leave me alone now.

FAK: Shut up. (*He hits her and walks away.*)

(CLAIRE *watches* FAK *disappear through the door to the pier.*)

***

Along the warehouse, in broad daylight.

(CHARLES *approaches* RODOLFE.)

CHARLES: I'm here to say good-bye. I have to go, quick, before it's too late. But I couldn't leave without saying good-bye.

RODOLFE: Shut up. I'm already half deaf and you're buzzing in my ears. I've already heard what I wanted to hear.

CHARLES: You're half deaf and half blind for everyone else, but I know that you can hear and see me, no need to fool me. You know what, I'm deaf and blind as you are to all this here, that's why I want to go when I still can. But to you, alone, I want to say good-bye, you alone will have heard my good-bye, and knowing that, I'll be okay.

RODOLFE: I don't want to hear your voice.

CHARLES: You'll hear it anyway.

RODOLFE: What do you want? I can't see very much and I can't hear very well. Who exactly are you?

CHARLES: I'm your son, Charles, Carlos.

RODOLFE: I don't know a thing about it, and neither do you, you know even less. Who can follow the water meanderings from the source to the sea and be sure of not making a wrong turn? There's no reason for me to waste my time listening to you.

CHARLES: Help me leave. I haven't done anything that deserves punishment yet. Do you think it's fair when I'm old enough to fuck women, buy suits and drive cars, old enough to be making money for all that, I spend these years and this money to support the death of an old woman and when she dies, there'll be nothing left for me? And to feed a girl for boys I don't even know and when they pick her up, all primped and preened, there'll be nothing left for me. These years are gone and so is my cash. That's why I'm leaving today, saying good-bye, and I'm asking your blessing like you taught me a son should ask his father when he leaves home.

RODOLFE: Ask your mother and leave me alone.

CHARLES: I don't want to ask my mother anything.

RODOLFE: You're right. She's a bitch. That bitch takes advantage of the fact I can barely walk and barely spit anymore, only half spit. That savage was wallowing in the swamp; I'm the one who fished her out like a tadpole from the pond, who washed and dressed her, who taught her everything, how to walk, eat, laugh, cry, taught her the earth was round and the sun spins around it, taught her to speak correctly, she only spoke obscene language, taught her religion, and once she was fed, dressed, and knew how to spit in a spittoon and wash her fingers in a finger bowl, the savage in her woke up and she works at my misfortune for no reason, for her fucking savage pleasure. You know, a healthy fruit can rot but a rotten fruit can never be healthy again.

CHARLES: So then you think it's okay I leave.

RODOLFE: Not at all, I don't think a thing at all, I'm too old and too stupid to think. I just want you to leave me the fuck alone.

CHARLES: And I don't want to be cursed. I don't care what the others think of me, but I know if you accept my good-bye without cursing me, I won't wander around my whole life unable to get rid of this curse like when kids are cursed by their fathers, you taught me that.

RODOLFE: Anyway, your mother will curse you so leave me alone and get lost.

CHARLES: I don't give a damn about my mother's curse.

RODOLFE: True. Women curse in the morning and suddenly bless at night, and when the morning comes they curse again, and bless one more time at noon, they're like a wind that blows in one direction and then another, leaving the trees all upright. But my curse is a pinch of salt I toss in the tea, and nothing will ever make it drinkable again.

CHARLES: That's why I don't want you to curse me.

RODOLFE: I'll do it anyway, I'll do it anyway, count on it.

CHARLES: Why? What do you want? Look at you, you can barely walk, you're half deaf and blind, life has completely broken you, and you're old. I admire the strong, imposing man, I admire the thirty-year-old man around you like a shadow, who I remember a little. But today, that man is only a shadow, and what actually exists is an old broken man whose pieces will never be put together again. But me, look at me, the pieces aren't broken yet, it's my old age that's around me like a shadow, but my time is now. You can't be hurt anymore. You don't have to hope to drive a car, you don't have to worry how to dress, you can forget about fucking a woman. We can't keep you from doing it, since you won't do it anyway. But, I can be hurt. And if the future has pity on the old fuck and forgets him, the old fuck can have pity on the ones who the future stalks like an enemy.

RODOLFE: I don't understand a word you're saying, the war and old age have left me half senile, I don't even know exactly who I am, so just tell me what you want.

CHARLES: You're my father, like it or not, and your old brain can't forget that.

RODOLFE: How can you be so sure I'm your father, when I'm not so sure myself? Anyway, mothers are mommies and daddies at the same time; a father is like a little storm over the ocean, no time to see where those damn drops rush off to. And anyway, I don't give a flying fuck.

CHARLES: Then I want you to remember me. Just that. I want to stay in somebody's memory like you taught me we had to stay in someone's memory so we wouldn't die, even in the memory of an old brain like yours. You can't refuse that. You can't deny me.

RODOLFE: Of course I can. I forget everything. I have no memory. Besides, I've already forgotten you.

CHARLES: Why do you wish me bad luck?

RODOLFE: Because I don't wish you anything.

(CHARLES exits.)

***

What is this house you make me enter, forming such an unusual building? What does it mean, the tremendous height of the different walls surrounding it? Where are you taking me?
- Marivaux

The highway. Afternoon.

(CLAIRE *finishes combing* MONIQUE*'s hair.*)
(CECILE *is in the corner, alone.*)

CLAIRE: (*To* MONIQUE *who stands up*) Where are you sneaking off to now?

MONIQUE: Looking for the police. Let go of me, you little brat, let me go.

CLAIRE: Don't go.

MONIQUE: I'll go, Christ! You can't stop me you little bag of dirt.

CLAIRE: What do you want to hurt us for, when it's all over for you? Why would you still want to hurt us?

MONIQUE: I'll hurt you as much as I can, all the pain I can imagine will be just for you.

CLAIRE: He killed himself; none of us had anything to do with it.

MONIQUE: Killed himself? I don't think so. Killed himself? I know him. He was bluffing. (*She cries.*) What am I going to do now? What am I going to do?

CLAIRE: Don't run off. It's a very long way, it takes hours and hours, you'll get lost, you'll go through streets, all alone in the middle of streets, your shoes will clack loud and wake people up, they'll watch you and surround you, they'll follow you for hours and hours and you'll be lost.

MONIQUE: Leave me alone. I'm crying.

CLAIRE: Don't run off, ma'am, don't run off. I'll look for some tires for your car myself and some gas for your tank and some towels for your tears, and when everything calms down, you'll go back in your car nice and easy, you'll know then who you hate and who you don't.

MONIQUE: Shut up. I'm crying.

CLAIRE: Night is falling very fast, ma'am, it's going to fall while you're getting lost in these completely lonely streets, and then you can cry and no one, no one will dry your eyes. Don't sneak off ma'am, don't sneak off. We'll leave you alone; you'll be in your own space with dignity, waiting for the day to go away and come back again, and you'll calm down ma'am, with dignity, in your own space.

MONIQUE: Let go of me.

CECILE: (*To* CLAIRE) Come here, help me, don't sit there doing nothing.

(CLAIRE *watches* MONIQUE *walk away*.)

("I call him loud-mouth, liar, cheat, because when he wakes up after a short nap he whines, already coveting another bed: If I was in your good graces, if only you'd allow yourself to be moved by my sadness and my disgust for life, just once; if at least you weren't so cruel that, out of pure spite, you deprive me of the final resting place which everyone has a right to; you would listen to my plea for one moment and let yourself be moved, you'd make it easy for me to get to that resting place, since I promise that as soon as I get there, I won't covet another, I'll stick to that one, I'll lay down in it and never leave it again, you'll never hear me complain again. But as soon as his prayer is granted, as soon as he has his fill, satisfied, after a short nap, he leaves with a vague regret, lifts his head, covets another bed and begs again.

It's the bitch that has man on a leash, the slave who cheats the master, the bird that locks the child in its cage. I don't want to talk to her, listen to her, give in to her, and never again shed another tear; now it's my turn to be mean and tough and heartless, I want to muzzle her like a badly trained mutt, fight her until she lies down when I tell her to, make her go where I tell her to, so we find out who obeys who.

I beat her with a stick to teach her respect, but I only toughened her up and made her insolent; I held her under icy water to teach her silence but I only piqued her curiosity; I pricked her with thorns so the evil and suffering she inflicted on me would pour out with her blood, but I only gave her a taste for suffering. She bangs on the door, she screams: let me out, take me into the world, don't leave me locked up like an old useless wife who you're ashamed of. But if I let her out, she inflicts me with rashes and burns like a woman's period, and if I don't let her out, then she casts a spell and my skin turns yellow, covered in pimples, and my stomach aches.

It's the slave I can't set free, the dog I can't slaughter; but on the contrary, I must hold onto her leash tight with my hands and my teeth, because her name is mine and I don't want the traces of my life among men erased, nor my reason for existing wiped out from this world," says Fak.)

***

CECILE: Carry me to the kitchen, come on, get moving, I don't want to stay here.

CLAIRE: You're too heavy, I can't carry you by myself.

CECILE: Idiot. (*Quietly*) Hide me, I don't want Rodolfe to see me, I can hear him snickering back there, go find my shawl and hide me underneath, I want to look like a little pile of rocks. (*Angry*) Clean up around me, it's disgusting, go find the bucket and clean.

CLAIRE: There's no water.

CECILE: You found some for your coffee and to do yourself up like a little slut. Go to the river with the bucket.

CLAIRE: It's too far, it's too heavy, it's too dirty. I don't want to.

CECILE: Who taught you to talk back? (*Quietly*) Call your brother.

CLAIRE: He took off.

CECILE: Bullshit. Call your brother.

CLAIRE: No, I don't want a brother anymore.

CECILE: What do you think you would be without him? Who fattened you up, little slut? (*Quietly*) I don't want to be dirty, I don't want to smell bad and people telling me I do. Some water, my treasure, my flower, my sun, bring me some water. (*Angry*) Call Rodolfe, right now, que llames a Rodolfo, te digo, idiota.

CLAIRE: What are you saying?

CECILE: Que venga pronto, no que no venga, que desaparezca, que se muera, ya bastante me jodio toda mi puta vida.

CLAIRE: Stop it, mama, stop it. (*She cries.*)

CECILE: Ese impotente me hizo echar raices en este pais de salvajes, ese castrado me metio en la cama de los salvajes, me hizo fornicar con las larvas, hizo que se acoplara la orquidea con el cardo, y heme aqui reventando en medio de esta mierda.

CLAIRE: (*Running, panicked*) Papa, papa, come quick. I don't understand anything she's saying.

CECILE: Quiero regresar a las Lomas Altas, no, no quiero regresar alla, el aire alla esta podrido y huele a mierda, alla he perdido todos mis colores y mis fuerzas y mi virilidad, alla me gastaron la vida, y a cambio me dieron una bolsa de guijarros que debo arrastrar noche y dia por el mar, por los puertos, hasta que me caiga de cansancio.

(CLAIRE *returns*, RODOLFE *in tow*.)

RODOLFE: Leave me the fuck alone, bastard.

CLAIRE: What is she saying, papa, what is she saying?

RODOLFE: I don't want to know.

CECILE: ¿Imanasqam Maria? ¿Imanasqam noqa wachuchikurqani supaywan, nina nawiyuqwan, wachachikuwananpaq? ¿Dolores, Mariapa maman, niykuway? ¿imanasqam supaywan wachuspa, Mariata wachana? ¿Imanasqam? ¿Niykuway Carmen? ¿imanasqam wachuchikurqani Doloresta wacha naypaq, paypas Mariata wachananpaq, Mariapas, qanra chuchumeka, hatun rakayuq, paypas wachananpaq?

RODOLFE: The Indian awakes. (*He smiles*.)

CLAIRE: What is she saying? What is she saying papa?

CECILE: Cheqnisqa kachun llapallan tuta, chay warmikunapa tutan, waytarukuspa, pantasqa supaywan wachuchikuna tuta, paykuna waytakurukuspa, satirachikuspa isqon killamanta anchata qaparinqaku qanra qocha patanpi; cheqnisqa kachun warmipa qaparitynin, chawpi tutapi warmi wawata wachakuspa; chay warmi wawakunapas, winaspa, waytarikunqaku, wachuchikunqaku, qaparinqaku. Cheqnisqa kachun llapa warmikunapa rakan, cheqnisqa kachun Runa Kamaq, cheqnispa warmita rurarqa, pantasqa, yarqasqa runapa pisqonwan satichikunanpaq.

RODOLFE: The Indian goes to sleep. (CECILE *looks at the sun, the sun slips down.*)

(CECILE *has stopped moving*, CLAIRE *runs off.*)
(RODOLFE, *suddenly furious, approaches* CECILE *and pulls her skirt down over her legs.*)
(MONIQUE's *silhouette moves away, in the distance.*)

***

Inside the warehouse, in the dark red light of evening.

(CLAIRE, *out of breath, stops* CHARLES *who is heading toward the pier.*)

CLAIRE: What if I told you I could make time and make money for you. What if I told you I was going to give you more time than you could ever need to succeed in life, Charlie, and the best way to make more money than you would ever need in your whole lifetime, and the way to be the best and the strongest against all the others?

I can do for you, Charlie, what no one else could ever do. I can take care of you like no one else ever will; I can be there for you, at your beck and call, what no one else has at their beck and call, that way you'll have all your time for everything else. What if I told you, Charlie, I can love you like no one else will ever love you?

You're wasting your time, Charlie, half making money, half looking for someone who loves you, while with me you could spend all your time on the money without bothering with the rest. I'd love you like no one else would ever love you, you'd only have one thing to look for and to find: only taking care of yourself and make your money.

Look at everyone else, Charlie, trying to find somebody to love, to love this way, that way, one here, some there, some a little more, some a little less, and some who charge a fee. With me there wouldn't be a fee, it would be a sure thing; you wouldn't need anything, not to look at me, not to talk to me, not to think about me, not to love me at all, only to have me at your beck and call and you could love whoever you wanted, and you charge the fee. So, Charlie, you'd just sit back and laugh watching everyone else. It would be stupid, Charlie, not to take the deal.

What if I told you I could love you, Charlie, like no one else will ever love you? I can love you, day or night, winter and summer, doesn't matter how and doesn't matter where, here or anywhere. What if I told you I love you so much, Charlie, it's good for you that I love you like that, and that I keep doing it and I could keep doing it, Charlie, like no one will love you ever?

(CLAIRE *watches* CHARLES *walk away, night.*)

***

On the pier.

(ABAD, CHARLES, FAK, *the Ak-47.*)
(FAK *tries with difficulty to pull* KOCH's *body toward the water.*)

CHARLES: (*To* FAK) He's heavy or are you just tired?

FAK: He's heavy.

CHARLES: When you die, the soul flies away and finds itself before God who judges and decides who goes to heaven and who goes to hell. He asks for your average yearly salary and you must bring either your pay stub or your tax return to prove your income. Everyone who can prove their salary exceeds a certain amount goes to heaven, and everyone else to hell. They also examine your clothes. (*Examining* KOCH's *suit*) It's an Armani.

(ABAD *picks up the AK-47, and puts it in semi-automatic position, fires a shot over the river.*)

The waves roar in response.

(FAK *shoves the body into the water.*)

Ship's horn in the distance.

FAK: I'm beat. (*He lies down and closes his eyes.*)

CHARLES: (*Watching* KOCH's *body floating on the water*) In heaven, there are rich villas guarded by Dobermans, with lawns and tennis courts; they serve cocktails before meals and even the angels, who are the waiters, are wearing shoes by Weston. In hell, you live in rusted shells of old abandoned cars (*He snickers.*) Nonsense.

FAK: Now I know why he wasn't that heavy; I forgot to put the stones back in his pockets. He must be floating.

(ABAD *fires over the river. He sets off a small storm.*)

It rains.

CHARLES: Maybe I can get a fake pay stub. (*He snickers, looks at* ABAD.)

FAK: (*Opening his eyes*) He's floating.

Clamor of birds taking flight, nearby.

(ABAD *points the weapon at* CHARLES *and fires*.)

END OF PLAY

NOTES TO WEST PIER

Translated by Marion Schoevaert
and Theresa M. Weber

1. Translation from Spanish and Quechua in Cecile's death:

> "Call Rodolfe, do as I say, idiot.
> So he comes right away; no, so he doesn't come, so he disappears, so he dies; he's pissed me off enough all my fucking life.
> That impotent made me plant roots in this country of savages, this eunuch pushed me into savages' beds, he made me fornicate with larvas, he made the orchid copulate with the dandelion, and here I am dying in the middle of this shit.
> I want to return to the High Hills, no, I don't want to go back there, the air is rotten and smells of shit; there, I lost my colors and my strength and my virility; I lost my life, and was given in exchange a little bag of stones that I must carry day and night on the sea, in ports, until I collapse from exhaustion.
> Why, Maria, tell me: why did you fornicate with a red-eyed jackal and give birth to me? Tell me, Dolores, mother of Maria, tell me why you fornicated with a jackal and gave birth to Maria? And why, tell me this, Carmen, did you fornicate and drop Dolores, who dropped Maria the whore, equipped with everything she needs for dropping, when it's her turn.
> Cursed be the night when women get all dressed up to fornicate with the errant jackal; and nine months later get undressed on some detested beach screaming; cursed be a woman's scream in the heart of the night, who gives birth to other women who'll get dressed up and get undressed and scream when it's their turn. Cursed be the instrument of woman's reproduction and cursed be the god who cursed the woman with man's errant instrument like a starving jackal."

2. Production Notes for *West Pier*

A priori, all language should be considered ironic, and each movement serious; in this way, things which are not meant to be serious will not be taken as such, and scenes which are meant to be funny will not become sad, and tragedy will be eliminated from the story.

So, in Monique's and Koch's first scene in the dark, in order to give a true sense of the scene, the focus must be, first and foremost, on two people trying to walk on slippery ground. Because this scene is, above all, about an unanswered question: who's following who? Who's leading who?

The text is, maybe, sometimes too long to play but the actors are always too slow. They have a tendency not just to say the words but also to weight them, to show them, to give them meaning. In fact, one should always say a text like a child with a strong need to piss, reciting a lesson: very fast, shifting from one leg to the other, and who, when he's finished, rushes off to do what was on his mind all along.

One should never try to deduce the characters' psychology from the meaning of what they're saying, but on the contrary, have them say the words according to what we deduce they are, based on what they do.

Naturally, the passages within quotes and parentheses, written like Romanesque monologues shouldn't be performed; nor are they for the programs. They each have their place to be read, between two scenes; and there they should stay because the play has been written to be both read and performed.

If there are cuts to be made, they are not necessarily in the long monologues. Of course, one could say: at the beginning of the monologue Charles is here, at the end he is there, let's hurry from one point to the other. This is a miscalculation, because Charles comes from nowhere and goes nowhere, will take his time anyway, and if we prevent him, we simply prevent him from existing; and what there is to see about Charles is precisely the time he takes to go from one point to another, and the approach he uses.

For the same reason, in Koch's first scene with Charles and Abad on the pier, the steps that Charles must take between Koch and Abad, and between Abad and Koch shouldn't be economized.

Charles is neither weak, nor soft, nor indecisive. He is simply "prevented"; I mean to say that the slight gap between him and life is the real cause of all his unfinished projects.

I don't see how one could avoid making Rodolfe monstrous; he's a monster because he's happy, which is never nice to see. Maybe, at the very end, like a murderer who ends up at some point bragging about his crime, he then finds himself surprised at his own happiness. So then, like the muzzle of a dog that is yanked from the garbage, briefly, he might seem familiar to us.

The worst that could happen to Koch is to make him tortured and deep when he's capricious and secretive. Koch's real depth, if he has any, comes from the many obstacles he puts up between what he reveals and his secret; so when we think we've discovered the heart of the problem, we can be certain that it's only another obstacle made up to keep us from penetrating further, so that it's not clear at all whether in the end there is a secret, only that Koch presents himself as an infinite number of pharaonic caskets encased one inside the other and made to deceive the eye; and to want to profane the infinite mystery of this tomb would probably lead to the discovery of a last box containing some dead ashes and devoid of meaning.

It would be best to conclude that Fak is Asian, of rather frail appearance, but with a fearsome strength; and one should be absolutely convinced, that he could if he wanted, with one sweep of his arm, wipe them all out. But he has a taste for game or competition or success; he jumps from one strategy to another and, it's on these terms, he should be characterized; because the play hinges on this and this alone. It would be better not to give Fak an ounce of emotion that he doesn't have or that we are far from understanding. Fak is real tough guy.

Cecile shouldn't be taken for an imbecile; everyone around her does. To take Cecile for an imbecile would be to take her for a mother, an aristocrat in exile, or an Indian who possesses, who knows what, magic powers; while she's only, as she says herself, a fly trapped in a closet, who will surely die before the door is opened.

If someone takes you for an imbecile, of the thousand ways that exist to take someone for an imbecile, I know of three possible responses:
- Adopt an unshakable dignity;
- Show to what extent you can play the imbecile. (It was an art that was a specialty of the Blacks in San Francisco's ghetto which was called "mau-mauing," and consisted of the following reasoning: the Whites take us for savages, let's give them a grand show of savages.)
- Cecile says: let's show to what extent I'm capable of being an imbecile, such an imbecile that I pretend, feet in shit, to adopt an unshakable dignity.

The real work of the actress who plays Cecile would be to show she's not doing what she seems to be doing, nor desiring what she's asking for; but she's like a mirror reflecting what we expect from her, and reflecting it with such powerful light that she dazzles the other actors.

In this infinite game of defense, Cecile expends infinite energy; sometimes, she loses the thread and she asks herself: where was I? And it's also in this game of infinite mystery that Koch finds some familiarity in her.

Claire runs after Monique; at the end they meet. Monique is one of these interminable deaths of the Theater, where the wounded hero accumulates reasons for his death just to avoid admitting he's dying for no reason. While Claire, who's impatient, who drinks coffee, who learns quickly, and immediately finds theatrical death more beautiful than life, is hurrying up just to be dragged through life, until the moment when life runs away from her with the little clap-clap of Charles' heels on the ground; and at the end of the play, she prepares for her death, no doubt, with the cursing and whining she saw in Monique's.

I've noticed that, though it would seem obvious to everyone that the role of a man should be played by a man, an old man by an old man, a young woman by a young woman, it is convention to consider anyone for the role of a black man; we dress him up either in a mask or with paint, or with a "reason" for being black—and of course, when we find the "reason" we can skirt around it. Therefore, to give it a closer look, based on his name and the mark he left in the snow in his first appearance, it seems to me that Abad is black-skinned, absolutely; that there is no reason he should be and that is why he absolutely is; and, if we skimp on this, then we can also skimp on the water, on the warehouse, Rodolfe, the sun and the play.

Abad refuses to speak to anyone else but Charles; and still he economizes on words, and he whispers in his ear. I didn't make him mute because it was easier, even though in effect it was, but because it was unavoidable. Abad is not a character in photonegative in the middle of the play; it is a play which is the photonegative of Abad.

So the actor who plays Abad should be chosen according to what he has to do and not according to what he's spared from doing. No need for him to know how to speak, no doubt; but when he's put in a corner, sheltered, his body emits steam. That is what he should be chosen for.

The worst that could happen to the play is to make it sentimental and not funny. No scene should be interpreted as a love scene, because no scene has been written as a love scene. They are scenes of business, exchange and trafficking, and they should be played as such. There is no tenderness in business and none should be added where there isn't any. The only passage that could be approached as a love scene is Monique's and Charles' dialogue the afternoon on the highway dealing with technical performance, brakes and number of cylinders in the jaguar. One should think that love, passion, tenderness, and I don't know what else, make their way by themselves; and by being too concerned with them one diminishes and ridicules them always.

IN THE SOLITUDE OF COTTON FIELDS

Translated by Amin Erfani

A deal is a commercial transaction of prohibited or strictly controlled goods, reached in neutral and indefinite spaces, not intended for that use, between purveyors and buyers, through tacit agreements, conventional signs, or innuendos—in order to avoid the risk of betrayal or fraud inherent to such an operation—at any time of the day or night, regardless of the official opening hours of accredited businesses, but rather after their closing time.

THE DEALER

If you walk outside, at this hour and in this place, it is because you desire something you do not have, and that thing, I can provide it to you; and if I have been in this place long before you, and will be here long after you, and even this hour when savage encounters between men and animals won't drive me away, it is because I have what is necessary to satisfy the desire that passes in front of me, and it is like a burden I must unload on whoever passes in front of me, man or animal.

That is why I approach you, despite this hour when ordinarily men and animals savagely pounce on each other, I approach you with open hands, my palms turned toward you, with the humility of someone who offers facing someone who buys, with the humility of someone who possesses facing someone who desires; and I see your desire like a light that turns on at a window at the very top of a building, in the twilight; I approach you like that twilight approaches that first light, slowly, respectfully, almost affectionately, leaving down in the street the animals and the men who pull on their leashes and savagely show their teeth to one another.

Not that I have guessed your desire, nor am I in a hurry to know; because a customer's desire is the most melancholy thing, which you covet like a little secret waiting to be pierced and you take your time to pierce it; like a gift wrapped up whose string you take your time to untie. But, then, ever since I've come to this place, I have desired all the things that all the men and all the animals might desire at this hour of darkness, which pull them out of their home despite the savage growls of unsatisfied animals and unsatisfied men; that's why I know better than the worried customer who for a time keeps his mystery to himself, like a little virgin raised to become a whore, and that what you will ask for, I already have it, and that all you have to do, is to ask it from me, without taking offense at the apparent injustice of being the one who asks facing the one who offers.

Since there is no real injustice on this earth other than the injustice of the earth itself, sterile from the cold or sterile from the heat and rarely fertile from the mild mix of the heat and the cold, there is no injustice for someone who walks on the same parcel of the earth in the same cold or in the same heat or in the same mild mix, and a man or an animal who can look another man or animal in the eye is his equal, because they walk on the same fine line, flat from latitude, slaves to the same cold and to the same heat, rich in the same way and in the same way poor; and the only real boundary, no matter how blurry, is between the customer and the salesman, both of whom possess desire and the object of desire, empty and full at the same time, with an injustice smaller still than the injustice of being male or female among men or animals. That is why I borrow humility for a time and lend you arrogance, so we won't give the same appearance, at this hour which ineluctably is the same for you and for me.

So tell me, melancholy virgin, at this moment when men and animals quietly growl, tell me the thing that you desire and that I can provide you and I will provide it to you, gently, almost respectfully, perhaps with affection; and then, after filling the void and flattening the peaks within us, we will walk away, one from the other, balanced on the thin and flat rope of our latitude, satisfied amid men and animals dissatisfied with being men and dissatisfied with being animals; but don't ask me to guess your desire; in order to satisfy everyone who passes in front of me while I stand here, I would need to enumerate everything in my possession, and no doubt the time required for this enumeration would dry out my heart and wear thin your hope.

THE CLIENT

I don't walk in a certain place at a certain hour; I walk, period, from one point to another, for personal business conducted at those points and not along the path between them. I don't know any twilight or any form of desire and I want to ignore the accidents on my path. I was going from that lit window, in my back, up there, to that other lit window, out there, in front of me, following a very straight line that goes through you because you put yourself here on purpose. And yet there is no way for someone who travels from a high point to another high point to avoid going down only to have to go back up again, with the absurdity of two movements that cancel each other, and at the risk, between them, of treading on trash thrown out the windows; the higher one lives, the healthier the air, but the harder the fall; and when the elevator leaves you down here, it condemns you to walk amid all the things nobody wanted up there, piles of rotting memories, like at the restaurant when the waiter brings you the check and enumerates to your disgusted ears all the meals you've started digesting a long time ago.

The darkness should have been thicker still, so I wouldn't see your face; only then, perhaps, I could have misunderstood the reason why you're here, why you moved off your path to place yourself in mine and why, in turn, I moved off mine to accommodate yours; but what darkness could be so thick to make you look less dark than itself? There is no moonless night that wouldn't look like noon if you walked into it, and that noon makes it clear that it wasn't the randomness of elevators that brought you down here, but an imprescriptible law of gravity, that is yours alone, that you conspicuously carry on your shoulders, like a bag that ties you down to this hour and to this place from where you try to assess, with a sigh, the heights of the buildings.

As to what I desire, if there were any desire I could remember, down here, in the darkness of the twilight, amid the growls of animals that don't even show their tails, other than the quite certain desire I have to see you rid yourself of humility and not offer me arrogance—because if I have a weakness for arrogance, I hate humility, in me and in others, and this exchange displeases me—, what I would desire, you certainly wouldn't have it. My desire, if I had any, if I revealed it to you, would burn your face, would make you pull away your hands with a cry and run away into the darkness, like a dog that runs so fast nobody sees its tail. But, no, the turmoil of this place and this hour makes me doubt that I ever had any desire to recall, no, or any offer to make, and you'll have to move away, so that I won't have to myself, move off my axis, cancel yourself, because that light up there, at the top of the building, undisturbed, continues to shine despite the approaching darkness; it tears a hole into the darkness like a lit match burning a hole into the piece of rag that tries to snuff it out.

THE DEALER

You are right to think that I come down from nowhere and have no intention of going up, but you would be wrong to believe that I feel any regret. I steer clear of elevators like a dog steers clear of water. Not that their doors refuse to open for me, or that I am repulsed by closing myself in them; but moving elevators tickle me and make me lose my dignity; and if I like to be tickled, I like not to be tickled as soon as my dignity demands it. There are elevators like some drugs, too much of them makes you float, never going up, never coming down, mistaking curves for straight lines, freezing the fire in its core. That said, during the time that I've spent in this place, I've learned to recognize those flames, far away, behind the windows, that look frozen like twilights during winter, but if you just approach them gently, perhaps affectionately, you'll remember that no glimmer remains forever cold, and my goal is not to put you out, but to shelter you from the wind, and dry up the humidity of the hour with the warmth of this flame.

Because, say what you will, the line you walked on, no matter how straight it was, became crooked when you saw me, and I grasped the exact moment when you saw me by the exact moment when your path became curved, and not curved to get away from me, but curved to come closer to me, otherwise we would have never met, and you would have gotten further away from me, because you were walking with the speed of someone who goes from one point to another; and I would have never caught up with you because I only move slowly, calmly, almost immovably, with the gait of someone who doesn't go from one point to another but who stays on an invariable spot, lying in wait for whoever passes in front of him and slightly alters his path. And if I say that you made a curve, no doubt you will claim that you moved off your path only to avoid me, and then I will claim in turn that you moved only to get closer to me, and surely it is because you never shifted from your path in the first place, and that a line is straight only relative to a plane, and that we move upon two distinct planes, and in the end what matters is the fact that you looked at me and that I caught that look or the other way around, and from then, no matter how absolute, the line on which you moved became relative and complex, neither straight nor curved, but fateful.

THE CLIENT

In any event, I do not have, for your pleasure, any illicit desire. My business, I conduct it at the accredited hours of daytime, in accredited places of business lit by electric light. Maybe I am a whore, if so, my brothel is not of this world; mine operates under legal light and closes its doors at night, stamped by the law and lit by electric light, because even sunlight isn't trustworthy and shows complicity. What do you expect from a man whose every step is accredited and stamped and lawful and flooded with electric light in every corner? And if I am here, mid-course, delayed, suspended, displaced, offside, off-life, provisional, practically absent, so to speak not here—because, do you say of a man traveling by plane over the Atlantic that he is in Greenland at a given time, and is he really? or in the tumultuous heart of the ocean?—and if I strayed off my path, although the straight line connecting my point of origin to my point of destination had no reason to become crooked all of a sudden,

I did so because you blocked my way, while being full of illicit intentions and assumptions about me being full of illicit intentions. But know that what I hate most in this world, even more than illicit intentions, even more than the illicit act itself, is the look that someone gives you assuming that you are full of illicit intentions and so used to them; not just the look itself, although so troubling it muddies the torrents on the mountains,—and you, your look rises up the mud at the bottom of a glass of water—but the sheer weight of your gaze violates my virginity, my innocence turned guilty, and the straight line supposed to bring me from one bright point to another bright point got twisted, because of you, a dark labyrinth in the dark territory where I have lost myself.

THE DEALER

You're trying to slip a thorn underneath the saddle of my horse, so he gets angry and loses control; but if my horse is nervous and wild at times, I hold him by a tight bridle so he doesn't lose control so easily; a thorn is no blade, and he knows the thickness of his skin, and he can stand the itch. That said, who can really predict the temper of a horse? Sometimes he can take a needle in his flank, sometimes a speck of dust under the harness makes him buck, run in circles, and throw his rider off his back.

Know then, if I speak to you, at this hour, in this way, gently, perhaps still with respect, it is not the way you do: by necessity, your language shows your fear, one that's short and sharp, foolish and flagrant, like a child who is scared of a possible beating from his father; me, my language belongs to those who don't show themselves, it's the language of this territory and this lapse of time when men pull on their leashes and pigs bang their heads against the fence; me, I hold my tongue by the bridle like a stallion, so he won't jump on the mare, because if I let the bridle go, if I slightly distended the pressure of my fingers and the traction of my arms, my words would throw me off and race toward the horizon, with the violence of an Arab horse who catches the smell of the desert and, then, nothing can hold him back anymore.

That is why, without knowing you, I have treated you correctly from the start, from the first step I took toward you, a correct step, humble and respectful, without knowing if anything in you deserves respect, without knowing anything about you and if the comparison between our two states allows me to be humble and you arrogant, I let you have arrogance because of the hour of twilight when we approached each other, because at that twilight hour when you approached me, correction is no longer mandatory, and is therefore necessary, at this hour when nothing is mandatory anymore except savage encounters in the darkness, and I could have fallen on you like a piece of rag falling on a candle flame, I could have grabbed you, by surprise, by the collar of your shirt. And this correction I offered you, however both necessary and arbitrary, binds you to me, if only because I could have stepped on you out of pride like a boot on a dirty paper, because I knew, seeing our respective size, which makes the main difference between us—and at this hour and in this place only size makes the difference—, we both know which one of us is the boot and which, the dirty paper.

THE CLIENT

If I did so, know that I would have desired not to look at you. A gaze wanders around, sets on random things, and believes it is in free and neutral territory, like a bee in a field of flowers, like a cow's muzzle in an enclosed pasture. But what can you do with your gaze? Looking at the sky makes me nostalgic, staring at the ground makes me sad, missing things and remembering that I don't have them are both equally unbearable. So, I must look straight ahead, at my own eye level, no matter the ground I walk on at that moment; that's why, a moment ago, as I was walking where I was walking and where I have now come to stop, my eyes must have eventually landed on all things laying still or walking at the same level as me; yet, because of the laws of distance and perspective, any man or animal is temporarily and approximately at the same level as me. Maybe you're right, the only difference between us, or the only injustice if you prefer, is that one is vaguely afraid of a possible beating from the other; and the only similarity, or the only justice if you prefer, is the ignorance of the degree of reciprocity of our fear, the degree of the future reality of those beatings, and the respective degree of their violence.

As a result all we do is duplicate ordinary encounters between men and animals, at hours and in places that are illicit and dark and invested by no law or electricity; and that's why, out of hatred of animals and out of hatred of men, I choose the law and the electric light and I am right to think that all natural lights and all non-filtered air and unregulated seasonal temperatures make the world hazardous; because there is no peace and no right in the natural elements, there is no business in illicit business, but only threats and escapes and beatings with nothing to buy and nothing to sell and no accepted currency and no price range, only the darkness, the darkness of men who approach each other; and if you approached me, it is because, in the end, you want to strike me; and if I asked you why you wanted to strike me, you would answer, only I know why, and it is for a secret reason you keep to yourself, and there's certainly no need for me to know. So, I won't ask you anything. Do you talk to a tile that's about to fall from a roof and smash your skull? It's like a bee landing on the wrong flower, the muzzle of a cow about to graze on the other side of the electric fence; you keep quiet, you run away, you regret, you wait, you do what you can, senseless motives, illicitness, darkness.

    I stepped into the stream of a stable where mysteries flow like animal wastes; and those mysteries and this darkness are yours, and they dictate the rule that when two men meet, one must always choose to be the one who strikes first ; and without a doubt, at this hour and in these places, one must approach any man or animal who comes in sight, and one must strike first and then say: I don't know if it was your intention to strike me, for some senseless and mysterious reason which in any event you wouldn't deem necessary to share with me, but, be that as it may, I preferred to do it first, and my reason, however senseless, at least is no secret: because of my presence and yours and the accidental meeting of our eyes, I sensed the floating possibility that you might strike me first, and I preferred to be the falling tile rather than the skull, the electric fence rather than the cow's muzzle.

    At the very least, if it were true that you, the salesman, own merchandise so mysterious that you refuse to show them to me or let me guess what they are, and that I, the buyer, have a desire so secret even I am not aware of it, and that in order for me to see that I have one, I would need to scratch my memory like a scab and make it bleed, if that is true, then why do you keep your merchandise to yourself, now that I have stopped, now that I am here, now that I am waiting? It's like a big sealed bag that you carry over your shoulders, like an ungraspable law of gravity that wouldn't exist and could only be by conforming to the shape of a desire; like those doormen at the striptease clubs who catch you by the elbow, when you go home at night, and whisper into your ear: she's here, tonight. But if you showed them to me, if you gave a name to your offer, licit or illicit goods, but named and therefore submitted to judgment at the very least, if you named them for me, I would be able to say no, and would stop feeling like a shaken tree, rattled to its roots by an unpredictable wind. Because I know how to say no, and I like saying no, I am able to blow you away with my nos, to make you discover all the ways there are to say no, which begin with all the ways there are to say yes, like the coquettes trying on all the dresses and all the shoes only to buy nothing in the end, and the pleasure they find in trying them on only comes from the pleasure they find in refusing them all. Make up your mind, show yourself: are you the brute stumping on the pavement or are you a businessman? If so, lay out your merchandise first, and then we'll take the time to look them over.

THE DEALER

It is because I want to be a businessman and no brute, but a real businessman, that I won't tell you what I possess or offer, because I cannot suffer a refusal, which is the one thing in the world a businessman dreads most, since it is a weapon he does not possess himself. So, I've never learned to say no, and I don't want to learn it; but all the kinds of yes, I know them: yes wait a little, wait a lot, wait with me an eternity; yes I have it, I will have it, I had it and will have it again, I never had it but I will have it for you. And if someone comes and says: let's imagine I confess to a desire and you have nothing to satisfy it? I will say, I have what it takes to satisfy it, and if someone says: still, imagine that you don't have it?—even while I'm imagining it, I still have it. And if someone says: let's agree that, in the end, my desire is so that you absolutely wouldn't even want to have the slightest idea of what it takes to satisfy it? Well, while I wouldn't even want this, despite everything, I have what it takes, still.

But the more a salesman is decent, the more the buyer is deviant; all a salesman wants is to satisfy a desire he doesn't already know, while the buyer always trades his desire for the primary satisfaction of refusing what is offered to him; his unspoken desire is elated by the refusal, and he gives up on his desire for the pleasure of humiliating the salesman. But I am not the kind of businessman who shows the price tag to satisfy his client's inclination for anger and indignation. I am not here to give pleasure, instead I am here to fill the void of desire, to recall desire, and force it to have a name, drag it on the ground and give it shape and weight, along with the necessary cruelty involved in giving shape and weight to desire. Because I see yours like saliva spilling at the corner of your lips before you swallow it back in, and I'll wait for it to spill over your chin, or wait for you to spit, and only then I will hand you a tissue to wipe yourself clean, because if I hand it too soon, I know you would refuse it from me, and this is the sort of refusal I do not care to suffer.

What every man or every animal dreads, at this hour when men walk at the same level as animals and when every animal walks at the same level as every man, it isn't suffering itself, because suffering can be measured, and his ability to inflict suffering can be measured; what he fears more than anything, it is the strangeness of suffering, and being forced to endure a suffering that is unfamiliar to him. And so the distance that will always keep brutes away from the young ladies who populate the world does not come from the respective assessment of their strengths, because then, the world will simply be divided between brutes and young ladies, every brute would jump on every young lady and the world would be simple; but what keeps the brute away from the young lady, and will keep him away for eternities, is the infinite mystery and the infinite strangeness of the weapons, like those little spray bottles that young ladies keep in their purses, that project liquid in the eyes of brutes and make them cry, and suddenly brutes are crying in front of young ladies, all dignity vanished, no longer man or animal, turned into nothing, only tears of shame shed over the soil of a field. That's why brutes and young ladies fear each other and are equally wary of each other, because we only inflict suffering that we can endure ourselves, and we only fear suffering that we can't inflict ourselves on others.

So, don't hold back, go ahead and tell me, I beg you, the object of your fever, of your gaze upon me, the reason, tell it to me; and if it is a matter of not wounding your pride, then, say it like you would say it to a tree, or in front of a prison wall, or in the solitude of a cotton field where you walk naked at night; tell it to me without even looking at me. Because the only real cruelty of this twilight hour when we stand together is not that one man wounds the other, maims him, tortures him, severs his limbs and his head, or makes him cry even; the true and terrible cruelty is the cruelty of a man or an animal who makes another man or animal incomplete, who interrupts him like an ellipsis in the middle of a sentence, who turns away despite setting his eyes on him, who turns the animal or the man into an error of his gaze, an error of his judgment, an error, like a letter you've started but crumble into a ball right after writing the date.

THE CLIENT

You are too strange a bandit, stealing nothing or waiting too long before stealing, an eccentric thief who sneaks into an orchard to shake the trees, but leaves without picking the fruits up. You are the person familiar with this place, and I am the foreigner; I am the one who's afraid and who's right to be afraid; I am the one who doesn't know you, who can't know you, who can only guess your silhouette in the darkness. It was your turn to guess and name something, and then perhaps with a nod of my head, I would have acquiesced, with a sign, you would have known; but I don't want my desire to be spilled for nothing, like blood on foreign land. You risk nothing, you know of me the apprehension and the hesitation and the suspicion; you know where I come from and you know where I'm going; you know these streets, you know this hour, you know your moves; me, I know nothing and, me, I risk everything. Facing you is like facing those transvestite men who dress like women who dress like men, in the end, nobody knows where the sex is.

Because you put your hand on me like a bandit on his victim or like the law on the bandit, and since then, I suffer from not knowing, not knowing my fate, not knowing if I am being arrested or an accomplice, not knowing what it is that I suffer from, I suffer from not knowing what wound you've inflicted on me and where my blood spills from. Perhaps you're not strange, but deviant; perhaps, you're just a servant of the law in disguise, whom the law makes in the image of the bandit in order to track him; perhaps, you're more loyal than I am after all. And so, for nothing, by accident, without having said anything, because I didn't know who you are, because I'm a foreigner who doesn't know the language, or the customs, or what is bad from what is proper, or right from wrong, like being blinded, lost, it's like I had asked you for something, like I had asked you for the worst possible thing, and that I was guilty of it. A desire like blood spilled out of me onto your feet, a desire I don't know and don't recognize, that only you know, and that only you judge.

If so, if you intend to trick me into action with the suspicious haste of a traitor, with or against you, so I become guilty either way, if so, then, at least acknowledge that I have not yet acted with you or against you, that I cannot be blamed for anything just yet, that I have been blameless up to this moment. Testify in my favor that I have found no enjoyment in the darkness, where you stopped me, and that I stopped here only because you put your hand on me; testify that I called out for light, that I didn't sneak into the darkness like a thief, by my own will, with illicit intentions, but that I was taken by surprise and cried out, like a child in bed whose nightlight suddenly turns off.

THE DEALER

If you believe that I harbor violent intentions toward you—and perhaps you are right to think I do—, don't hurry and give a gender and a name to its violence. You were born with the belief that a man's sex hides in a specific place and that it stays there, and you cautiously keep that belief to yourself; but me, I know,—although born the same way as you—, that during the time a man spends waiting and forgetting and sitting in solitude, his sex slowly travels from one place to another, never hidden in a specific place, but exposed where you don't look for it; and after the time he spends learning to sit and rest quietly in his solitude, no sex resembles any other, no more than a man's sex resembles a woman's; there is no disguise for a thing like that, but a soft hesitation of the things themselves, like the intermediate seasons that aren't summer disguised as winter, or winter as summer.

That said, a supposition is not worth panicking for; you must keep your imagination like your little fiancée: if it's all right to see her wander off, it's foolish to let her lose her sense of propriety. I am not deviant, but curious, I put my hand on your arm by sheer curiosity, in order to understand if a flesh resembling that of a featherless chicken carries the warmth of the living chicken or the cold of the dead chicken, and now, I know. You suffer, if I may say so without offending you, from the cold, like a half-bald live chicken, like the hen suffering, in the strict sense of the term, from balding ringworm; and when I was a child, I used to run behind the chickens in the barnyard to grope them, by sheer curiosity, and see if their temperature was the temperature of the dead or the living. Today as I touched you, I felt in you the coldness of death, but I also felt that you were suffering from the cold, only like a living person could suffer. That's why I offered you my coat, to cover your shoulders, since I don't suffer from the cold myself. And I have never suffered from it, so much so that I have suffered from not knowing what it feels to suffer from it, so much so that the only dream I had when I was a child—one of those dreams that are not ambitions but additional prisons, the moment when a child sees his first prison, like children born slaves who believe they descend from their masters—, the dream I had was to discover snow and frost, discover the cold from which you suffer.

If I lent you only my coat, it is not that I don't know that you suffer from the cold not just in the top part of your body, but, to say so without offending you, from the top to the bottom, and perhaps a little beyond; and for me, I've always thought that it is important to give someone who's cold the article of clothing that corresponds to the part of his body where he feels cold, at the risk of finding yourself naked from the top to the bottom and perhaps a little beyond; and my mother, who was not greedy but blessed with a sense of propriety, used to tell me that although it is commendable to offer your shirt or your coat or whatever covers the top part of your body, you must always hesitate for a long time before offering your shoes, and under no circumstances is it proper to give away your pants.

And the same way I know—without understanding why and yet with absolute certainty—that the land you and I and everyone else stand on, it itself stands in balance on the tip of a bull's horn and is kept in position by the hand of providence, in the same way, without really knowing why and yet without hesitation, I try to stay within the boundaries of what is proper and to avoid impropriety, like a child must avoid leaning over the roof's edge even before he grasps the law of fallen bodies. The same way the child believes he is forbidden to lean over the roof's edge only to be kept from flying away, I used to believe for a long time that a boy is forbidden to give away his pants only to avoid revealing the enthusiasm or the torpor of his feelings. But today as I understand more things, and recognize more the things that I don't understand, and have spent so much time in this place at this hour, and seen so many people pass by, and looked at them and sometimes put my hand on their arm, many times without understanding anything and without wanting to understand anything, but also without missing the opportunity to look at them and try to put my hand on their arm—because it is easier to catch a passerby than a chicken in a barnyard—, now I realize that there is nothing improper in the enthusiasm or the torpor that needs to be hidden, and that you always follow the rule without knowing why.

Besides, if I may say so without offending you, I covered your shoulders with my coat with the hope that it gives you an appearance more familiar to my eyes. Too much strangeness makes me shy, and, earlier, as I watched you come toward me, I wondered why a man who is not sick dresses like a chicken sick from the ringworm, losing feathers as he wanders around in the barnyard, with random feathers standing up on his back at the whim of his sickness; and because I am shy, I would've probably continued to scratch my head and stepped away to avoid you, if

I hadn't seen in your eyes staring at me the spark of someone who was going, in the strict sense of the term, to ask for something, and that spark distracted me from your clothing.

THE CLIENT

What do you hope to get from me? Every move you make, I take it for a strike, but it ends up being a caress; it is worrisome to be caressed when you're supposed to be hit. At a minimum, if you want me to stick around, I expect you to be suspicious of me. Since you randomly claim to sell something, why don't you first question that I have enough to pay? My pockets, perhaps, are empty; it would have been honest of you to ask, first, that I put my money on the counter, like you do with shady clients. You didn't ask me that: what pleasure do you take in being cheated? I didn't come in this place to seek tenderness; tenderness looks into details, it attacks by bits, cuts your strength into pieces, like a corpse at the doctor's office. I need my integrity; malice, at least, will keep me whole. Get mad: otherwise, where will I find my strength? Get mad: we'll stick to our business, and we'll both know we're dealing in the same business. Because, if I understand where I take my pleasure from, I do not understand from where you take yours.

THE DEALER

If I doubted for a second that you have what's needed to pay for what you're after, I would have stepped away the moment you approached me. Vulgar businesses ask their clients for proof of solvency, but luxury boutiques guess and don't ask anything, never bend down to verify the amount on the check or the conformity of the signature. There are things to sell and things to buy such that the question is not asked whether the buyer can afford the price or how long it will take him to decide. So, I exercise patience, because there is no point in offending a man who is walking away when you know he is going to backtrack. You can't backtrack on insult, but you can backtrack on kindness, and it is better to overuse the latter than to use the former just once. That's why I will not get mad so quickly, because I have the time not to get mad, and I have the time to get mad, and perhaps I will get mad when all this time runs out.

THE CLIENT

What if—as a hypothesis—I admitted to using arrogance—without inclination for it—only because you asked me to use it, when you approached me full of intentions, which were impossible for me to guess—because I'm not good at guessing—but which hold me back here? What if, as a hypothesis, I told you that what holds me back here is the uncertainty I feel regarding your intentions, and the interest I take in them? In the strangeness of this hour and the strangeness of this place and the strangeness of your advances toward me, I would have advanced toward you, moved according to the indelible movement innate to all things as long as no opposite movement is impressed against them. What if I approached you with immobility? Pulled down, not by my own will, but by the attraction that kings feel when they go slumming in the taverns, or the child sneaking into the basement, the attraction of the small and solitary object toward the obscure and impassible mass that sits in the shadows; I would have come to you, calmly measuring the softness of the rhythm of my blood in my veins, wondering if that softness was going to get aroused or run completely dry; slowly perhaps, but full of hope, stripped of any desire that could be said out loud, ready to be satisfied with any offer, because, whatever the offer, it would have been like the furrows of a barren field abandoned for too long, it makes no difference what seeds fall on them; prepared to be satisfied with anything, in the strangeness of us approaching each other, I would have thought from a distance that you were approaching me, I would have thought from a distance that you were looking at me; and then, I would have approached you, I would have looked at you, I would have come closer to you, expecting from you—too many things—too many things, not that you could have guessed, because me, I am not good at it, me, I can't guess, but I expected from you the taste of desire, the idea of desire, the object, the price, and the satisfaction.

THE DEALER

There is no shame in forgetting at night what you will remember in the morning; the night is the time for forgetting, for confusion, for desires so heated that they turn into vapor. But the morning picks them up like a big cloud forming above the bed, and it would be foolish not to plan at night for the morning rain. So if, as a hypothesis, you told me that you were, for the moment, stripped of any desire to be said out loud, because you feel tired or forgetful or because of an excess of desire that makes you forgetful, I would, as a hypothesis, tell you not to tire yourself out anymore and borrow somebody else's desire. A desire is stolen, not invented; so one man's coat can as easily keep another man warm; and it is easier to borrow a desire than an article of clothing. Given that I must sell, at any price, and that, at any price, you must buy, then buy something for someone else—any desire will do, one that you find laying around on the ground and that you pick up—; one that would make happy and satisfy whoever it is that wakes up next to you in your bed, for example, a little fiancée who will wake up in the morning desiring something that you don't have yet, that you will find pleasure in offering her, that you will be happy to possess because you will have bought it from me. It's the merchant's good fortune that there are so many different people who have become so many times engaged to so many different things in so many different ways, because one man's memory is relayed by another man's memory. And the merchandise you are going to buy from me could be useful to somebody else if, as a hypothesis, you find no use for it yourself.

THE CLIENT

The rule says that a man who meets another man will eventually tap on his shoulder and talk to him about women; the rule says that the memory of a woman should be used as the last resort for the tired soldier; the rule says that, your rule; I will not submit to it. I don't want us to find peace in the absence of women, or in the memory of an absence, or in the memory of anything whatsoever. Memories disgust me, the absent ones too; over digested food I prefer meals left untouched. I don't want peace that comes out of nowhere; I don't want us to find peace.

But a dog's gaze contains nothing but the presumption that everything around him is dog. So, you pretend that the world you and I stand on is kept in balance on the tip of a bull's horn by the hand of providence; but I know that the world floats laying on the back of three whales; and that there is no providence or balance, just the whim of three half-witted monsters. Our worlds are not the same, and our strangeness mixes into our nature like grape into wine. No, I will not lift my leg in front of you, in the same place as you; I am not pulled down by the same gravity as you; I am not born from the same female. Because it is not in the morning that I wake up, and it is not in a bed that I sleep.

THE DEALER

Don't get mad, little man, don't get mad. I'm just a poor salesman who doesn't know this piece of land where I wait to sell, I know nothing more than what my mother taught me; and since she knew nothing, or almost nothing, I know nothing either, or almost. But a good salesman tries to say what the buyer wants to hear, and in order to guess, he must lick him a little to catch a whiff of him. You, your smell wasn't familiar to me, and so you are right, we weren't born from the same mother. But to approach you, I assumed that you too must have been born from a mother, like me, and that your mother gave you countless brothers, like mine, like a bout of hiccups after a big meal, and that what brings us together, in spite of everything, is the lack of scarcity that defines us both. And at least I hung on to what we have in common, because you can travel far into the desert as long as you keep a point of reference somewhere. But if I am mistaken, if you weren't born from a mother, if nobody gave you brothers, if you don't have a little fiancée who wakes up in the morning next to you in your bed, little man, I apologize to you.

Two men who meet have no choice but to fight, with the violence of enmity or the tenderness of fraternity. And, in the end, in the desert of this hour, if they choose to remember something that isn't there, something from the past or from a dream, something that's missing, it is because you can't directly face too much strangeness. In the face of mystery, it's best to open up, and expose yourself completely, and force the mystery to expose itself in return. Memories are secret weapons that a man keeps on himself when he is stripped of everything else, they are the last honesty that compels honesty in return; the very last nakedness. I gain no glory or shame from who I am, but since you are a stranger, and more of a stranger at every passing moment, then, like the coat I took off my shoulders and offered you, like the disarmed hands I showed you, whether I am dog and you human, whether I am dog and you something other than dog, whatever is my race and whatever is yours, at least I lay mine bare before your eyes, I let you touch it, let you grope me and get accustomed to me, like a man consenting to be frisked and exposing his weapons.

That is why, prudently, gravely, quietly, I suggest that you look at me with friendship, because business is better conducted under the guise of familiarity. I am not here to cheat you, and I don't ask for anything you don't want to give. The only companionship worth seeking never expects you to act in a certain way, but not to act; I offer you immobility, infinite patience, the blind injustice of friendship. Because there is no justice between people who do not know each other, and no friendship between people who do know each other, the same way there are no bridges without ravines. My mother always told me that it is foolish to decline an umbrella when you know it is about to rain.

THE CLIENT

I preferred you deviant rather than friendly. Friendship is greedier than treachery. If it were feelings I had needed, I would have told you, asked you for the price, and paid for it. But you don't trade feelings for feelings. It's fake business, conducted with fake currency, it's poor people's business that fakes real business. Do you trade a bag of rice for a bag of rice? You have nothing to offer, that's why you lay your feelings over the counter, like bad businesses do when they offer rebates on junk, and after that, it's too late to complain about the product. I have no feelings to offer you in return; of that currency, I am short, I didn't think of bringing any with me, you can search me. So, keep your hand in your pocket, keep your mother in your family, keep your memories for your solitude, that's the least you could do.

I will never seek the familiarity that you're trying to sneak between us. I didn't want your hand on my arm, I didn't want your coat on my shoulders, I don't want to risk being mistaken for you. Because you should know that if you were surprised earlier by my clothing, and you didn't find it necessary to hide your surprise, my surprise was at least as great as yours when I saw you approaching me. But in foreign lands, the foreigner falls into the habit of masking his surprise, thinking everything strange is local custom, and that he would be better off going along with them, as one does with the weather or the local dishes. But if I were to bring you among my kind, then you would be a foreigner yourself, forced to mask your surprise in return, and us autochthones free to show you ours, and everyone would gather around you and point the finger at you, everyone would take you for a freak show and ask me where to get their tickets.

You are not here for business. You've come here to loiter, to beg at first and then to steal, like someone who declares war after the negotiations. As for desires, I had them, they fell to the ground, around us, and got stepped on; the big ones, the small ones, the complicated ones, the easy ones, all you had to do was to bend down and pick them up by the handful; but you let them roll into the gutter, because even the small ones, even the easy ones, you don't have what is necessary to satisfy them. You are poor and you come here, without inclination, because of your poverty, necessity, and ignorance. I won't act like I'm buying pious pictures or paying for a lousy guitar tune at a street corner. I give handouts if I want to, or I pay the price of things. But let the beggars beg, let them dare hold out a hand; and let the robbers rob.

I don't want to insult you or to please you; I don't want to be good or bad, to hit you or to be hit by you, to be seduced, or to try to seduce you. I want to be zero. I dread cordiality, I find no vocation in collegiality, and more than the violence of strikes, I fear the violence of camaraderie. Let us be two zeros, well-rounded and impenetrable one to the other, provisionally juxtaposed, each rolling away in a different direction. Here, we are alone, in the infinite solitude of this hour and this place, which is no definable hour or place, because there is no reason for you to meet me here and no reason for me to meet you here and no reason for cordiality and no reasonable number that precedes us and gives us meaning, let us be two simple, solitary, and proud zeroes.

THE DEALER

But now it is too late: your bill is up and you're going to have to pay. It's fair to steal from someone who refuses to give and hoards in his coffers with jealousy and for his solitary pleasure, but it's vulgar to steal when everything is for sale and everything could be bought. And if it is provisionally acceptable to owe someone—just a fair contractual delay—, it is obscene to give away things and obscene to receive them for free. We found each other here for business, not for war, so it would be unfair to have a loser and a winner. You won't walk away like a thief, your pockets full, you forget the dog who's watching over the street and who's going to bite your ass.

Since you've come here, in the midst of hostilities between angry men and animals, to seek nothing tangible, and since for whatever obscure reason you wish to get hurt, you will have to pay up and empty your pockets before turning your back, so that we owe each other nothing and that we gave each other nothing. Beware of the merchant: the merchant who is robbed is more jealous than the looted landlord; beware of the merchant: his tongue gives the appearance of respect and tenderness, the appearance of humility, the appearance of love, the appearance only.

THE CLIENT

What have you lost, exactly, that I have not gained? Because, no matter how much I dig through my memories, I have gained nothing. I would gladly pay the price for things, but I don't pay for the wind, for the darkness, for the nothingness between us. If you have lost something, if your fortune diminished after you met me, then where is the thing that's missing to us both? Show me. No, I didn't enjoy anything. No, I won't pay for anything.

THE DEALER

If you want to know what was added to your bill right from the beginning, and what you will have to pay before you turn your back and walk away, I will tell you, it is the time spent waiting, and the patience, and the article the salesman made for his client, and the hope to sell, the hope especially, that makes any man who approaches any other man with a request in his eyes someone already in debt. For the promise to sell I'll withhold the promise to buy, there's also the penalty to pay for who breaks the promise.

THE CLIENT

You and I, we are not lost in the middle of the fields. If I called in this direction, toward this wall, up there, toward the sky, you'll see lights turning on, steps approaching, help coming. If it is hard to hate in solitude, it becomes a pleasure in the presence of others. You attack men instead of women, because you are scared of the screams of women, and you presume that men will find it undignified to scream; you count on the dignity and the vanity and the mutism of men. I give up that dignity. If you want to hurt me, I will call out, I will scream, I will ask for help, I will make you hear all the ways there are to call for help, because I know them all.

THE DEALER

If it isn't the dishonor of flight that keeps you here, why don't you flee? Flight is a subtle way to fight; you are subtle; you should flee. You are like those fat ladies in the teashops squeezing between tables and knocking over teapots: you drag your ass behind you like a sin you repent for, you turn in every direction to act like your ass doesn't exist. But no matter what, somebody will still bite it.

THE CLIENT

I don't belong to the race of those who attack first. I ask for more time. Perhaps, in the end, it's better we pick a fight rather than bite each other. I ask for more time. I don't want to get injured like a distracted dog. Come with me; let's look for people, because our solitude is wearing us out.

THE DEALER

There is this coat you didn't take when I offered it to you, and now, you have no choice but to bend down and pick it up.

THE CLIENT

If I spat on something, however, I did so on generalities, and an article of clothing is nothing but an article of clothing; and if I spat in your direction, it wasn't against you, and you didn't have to move to dodge my spit; and if you moved on purpose so it lands on your face, because you like it, because you're a pervert, or because you planned it, the fact still remains that I showed contempt only to this piece of rag, and that a piece of rag holds no grudge. No, I will not bend my back before you, impossible, I don't have the flexibility for a freak show. There are movements a man can't do, like licking his own ass. I will not pay for a temptation I didn't have.

THE DEALER

It's improper for a man to let another man insult his clothing. Because if the real injustice in this world is the circumstances of a man's birth, the place and the hour, the only justice left is his clothing. A man's clothes, more than himself, are the most sacred thing: they are him without the suffering; the equilibrium point where justice and injustice balance out, and that point shouldn't be mistreated. That's why a man must be judged by his clothes, not by his face, or his arms, or his skin. If it is normal to spit on the circumstances of a man's birth, it is dangerous to spit on his rebellion.

THE CLIENT

Well then, I offer you equality. A coat in the dust, I pay it with a coat in the dust. Let us be equal, equal in our pride, equal in our weaknesses, equally disarmed, suffering equally from the cold and the heat. Your partial nakedness, your half humiliation, I pay it with half of mine. The other half we will keep to ourselves, that's enough for us to dare look at each other, and to forget what we've lost because of inadvertence, of risk, of hope, of distraction, of chance. And me, I'll still have the persistent fret of someone who's in debt and has already paid.

THE DEALER

Why is it that, what you ask so abstractly, so intangibly, at this hour of the night, why is it that, what you would have asked from somebody else, you won't ask it from me?

THE CLIENT

Beware of the client: he seems to look for one thing when in fact he wants something else, something the salesman can't guess, but that the client will finally get.

THE DEALER

If you ran away, I would follow you; if you got knocked out by my punches, I would stay beside you and wake you up; and if you decided not to wake up, I would stay by you in your sleep, in your unconscious, and beyond. But I don't wish to fight you.

THE CLIENT

I am not afraid to fight, but I am afraid of the rules that I don't understand.

THE DEALER

There are no rules; there are only means; there are only weapons.

THE CLIENT

Try to reach me, you won't be able to; try to wound me: when blood spills, then, it will from both sides and, inescapably, blood will unite us—like two Indians, by the fire, exchanging blood in the midst of wild animals. There is no love, there is no love. No, you won't reach anything that wasn't already reached, because a man dies first, and then seeks his death, and finally finds it, by chance, on the hazardous road between one light and another light, and says: so, that's all it was.

THE DEALER

Please, in the racket of this night, have you not told me something, anything, that you desire, and that I would have missed?

THE CLIENT

I told you nothing; I told you nothing. And you, have you not offered me something, anything, in the night, in this darkness so thick that it takes too long for the eyes to get accustomed to it, and that I have not guessed?

THE DEALER

Nothing.

THE CLIENT

Then, what weapon?

TABATABA

Translated by Amin Erfani

CHARACTERS.
MAÏMOUNA, older sister.
LITTLE ABOU, younger brother.
HARLEY DAVIDSON, motorcycle.

The inner courtyard of a house.
Eleven o'clock at night.
One hundred and four degrees.

MAÏMOUNA: Why don't you go out, at night, when all the boys your age are already out in the streets, wearing shirts, the crease of their pants ironed out, prowling around the girls? All Tabataba is out, all Tabataba is primped up, the boys flirt with the girls and the girls spent all day doing their hair and me, my brother's got grease all over his paws and he's fiddling with his machine. Shame on me, people are going to think I don't know how to iron a shirt.

In the morning, instead of taking apart the machine's engine to put it back together in the evening, if you gave me your shirt to wash, your jacket to iron, the button of your pants to sew back on, I would not be humiliated in the evening when the other boys come and ask: where's he, little Abou, where's he, your brother, where's our pal, we want to go out with him? Shame on me. He's right here, in the courtyard, with the dogs and the old ladies and the chickens, with a nasty old rag in his hand. Wash up your mop or I'll slap you; make dreadlocks, braid your hair, shave your skull; give me your shirt; stop being my shame, in the evening, when the women next door come, with their stuck-up faces, Fatoumata especially, and ask: and your brother? Where's he then, our darling? Where's he, little Abou? What can I tell them?: he's in engine oil, he smells like an old machine, there're buttons missing on his pants? Shame on me.

Let go of this rag, pull your head out of this machine's butt. Do you think a girl would want to ride on this, after spending all afternoon doing her hair? You don't even use it to get out, you only use it to stay in. How does that make me look, a filthy brother among the old ladies, bent over his machine at the hour when everybody is out? How does that make me look, at this hour of the evening and in this heat, when you should be drinking beer in the juke joints, when you should be prowling around those stuck-up women next door? You're the disgrace of this courtyard.

The older sister feels responsible for her brother. I taught you how to wash yourself, I washed you enough times myself, picaninny, wiped you, bathed you, dived you in the basin, and now your hands are white with filth and you smell like a beast; just the sight of you makes my dress filthy, I'm tired of being your sister and I'm going to slap you. The hour has come, it is hot, tell me where your shirt is, let me comb your hair, and I'll spray you with *Paris by Night*. Raise your head, little Abou. A sister whose brother doesn't go out is the laughing stock of the women next door. Out with you, my shame and my humiliation, run the streets of Tabataba, honor me: drink beer and fuck the girls.

LITTLE ABOU: I don't want to walk in the streets of Tabataba, they are full of dog shit; I don't want to drink beer in the juke joints, they're not even cold and they're bootlegged.

I don't like the women next door, they smell like chicken, and I don't like the way they do their hair and the way they dress, I prefer them in the morning when they prepare the meal. And as soon as night comes, I don't like my pals anymore. I like my bike and my paws full of grease, and this filthy rag; I prefer my pants with no buttons on them and my shirt wrinkled up; I like the old courtyard and the old people and the goats; a goat smells like a goat, I don't want to smell like chicken, I want to smell like me, I want to choose my filth and stay in the courtyard. Leave my pals alone and forget about the women next door. Don't stay here, I don't need you. Don't look at me like that, like you're going to give me a bath or a slap; I'm not a picaninny anymore, I'm too old, I'm not going to climb on your back. Go away, Maïmouna; when it gets hot like this, it makes me want to kill.

MAÏMOUNA: Who do you think you are, little shithead, to think you can fight nature? I'm not asking you what you like, I'm not asking you what you want. Even the stones mate with one another, there's no escaping that. Even if you don't want to, get out anyway, or I'll slap you.

You stay here, smoking like a whore at the police precinct. Who taught you to smoke by yourself? men smoke in the juke joint, drink beer and fondle the girls, but someone who smokes all alone is vicious; shame on me, they're going to think I made you vicious, they're going to think I didn't teach you life or anything, they're going to think I didn't fulfill my duties as the older sister.

And yet, when you were little, I did spend them, those evenings, slapping you around, teaching you to be prepared, talking to you about women, you looked like you got it. You were seven, I drew a picture for you on your school notebook, I even let you touch me so you won't be too surprised the first time; I explained to you: it's here, like this, inside, outside, that's it, it's simple, men, women, life, the whole mess, there's nothing more to learn, there's nothing more to know. You looked like you got it; shame on me, you got nothing at all. And at the hour when you should be out rubbing yourself against the women next door, you're in the courtyard with the old people and you're rubbing this machine.

I should have hit you more often. I should have been suspicious. I should have known that you're vicious. At the age when the boys were checking out the girls who went to swim, you, I remember this very well, you preferred climbing on the back of trucks and inhale exhaust fumes, and you came back home coughing, with a headache, dopey like an American. And I can cry now: it's too late. You stay in your corner with your vice, you leave me in mine with my disgrace.

And yet, you're so beautiful, little Abou, that I would want to cry. If you let me, little frog, I would make you so beautiful that the women next door would turn gray, especially Fatoumata. If I made you braids, if I blackened your skin with cream, if you let me spray on you *Paris by Night*, and iron your shirt, sew up your pants and polish your shoes, little Abou, I would feel so proud in the streets of Tabataba. Let go of that mean rag full of grease, it's going to make me cry.

What do you have against the women next door? It's true, they're not very pretty, and you should expect better, but they spent so much of them, those hours, doing their hair, putting on perfume, trying to doll up for you, Fatoumata especially; and now they are here, the stuck-up women, prowling by the front door, waiting for you to come out. They're as good as any, until something better comes along. If you don't like the women next door, then go drink beer with your pals and then, go and pick up a whore. But it's hot, it's late, you must hurry and get out; all Tabataba is out, you have no right to hold me in my shame.

LITTLE ABOU: Maïmouna, my sister, you're already not worth much, but soon, you won't be worth a dime. Who are you to tell me what to do, and whom I should rub against, and what I should prowl around? You're old and you're not married. At your age, you should have settled down, serving an old man at the table, and wiping the butts of other picaninnies than me. At your age, you should have mated long ago, and you're worth nothing yourself, and you're lecturing me.

Soon you'll be so worn out by the nights of Tabataba that no reasonable man would even want to be with you. Stop acting young. How much longer will it take before you stop acting young? What does a boy look like when his older sister acts young, and stays young, and she never decides to stop being young? Find yourself a lover and let me grow old.

At this hour, instead of being primped up and perfumed like a widow, you should be in the home of a man who's yours, who's very rich and very old, ironing his shirts and sewing up his pants.

But you prefer spending the day doing your hair like a damsel. What's she worth, a girl who talks to her little brother about drinking beer, dealing in the juke joints, and picking up whores? Boys are allowed to do those things but girls have no right to talk about them. Shame on you, Maïmouna, because of your language and your solitude.

MAÏMOUNA: (*she crouches and cries*) I don't want a lover, I don't want a husband. A lover, it's like the sun, the more it heats up, the more it turns everything around you into a desert. I don't want to be like a little succulent plant all alone in the middle of a desert of stones.

LITTLE ABOU: So why do you bother me, Maïmouna, and why would you want me to do what even you don't want to do? You see, there's no use going out, walking in dog shit in the streets of Tabataba.

MAÏMOUNA: But life, little Abou? Everything I taught you, women, men, love, all that mess? You're not young anymore and you're not already old, little Abou; you can't fight nature. Shame on us: the women next door keep laughing and your pals knock at the door.

LITTLE ABOU: Let me be old and smoke in peace in my corner; you do what you want.

MAÏMOUNA: With no woman around, little Abou, who will iron your shirts? When you get very old, who will make your meal?

LITTLE ABOU: You make my meals yourself, and I don't want anybody to iron my shirts.

MAÏMOUNA: Give me that rag, little prick; this machine is disgusting, I'm going to rub it with you.

BACK TO THE DESERT

Translated by Andy Bragen

Why grow the branches now the root is wither'd?
Why wither not the leaves that want their sap?
(Shakespeare: *Richard III*, II, 2)

CHARACTERS:

MATHILDE SERPENOISE
ADRIEN, her brother, manufacturer

MATTHIEU, Adrien's son
FATIMA, Mathilde's daughter
EDOUARD, Mathilde's son.

MARIE RÓZERIEULLES, Adrien's first wife, deceased.
MARTHE, her sister, Adrien's second wife.

MAAME QUEULEU, live-in housekeeper.
AZIZ, servant

THE BIG BLACK PARATROOPER

SAÏFI, café owner.
PLANTIÈRES, Police chief
BORNY, Lawyer,
SABLON, County Commissioner

PLACE:
A provincial town in Eastern France, in the early sixties.

I SOBH

1

A wall enclosing the garden.
By the open front door.
Early morning.

MAAME QUEULEU: Aziz, hurry up and come in. We've got work to do. Mathilde, the master's sister, is coming back from Algeria with her children. We need to prepare for her arrival. I can't do it alone.

AZIZ: I'm coming, Maame Queuleu. But I thought I heard footsteps and voices, and that seemed odd so early in the morning on this street.

MAAME QUEULEU: The streets are dangerous. Get in quick. I don't like leaving the door open.

AZIZ: هَاد النَهَارْ طَالِعْ مَا فِي بَائِنْش

MATHILDE enters.

MATHILDE: عَلاَّشْ غَادِي يكُونْ نَهَارْ خَايبْ ؟

AZIZ: . . . إِذَا كَانِتْ الأُخْت حُمَارَه بْحَالْ خُوهَا ، بَايْنَهْ

MATHILDE: ! أَنَا عَارْفتْهَا مِشْ بْحَالْ خُوهَا

AZIZ: How would you know?
و كِيفْ تَعْرِفهاً ؟

MATHILDE: . . . . أَنَا هِيَّ خْتُو

FATIMA and EDOUARD enter with bags.

MAAME QUEULEU: Come on in, Aziz. Stop loafing by the door. (*To* MATHILDE.) Who are you? What do you want?

MATHILDE: Let me in, Maame Queuleu. It's me, Mathilde.

2

In the entrance hall. A broad staircase.

MATHILDE: Who's that old woman coming down the stairs?

MAAME QUEULEU: It's Marthe.

MATHILDE: Who?

MAAME QUEULEU: Marie's sister, Marthe.

MATHILDE: What's she doing here so early, dressed like that?

ADRIEN *enters, from the top of the stairs.*

ADRIEN: Mathilde, my dear sister, you've come back to our good little town. Have you come with good intentions? Now that age has mellowed us, we should try to avoid quarreling during your very short visit. During the fifteen years you've been gone, I've grown used to not quarreling. It would be hard to start up again.

MATHILDE: Adrien, my brother, my intentions are good. And if age has mellowed you, I'm happy to hear it: life will be easier during my very long stay. In my case, age, instead of mellowing me, has put me on edge, and between your calm and my nerves, everything should be fine.

ADRIEN: You wanted to escape the war, so naturally you came back to your roots, to your childhood home. You did the right thing. Soon, the war will be over. Soon you'll return to Algeria, to sunny Algeria. You'll have borne these uncertain times, which affect us all, here in the safety of this home.

MATHILDE: My roots? What roots? I'm not a tree. I have feet, and they aren't meant for the soil. As for the war, my dear Adrien, I couldn't give a damn. I'm not here to escape the war. On the contrary, I've brought it with me, to this good little town, where I have some old scores to settle. And if it's taken me so long to come back and settle these scores, it's because too much misfortune had softened my resolve. But fifteen years without hardship has brought back the memories, and the rancor, and the faces of my enemies.

ADRIEN: Enemies, my dear sister? You? In this good little town? Distance has fed your imagination, which was never lacking. Loneliness, and Algeria's hot sun, have fried your brain. But if, as I believe, you've simply come to look over your inheritance and then leave, go ahead, look around, see how well I've taken care of things, admire how I've improved the place. And once you've had a good look, touched and evaluated everything, we'll prepare for your departure.

MATHILDE: But I didn't come here to leave, Adrien. I've come with baggage and children. I've come back to this house because I own it. Improved, or destroyed, I will always own it. I want to settle down in the place I own.

ADRIEN: You own, my dear Mathilde, you own: wonderful.. I've paid you rent, I've improved its value considerably. So you own it. Very well. But don't start upsetting me, don't start in with your tricks. Why don't you make an effort? Let's start over with our hellos. We've gotten off on the wrong foot.

MATHILDE: Then let's start over, my dear Adrien. Let's start over.

ADRIEN: Mathilde, my sister, do you think I'm going to let you strut around here like you own the place, rummaging through drawers and running your hands over everything like the mistress of the house? You can't abandon a fallow field and wait under cover for some imbecile to cultivate it, then return at harvest-time and claim the crop. The house may be yours, but its prosperity is mine and believe me, I won't abandon my share. You too took your share. You left me the factory because you were incapable, and you chose the house out of laziness. You abandoned this house to run I don't know where from I don't know what; and now the house has taken on its own ways without you. It has its own peculiar smells, it has its habits, it has its traditions, it recognizes its masters. Don't treat it badly; I'll defend it if you've come to plunder.

MATHILDE: Why would I plunder my own house, since I intend to live in it? I gather, from the prosperity I see around me, that your factory is flourishing. It's producing serious profits, transforming the bankers into the best friends you've ever had. If you were poor I'd ask you to pack your bags, but since you're rich I won't drive you out. I'll make the best of you, and your son, and everything else. But I won't forget that I own the bed where I sleep and the table where I eat, that the order and disorder I bring to the living rooms will be a fair and appropriate order and disorder. Besides, it was time for me to return. This house lacks women.

ADRIEN: Oh no my dear Mathilde, it doesn't lack women. There will always be too many. This house is a man's house, and the women who pass through are invited in and forgotten. Our father built it, and who honors his wife's memory? I'm the one who's kept it going. Who, my poor Mathilde, honors your memory? Act like a guest in your own house. You may think you'll jump back in bed as if you never left, but I'm not convinced your bed will even recognize you.

MATHILDE: And I know, that even after fifteen years, or another ten years after that, after years and years of sleeping elsewhere, I'll enter my room with eyes shut, I'll lay on my bed like I've always lain there, and my bed will recognize me right away. And if it doesn't recognize me, I'll shake it up until it surrenders.

ADRIEN: I knew it: you've come back to do harm. You're here to avenge your misfortune. You've always had misfortune to avenge; you attract it, it searches you out, you pursue misfortune for the pleasure of spite. You are harsh and you have a withered heart.

MATHILDE: Adrien, you're losing your temper. If you've never hurt me, why should I want revenge? Adrien, we still haven't said hello. Let's try again.

ADRIEN: I'm done trying.

He approaches MATHILDE

MARTHE *and* MAAME QUEULEU *enter.*

MARTHE: (*To* MAAME QUEULEU) Who is this lady?

MAAME QUEULEU: It's Mathilde.

MARTHE: Blessed Virgin, how she's grown up!

ADRIEN: I've forgotten your children's names.

MATHILDE: The boy is Edouard, and the girl, Fatima.

ADRIEN: Fatima? Are you crazy? We need to change that, we need to find her another name. Fatima! What am I supposed to say when they ask me her name? I don't want to be the butt of jokes.

MATHILDE: Nobody's changing anything. A name isn't invented, the cradle gives it its shape, it's trapped in the air that a child breathes. If she'd been born in Hong-Kong, I would've named her Tsouei Tai, I would've named her Shadémia if she'd been born in Bamako, and, if I'd given birth in Amecameca, her name would be Iztaccihuatl. Who would've stopped me? You can't stamp a newborn child for exportation right from the outset.

ADRIEN: At least while you're here, at least in front of friends, call her Caroline.

MATHILDE: Fatima, come greet your Uncle. Edouard, come here.

MARTHE How they've grown! Do they know how to read? Have they read the bible? This little girl is nearly grown up; has she performed her devotions at Notre-Dame de la Salette? Do they know about Mama Rosa, the saint?

MATHILDE: Adrien, did you really marry that?

ADRIEN: What?

MATHILDE: That thing, behind you. You must know what it is that you've married.

ADRIEN: Yes, I did marry her.

MATHILDE: Still such a monkey, Adrien. Marrying that, after having married the sister. Marie, poor Marie. All that was beautiful and soft, fragile, tender and noble in Marie has shriveled up in that thing.

ADRIEN: Having this one in sight has kept me from feeling remorse for the other one.

MATHILDE: What does your son have to say about it? Poor Mathieu.

ADRIEN: My son says nothing. Ever. At least not in front of me. He's not poor and doesn't need your pity.

MATHILDE: And you sleep in the same bed with her? She drinks, doesn't she? I can see it in her face.

ADRIEN: I don't know. Maybe. It seems like it. Not in front of me, anyway.

MATHILDE: You're thicker than a gorilla, Adrien. You prefer caricatures, you prefer cheap imitations, ugliness over all that is beautiful and noble. I'll never see her as your wife. Marie is dead, you no longer have a wife.

ADRIEN: And you no more have a husband than I a wife. Where did those two pop out from? Even you don't know. Don't you lecture me, Mathilde. We are brother and sister, completely. Hello, Mathilde, my sister.

MATHILDE: Hello Adrien.

ADRIEN: I thought I'd find you with darkened skin, wrinkled like an old Arab. How'd you pull it off, under that Goddamned Algerian sun, how did you remain so smooth and white?

MATHILDE: We have our ways, my brother. We've always had our ways. And Adrien, are you still spending your life padding around barefoot? What do you do when you go out?

ADRIEN: I don't go out, Mathilde, I don't go out.

Enter MATHIEU

Maame Queuleu, Aziz, let's prepare the rooms. Mathilde will share her room with her daughter, and her son will be with mine, in my son's room.

MATHIEU: I don't want that boy in my room. I don't want anyone in my room. It's my room.

ADRIEN *slaps* MATHIEU

EDOUARD: It's not your room, you dumbass. Come on, Mother, let's get settled.

3 THE SECRET IN THE CLOSET

MATHILDE's *bedroom*
A bed, a closet
MATHILDE *is in bed.*
FATIMA *enters.*

FATIMA: Mom, I met someone in the garden, someone I've never seen who reminds me of someone, someone whose name I dare not say, because this someone has forbidden me to do so. Mom, mom get up! Strange things are happening in this house, and I hate it here.

Mom, come with me. This someone disappeared with the first ray of morning, a tiny ray, dawn's very first light. Come with me, I bet the grass is still trampled, and maybe a thread of clothing is still caught on the tree trunk, because this someone leaned up against it. Mom, this house is full of secrets, and it scares me.

MATHILDE: I don't want to move. I've spent hours warming these sheets, and I'm not moving until breakfast. Come here next to me; it's warm here, snuggle up. We have hours to go until breakfast, but my hunger is already tormenting me. Better we spend our time sleeping. Speak to me after coffee.

FATIMA: I can't sleep. This house is a bad house. I don't feel well here.

MATHILDE: You should've seen it in Marie's day. Come lie next to me under the covers, and I'll tell you how kind Marie was. I'll tell you Marie's story: my friend, lovely Marie who made this house so pleasant and warm. I'll tell you all about her until you fall asleep.

FATIMA: All you think about is sleeping and bringing up old memories, but so much is happening here.

MATHILDE: What do you mean all I think about is sleeping? I was only now falling asleep after a night of insomnia.

FATIMA: You always say that, but you start snoring as soon as you near a bed.

MATHILDE: Me? Snore? I didn't hear anything. It always feels like autumn here, those filthy little rainstorms clog up the nose.

FATIMA: Mom, I'm telling you, I met someone. Come with me, or else you won't believe me; the garden grass will straighten, and the wind and the dew will tidy the tree trunk. I want you to believe me. Get up, put on a dress.

MATHILDE: What's that look for, Fatima? Tell me your secret, tell me; it's swelling your face, it's oozing out your ears, tell me, or you're going to explode.

FATIMA: Secrets shouldn't be told.

MATHILDE: I command you to tell me. I know all about these secrets, these night meetings in the garden, then nine months later, it's no longer a secret, but a scandal. Speak to me, who is this man? What has he done to you? Speak up. I order you to tell me; if you don't tell me, who will ease you of your secret?

FATIMA: I didn't say it was a man.

MATHILDE: Did you talk to each other? What did you say? Is it a ghost you can talk to?

FATIMA: I didn't speak, because I was too scared.

MATHILDE: Can you tell me what it said to you? Was this ghost as silent as you?

FATIMA: It spoke to me.

MATHILDE: Tell me its name.

FATIMA: Never.

MATHILDE: Then go say it in the closet, that'll ease your mind; tell it to the dresses, I don't need to know. But you'll be ill if you hold it in any longer.

FATIMA *encloses herself in the closet, then comes out.*

Already?

FATIMA: It wasn't a long secret.

MATHILDE: You're not blushing like before. But why such a big deal for such a small secret?

FATIMA: I said it wasn't long, I didn't say it was small.

MATHILDE: I'll put on a dress and go with you. But do you think you can keep living like a savage here? Do you think we can keep living like before?

MATHILDE *opens the closet.*

FATIMA: Mom, I didn't want this thing to happen to me.

MATHILDE: What name did you say?

FATIMA: I didn't say any name.

MATHILDE: I heard a name.

FATIMA: I didn't open my mouth, I waited there in silence.

MATHILDE: In the pleats of my dresses I heard a name.

FATIMA: What would a name be doing in your dresses? You're dreaming, mom, you're making fun of me. You don't believe me.

MATHILDE: I believe you. We'll stay together, we won't leave each other's side. I'm scared too. Come closer, Fatima. Let's get under the covers.

FATIMA: You're trembling, mom. You seem cold.

MATHILDE: Marie.

FATIMA: What? Why did you say that?

MATHILDE: Marie. That's the name I heard rustling in the dresses.

4 MATTHIEU JOINS UP

In the garden

ADRIEN: (*jumping in front of* MATHIEU) Where are you going? It's early. You haven't had breakfast. Where are you going with that scheming look on your face?

MATHIEU: I'm going out.

ADRIEN: Going out, Mathieu, my boy? Going out where? Where would you be going?

MATHIEU: I'm going out of the house, I'm going out of the garden, I'm going all the way out.

ADRIEN: Why in hell would you want to go out? Do you need something? Aziz will get it for you.

MATHIEU: I need to get out, and Aziz can't do that for me.

ADRIEN: Aziz can do everything for you except be my son. I want to know why my son has such a scheming look this early in the morning.

MATHIEU: Isn't it natural for a person my age to go out without it being part of some scheme?

ADRIEN: No, it's not natural. Do you want to go to the factory? I'll take you there in a moment. Do you want to go to church? If you've been born again we'll drive there after breakfast.

Where else could you want to go? Where'd you come up with this funny idea?

MATHIEU: I want to go to town.

ADRIEN: You're already in town, Matthieu my boy. Our house is smack in the center of town, you can't be more in town than you are in this house.

MATHIEU: I want to get some air.

ADRIEN: So stretch out in the garden, under the trees. I'll have them bring your coffee there. The freshest air in town is in this garden.

MATHIEU: I want to go away

ADRIEN: So go away, to the edge of the garden. And lose that scheming smirk, or tell me what's on your mind.

MATHIEU: What's on my mind is leaving this house, leaving this town, leaving this country and joining the army.

ADRIEN: One more time, Matthieu my boy, because my head's muddled from your aunt's screams this morning.

MATHIEU: I want to join the army, leave for Algeria, and wage war.

ADRIEN: Who told you there was a war in Algeria?

MATHIEU: I don't want to sleep in the same room as Edouard anymore, I don't want to keep bumping into him anymore, all day and all night. I want to go to Algeria because that's the only place I won't run into him, since he just left there.

ADRIEN: Who told you Algeria existed? You've never left home.

MATHIEU: No, I've never left, and Edouard has been making fun of me because I don't know about the world.

ADRIEN: The world is here, my boy, and you know it very well. You walk around here every day, and there is nothing else to know. Look at my feet, Mathieu, here is the center of the world. Beyond is the world's edge, and if you go to the edge too often, you'll fall off.

MATHIEU: I want to travel.

ADRIEN: Travel from your bedroom to the living room, from the living room to the attic, from the attic to the garden. Mathieu, my boy, you're all mixed up this morning.

MATHIEU: I want to join the army.

ADRIEN: They won't take you. You have flat feet.

MATHIEU: I don't have flat feet.

ADRIEN: Who told you that? I have flat feet, that means you do too. Some things a father knows better than a son.

MATHIEU: Flat feet or no, I want to be a soldier, to parachute into Algeria and fight the enemy. Daddy, I want to be a paratrooper. I want to have my hair buzzed short. I want to wear fatigues. I want to have a knife holstered to my leg, and a pistol in my belt; I want to leap out the wide-open door of an airplane, glide in the air, soar above the ground, sing between heaven and earth.

ADRIEN: I'm going to fire Aziz and set Edouard straight.

MATHIEU: I want children to admire me, boys to envy me, women to pick me up. I want the enemy to fear me. I want to be a hero, risk my life, dodge attacks, be wounded, suffer without complaint, bleed.

ADRIEN: Be a hero here, where I can keep an eye on you. Haven't I been one, since your aunt arrived? Haven't I always been one, raising you, and building your inheritance?

MATHIEU: I don't want an inheritance. I want to die with beautiful words on my lips.

ADRIEN: What words?

MATHIEU: I don't know yet.

ADRIEN: You know nothing. Over that wall is jungle. You mustn't climb it without your father's protection.

MATHIEU: I don't want my father's protection anymore. I don't want to be slapped. I want to be a man who hits other men. I want comrades to drink and fight with; I want enemies to kill and conquer; I want to go to Algeria.

ADRIEN: Your enemies are in your own house. Your comrades are your father; if you want to drink, drink; and I won't slap you anymore. Besides, Algeria doesn't exist, and you look like an idiot.

MATTHIEU: Edouard told me about Algeria.

ADRIEN: Edouard is a compulsive liar. He's twisted your head.

MATHIEU: I've heard you talk about the war too.

ADRIEN: It's over, we won, everything's quiet in the boonies, everyone's gone back to work.

MATHIEU: I want to go to Paris. I'm tired of living in the countryside We always the same faces, and nothing ever happens.

ADRIEN: Nothing? You call this nothing? Your aunt and cousins come to town and you think that's nothing? Mathieu, my boy, the French countryside is the only place in the world where people live well. The whole world envies our countryside, its stillness and steeples, its peace, its wine, its prosperity. Here in the country we have everything a man could desire. Unless he's crazy. Unless he prefers misery to opulence, hunger and thirst to satisfaction, danger and fear to security. Are you crazy, Matthieu, my boy? Do I need to knock some sense into you? What's all this talk of travel anyway? You don't speak other languages. You weren't even able to learn Latin.

MATHIEU: I'll learn foreign languages.

ADRIEN: A true Frenchman doesn't learn languages. He's happy with his own, which is more than good enough: complete, balanced, easy on the ears. The whole world envies our language.

MATHIEU: And I envy the whole world.

ADRIEN: Wipe that scheming smirk off your face.

He slaps him.

> There's still a little left.

He slaps him again.

> Finally, I get my son back.

MATHIEU: It doesn't matter: I will be a soldier.

ADRIEN: What's that?

MATHIEU: Do I really have flat feet?

ADRIEN: Of course you do. I said so, didn't I? Look at mine. Is that what's bothering you? We can live with that, Mathieu. Only don't wear shoes so often and that way you won't suffer. Otherwise Mathieu, you're an ordinary man, an absolutely ordinary man.

MATHIEU: I'd like to be extraordinary.

ADRIEN: Don't be stupid. There are more extraordinary people every day. Soon it will be extraordinary to be ordinary. So sit tight, you don't need to do a thing.

They exit.

II

5

Hallway; a door cracked open.
Exit ADRIEN, *followed by some men, separately,* PLANTIÈRES *remains alone in the hallway.*
Enter EDOUARD *who pinions* PLANTIÈRES.
Enter MATHILDE, *scissors in hand.*

PLANTIÈRES: Who are you? What do you want from me?

MATHILDE: I'm Mathilde and I'm here to shave your head. I'm going to chop off every last strand of your hair. You'll leave here with a smooth skull, looking like a woman who's slept with the enemy. You'll see what fun it is to walk the streets with your head bruised and white, bare, the worst sort of nakedness. You'll know the creeping rhythm, the endless, unbearably slow rhythm of hair growth. You'll look in the mirror in the morning and you'll see a horrid old man, a repulsive stranger, an ape who apes your airs. You'll see just how hard it is to dress up a skull. You'll search for hats, and they'll all seem awful to you. You'll dream of wigs and hoods. You'll loathe the passers-by in the street—they'll look so pretty to you with their curls, with their beautifully mussed hairdos, and over those long months, all of your thoughts and dreams, your desires and hatreds, your energy, your entire life will be fixated on this stupid little thing: the lack of hair on your head. You'll try to make it grow faster, you'll tug on the first sprouts to speed things up. But you'll see that it won't speed up, that it has an unbearably slow rhythm, that the days get so long, weeks so long, months so long, with an obscene skull on your shoulders, that you'll wish we'd chopped off your balls instead.

PLANTIÈRES: Who is this little snot who's brutalizing my arms? I'm an honorable man. I'm a respected man, because I deserve respect. My career is without stain, my family life perfect, my reputation in this town considerable. I'm not the kind who cruises the streets alone at night, who gets attacked by punks. I leave my house to go to friends' houses, to headquarters, or to church. Are even friends' houses no longer safe? Should I be afraid of leaving home? Should I worry that violence will soon come to my house? What do you have against my hair? What did it do to you? Soon enough, I'll be old, and it'll fall out on its own. I want it to fall out on its own, I don't want it touched.

MATHILDE: I didn't want mine touched either. But you threw me to the mob, you pointed your finger at me. Your lies drove them to spit at me. You branded me a traitor. You. And even if you've forgotten, even if time has passed, I haven't forgotten.

PLANTIÈRES: What are you talking about, and who do you think I am? Something happened to you, long ago, very long ago, and you think I'm someone else. I don't know you, and I've never seen you, and you don't know me either. Did you climb in through the window, you and this little snot who's bruising my arms? Are you burglars? You should know I'm not the owner of this house. I can't do anything for you, except stay out of your way and not call for help. Are you a servant? If so, let it be known that you've already lost your position. But more likely you're the inevitable crazy old aunt, whom they've stashed in the attic. How'd you get out of your room? Help! Help! Tell this brute to let me go!

MATHILDE: I'm no longer old, and I've never been a servant. I'm Mathilde, and this is my house. It's mine, and there is no reason for you to feel safe here. I know you. I recognize you. Fifteen years has fattened you up, it has improved your wardrobe, put glasses on your face, and rings on your fingers. Had a hundred years lapsed from the day you condemned me to exile by pointing your finger, to today, when you'll be punished, had three centuries passed, I would've recognized you.

PLANTIÈRES: You don't even know my name.

MATHILDE: What do I care about your name? It's your hair I'm after.

PLANTIÈRES: I'm going to tell you, and you need to believe me, you're making a mistake. I have a big family; I have at least seven brothers who all look like me; I have hundreds of cousins you could mistake me for, because in my family we intermarry, and each newborn resembles every other, to the point where mothers can't tell them apart. You're searching for someone else. Take a good look at me, there's not much light here. Do you recognize this cheek? And this little scar under the ear, have you already seen it? Do you recognize the shape of the nose? Take a good look. You're making a mistake. You're making a mistake. I'm not the one you're out to get.

MATHILDE *shaves his head.*

MATHILDE: It is you. You're the one.

Exit MATHILDE *and* EDOUARD

PLANTIÈRES: Adrien, help!

Enter ADRIEN

> Mr. Serpenoise, you've come too late. Mr. Serpenoise, I will no longer address you by your first name, you're no longer a friend, you're no longer one of us, you're no longer welcome at headquarters, you don't have the right to ask for any more favors. What? You're smiling? I saw that smile, that nasty smirk on your face. Don't look at me. Be polite, and turn away. Look at your feet. Mr. Serpenoise, do you think your bare feet, which you stroll around on in polite company, are any less ridiculous than my head? What is the meaning of this behavior? At least put on socks, at least wear slippers. And you allow yourself a smile. I thought I was at a friend's house, I thought I was with my set, I thought we were among friends. You've tricked us. You waited a long while before revealing yourself. You're from a family of lunatics. A hysterical sister, a child mute and practically Mongoloid, a sick niece and nephew, depressives, epileptics: how could we, the polite company this town, think you'd be able to escape your family's degeneracy? And now you snicker, you show your true colors, you have betrayed me Mr. Serpenoise. And to think we've been holding these dangerous meetings at your place, at the home of a lunatic and a traitor. I'm going to denounce you, you'll no longer be welcome, and we'll no longer come here. You'll be banished from the Office of Social Action which stupidly trusted you, and maybe you'll even be punished. You'll pay for this, Serpenoise. You are a traitor.

ADRIEN: Calm down, Plantières. I didn't smirk. It was a grimace of shame, because my family weighs me down. But what can I do? I'm not responsible for my sister, I can't kill her. With your help, Plantières, I've done everything possible to drive her away. But still, I can't kill her. I'll make amends for this terrible accident.

PLANTIÈRES: What about my wife? And my kids? And my colleagues at headquarters?

ADRIEN: Go to the country for a few weeks, go to my country house. That Mathilde. I would kill her, and her kids too. Yes, I could be an assassin, but I swear to you Archibald, I'm not a traitor.

PLANTIÈRES: Yes, you betrayed me, Adrien.

ADRIEN: I swear to you I didn't; no, I never said a word.

PLANTIÈRES: Then how could she have known? You asked me to accuse her of consorting with the enemy, I was crazy to give in, and it should've been our secret. Serpenoise, you talked. There is no other way.

ADRIEN: I didn't speak, I swear on my beloved son's life. Only you and I knew. And Marie.

PLANTIÈRES: Marie is dead.

ADRIEN: Yes, Marie is dead. Plantières, avenge yourself, and I know the way. You're the police chief, join with Borny the lawyer, and Sablon, the county commissioner. Mathilde's daughter is crazy, she thinks she sees ghosts in the garden at night. Isn't that a perfect reason to lock her up? We slip into the garden one night and hide. We witness her madness. And you will be avenged, my poor Archibald, and so will I.

They exit.

6 Zohr

In the living room.
MAAME QUEULEU *and* MATHILDE *enter.*

MAAME QUEULEU: Come on now, Mathilde, come on. Make peace with your brother. Your bickering is turning this house into a living Hell. And my God, for what? Because such and such an object was in such and such a place, and you didn't want it there any more; because Monsieur doesn't like the way you dress, because you don't like him walking around barefoot. Are you both still children? Can't you compromise? Don't you know that growing up is all about finding common ground, dropping your stubbornness, and making do with what you have? Grow up, Mathilde, the time has come. Quarrels bring wrinkles, ugly wrinkles, do you want to be covered with ugly wrinkles, wrinkled by trifles you'll have forgotten within the hour? I'll help you to find common ground, Mathilde, I know my way around: Monsieur gets up at six and you at ten. Both of you: get up at eight. You hate pork, and Monsieur likes nothing but roast; I'll make veal roast. Life would be simple if you wanted it that way. Make peace, Mathilde, because this house is becoming unbearable.

MATHILDE: Why should I make peace, since I'm not angry?

MAAME QUEULEU: Quiet. Even from here, I can hear your brother's voice, raised in anger. What have you done to him? Why does the morning always start with angry growls, and the evenings close with pouting? Is that your blood's rhythm? It's not mine. It's not mine. I'll never get used to it. One fit of fury like yours would leave me ill and used up, but your anger seems to rally you and give you strength. Your energy tires me more than the housework. Exert yourself in other ways, Mathilde; embroider, take up sewing or woodwork; and Monsieur should pay more attention to his factory, because I hear in town that it has been going to wrack and ruin ever since your return. Do you want to be ruined? Speak to me, Mathilde. Your silence scares me.

MATHILDE: Embroidery, Maame Queuleu? Can you picture me stitching? Quiet, I hear him coming.

MAAME QUEULEU: Have pity on us, Mathilde.

Enter MARTHE

MARTHE: I've calmed him, thank God. I know an invocation that demons particularly despise. I flung it at him, and one two three, the demon rushed away, and now my Adrien is gentle and tired, because demons are tiring.

MATHILDE: That woman is already boozed-up, so early in the morning. Why can't she drink tea like the rest of us? They should cart her off to the loony bin.

MARTHE: Dear Mathilde, we must be nice to my Adrien. He's but a child. He's clumsy, but he loves you so, and you so deserve his love.

MATHILDE: Maame Queuleu, can't you get rid of that woman?

MARTHE: (*To* MAAME QUEULEU) Bring us something to drink, to celebrate the peaceful reunion of these two angels.

MAAME QUEULEU: We can't hear your brother anymore. It seems like he's calmed down.

Enter ADRIEN

MAAME QUEULEU: Adrien, your sister is ready to kiss you.

ADRIEN: I'll kiss her later.

MAAME QUEULEU: Why not now?

ADRIEN: First, I have a couple of things to say. Thanks to her, I've had a falling out with my friends. She insults and brutalizes them, and now they don't dar come here anymore, and when I run into them, they glare at me with looks full of scorn. Why should I be blamed for the craziness of this woman? I'm tired of paying the price for her.

MATHILDE: Everything about them irritates me, Maame Queuleu, and I can't stand it. Adrien sets me off too. The sound of his footsteps in the hallway, the way he coughs, the way he says: my boy; their secret little meetings where women aren't allowed. They lock me out of a room for hours in my very own house? They plot and scheme right beside me? I'll unhinge all the doors, I want to see all things at all times; I want to go wherever I please, whenever I please.

MAAME QUEULEU: Mathilde, you promised.

MATHILDE: In a moment, Maame Queuleu.

ADRIEN: They say in town that she walks naked on the balcony.

MAAME QUEULEU: Come on now, Mathilde, naked on the balcony!

ADRIEN: They say it.

MAAME QUEULEU: People will say just about anything.

ADRIEN: If people say she walks naked on the balcony, it's like I've seen it myself. People don't say that about me or you, Maame Queuleu. She was young when she went wrong. It's the call of nature, she's not going to miraculously become a lady late in life.

MARTHE: A miracle is always possible. We must have faith.

MATHILDE: Went wrong, Maame Queuleu? And that son of his? What else is he but an enormous, gargantuan error? What was the point of producing that? What gives him the right to burden my home with his useless progeny, that lazy thing, lolling about all day in the garden or the living room? He was enough of a burden, I didn't need a double bumping into me in the hallways, a second Adrien, a cheap copy of the first. Why, ask him why he needed to marry, Maame Queuleu, and why he produced a child.

ADRIEN: Ask her, Maame Queuleu, why she produced two.

MATHILDE: Tell him I didn't do it, it was done to me.

ADRIEN: Her son lurks in the Arab cafes in the gutters of town; everyone knows it. It's the call of blood. The Algerian sun beat down on my sister's head and it turned her Arab, her son too. I don't want her son dragging mine through the gutters, I don't want Matthieu lurking in Arab cafes.

MARTHE: They say in town that the Arabs give poisoned sweets to young boys and young girls and then spirit them off to Marrakesh brothels.

ADRIEN: And she's going to top it off by denouncing my son to the draft board. She's been seen prowling around town. She's more than capable of it, since she wants the factory, and she'll send my son to be massacred in Algeria. But the factory: never, never!

MAAME QUEULEU: Are you done yet? Mathilde, you're the eldest. Kiss your brother; do this for me.

MATHILDE: I'll kiss him right away, Maame Queuleu. But did you know he hit me? Just this morning, while I was drinking my tea, he hit me and even shattered the teapot. Should I have to put up with that?

MARTHE: That was when the devil possessed him.

MAAME QUEULEU: (*To* ADRIEN) Did you really hit her? Why did you do that?

ADRIEN: I don't remember, but if I did, I must've had a good reason. I don't hit people willy-nilly.

MAAME QUEULEU: Is that it? So kiss and make up. Adrien, you promised.

ADRIEN: Right away, soon, in a moment. But one more thing: Maame Queuleu, did you know that yesterday she hit my wife? My poor Marthe, she hit her.

MARTHE: No, no, she didn't hit me.

ADRIEN: I saw it, I heard the blow, she bore the mark for several hours.

MARTHE: She didn't hit me, she punished me because I'm mean. It was for my own good, and I'm glad for it.

MATHILDE: Idiot.

ADRIEN: (*To* MATHILDE) What did you say?

He approaches MATHILDE.

MAAME QUEULEU: Fine, beat on each other, disfigure, pluck out each other's eyes, just get it over with. I'll get you a knife, if only to speed things up. Aziz, bring me the big kitchen knife, better make it two for good measure; I sharpened them this morning, that'll speed things up. Tear, claw, go ahead and kill each other, only shut up, or else I'll cut your tongues out myself, slice them from the roots deep in your throats, quiet your voices once and for all. You'll fight in silence. No one'll know about it, and we'll get on with life. You fight only with words, useless words that damage everyone but yourselves. If only I were deaf, none of this would bother me. Fighting doesn't bother me, but do it in silence, so those of us around you don't feel the wounds in our bodies and heads. Every day your voices get louder and shriller, they cut through the walls, they sour milk in the kitchen. We can't wait for nighttime when you sulk; at least then we can work. May the sun sink earlier and earlier, so they may hate each other in silence. I give up.

MATHILDE: (*To* ADRIEN) I said: idiot. She's dead drunk. She's about to throw up on my rug.

ADRIEN *hits* MATHILDE.

MAAME QUEULEU: Aziz, Aziz!

MATHILDE *hits* ADRIEN

Edouard, Aziz, help!

Enter AZIZ

Aziz, separate them. Let's go, hurry up. What are you waiting for, Aziz? Get a move on.

AZIZ: No, I don't want to get a move on. I'm not paid to get a move on. If

I do, I'll be blamed, and if I don't, I'll still be blamed, so I'd rather do nothing. I'll take the blame, but at least I won't be tired.

MAAME QUEULEU: Aziz, look at them.

AZIZ: I see them, Maame Queuleu, I see them. But who cares if they're fighting, and what's it got to do with me? They don't even see me, they're so full of hatred they see nothing else. And when their anger subsides, I'll be the last thing they see, after the vases they've smashed. So let them beat each other up, and once they've calmed down, Aziz will pick up the pieces.

Enter EDOUARD

MAAME QUEULEU: Edouard, please, I'm going to lose my mind.

EDOUARD *restrains his mother.* AZIZ *restrains* ADRIEN.

ADRIEN: You lunatic. Do you think you can defy the world? Who are you to provoke honorable people? Who do you think you are, criticizing others, accusing, slandering, wounding the entire world? You're nothing but a woman, a woman without money, a single mother, forever unwed, and soon you'll be banished from society, they'll spit on you, they'll lock you away in a secret room and pretend you never existed. What claim has brought you here? Yes, it's true, to pay for your sin, our father made you sup on your knees for a year, but no, it seems the penalty wasn't severe enough. Now once again you should eat from our table on your knees, on your knees you should speak to me, on your knees before my wife, before Maame Queuleu, before your children. Who do you think you are, who do you think we are, constantly cursing and defying us?

MATHILDE: I do defy you, Adrien; and along with you, your son, and that thing you call your wife. I do defy you, all of you in this house, and I defy the garden that surrounds it, and the tree where my daughter shames herself, and the wall which encloses the garden. I defy you, the air you breathe, the rain that falls on your heads, the ground where you walk; I defy this town, each of its streets and each of its houses, I defy the river that flows through it, the canal and the barges on the canal, I defy the sky above our heads, the birds in the sky, the dead in the earth, the dead mixed in with the soil and the infants in the bellies of their mothers. I defy, because I know I'm stronger than all of you, Adrien.

AZIZ *restrains* ADRIEN, EDOUARD *restrains* MATHILDE, *but they escape and go back at it.*

MATHILDE: If the factory doesn't belong to me, it's because I didn't want it, because a factory falls into bankruptcy faster than a house falls to ruin, and this house will stand beyond my death, beyond the deaths of my children, while your child will wander through deserted leaking warehouses saying: this is mine, this is mine. No, the factory doesn't belong to me, but this house is mine, and because it's mine, I've decided that you will leave it tomorrow. You'll take your baggage, your son, and everything, everything else, and move to the warehouse, to your office with its cracking walls, with its jumbled stockpile of rot. Tomorrow, I will be home.

ADRIEN: What rot? What cracks in the walls? What ruins? My business is booming. Do you think I need this house? I don't. The only reason I liked living here is because of our father, in memory of him, out of love for him.

MATHILDE: Our father? Out of love for our father? I tossed the memory of our father in the trash a good long time ago.

ADRIEN: Don't touch that, Mathilde. At least respect his memory. That, at least, don't soil.

MATHILDE: I won't soil it, since it was already filthy enough without my help.

ADRIEN: I'll kill her.

EDOUARD: (*Restraining* MATHILDE) Stop it, mother. Come now, let's go.

AZIZ: (*Restraining* ADRIEN) Monsieur, Madame is very angry. She doesn't know what she's saying. Nobody would speak of their father that way, if they knew what they were saying.

They exit, then MATHILDE *and* ADRIEN *escape and go back at it.*

ADRIEN: (*Held back by* AZIZ) You'll pay for that, you old bitch, for that you'll pay.

MATHILDE: I've got what it takes to pay, but I'll pay nothing.

AZIZ: Monsieur, my arms ache from restraining you. Do I need to knock you out?

He restrains ADRIEN

ADRIEN: I'll kill her.

ADRIEN *and* AZIZ *exit.*

EDOUARD: Mother, if it has to be done, I'll drag you out of here.

MATHILDE: Tomorrow, I'll kick him out.

EDOUARD *and* MATHILDE *exit.*

MAAME QUEULEU: My poor child, we are quite miserable. They loved each other so much when they were small.

MARTHE: Bring me a drink, I'm so tired. Josephine, please go get me a bottle of port.

MAAME QUEULEU: It's still too early, dear girl.

MARTHE: Josephine, my good friend. If you weren't here, the world would crumble. Take me away from this hell, I implore you. You're a saint. When we're both dead, when you're in heaven and me in hell because of all the bad things I've done, throw me a rope, pull me up to you, because if you don't do it, who will? My sister Marie won't even look at me, the others have too many worries to remember me, and Aziz, noble Aziz, will be in limbo since he wasn't baptized, and there's no contact between hell and limbo. I don't want to be forgotten in hell for eternity like I've been forgotten during my short life. Promise me you'll pull me up to you, Josephine.

MAAME QUEULEU: I don't know, my poor dear, I don't know if heaven even exists.

MARTHE: What are you saying?

MAAME QUEULEU: If it existed, there'd be some sign of it here, some small imprint, the shadow of heaven on earth, some scraps, a small shimmer. But there's nothing, nothing but the scraps of hell.

MARTHE: Let's have a drink.

They exit.

7

From far off, the lewd song of paratroopers marching in time.

ADRIEN: (*To the audience*) Mathilde says I'm not really a man, but an ape. Maybe I'm like everyone else: halfway between ape and man. Maybe I'm a little more ape-like than she is, and maybe Mathilde is a little more human than me; no doubt she's craftier, but I hit harder. Like an old ape sitting at a man's feet gazing up at him, I feel at ease in my ape skin. I'm not interested in acting human, I'm not about to start now. I don't even know how it's done, I've seen it far too rarely.

When my son was born, I built high walls all around the house. I didn't want this ape's son to see the forest, and the insects, and the wild animals, the traps and the hunters. I slip on my shoes only to escort him on field trips, to protect him out in the jungle. The happiest apes are raised in a cage, with a good keeper. They die believing the entire world is like their cage. All the better for them—one more monkey saved. My own little baboon, at least I will have protected him.

Secretly, apes love watching men, and, secretly, men cannot help but gaze at apes. They're from the same family, at different stages, and neither one knows who's ahead of whom, no one knows who tends towards the other, since the ape boundlessly tends toward man, and man boundlessly towards the ape. Man has greater need to watch apes than other men, and the ape greater need to watch men. So they gaze at each other, get jealous, fight, gash with claws, and slug each other in the snouts, but they never leave each other, not even in spirit, they never tire of staring.

When Buddha visited the apes, he sat down one evening among them and told them: Apes, behave yourselves, act like humans, not like apes. This way, one morning you'll wake up human. So the naive apes acted human: they tried to behave like they thought a human should. But the apes were too kind, too dumb. And now each night they hope, they go to bed with a soft, gentle smile of hope. And each morning, they cry.

I am an aggressive and brutal ape, and I don't believe in Buddha's stories. I don't want to spend the night hoping, because I don't want to cry in the morning.

III 'ICHÂ

8

The garden. Night.
Enter FATIMA *and* MATHIEU.

FATIMA: Go away, Mathieu. Stop squeezing me. Lucky you—any pretext—since I got here, always squeezing and touching me. Don't forget we're cousins, and you can't touch me the way you're touching me when you're from the same family.

MATHIEU: We're not from the same family. Families only exist for inheritance, from father to son. You won't inherit from my father and I won't inherit from you, so if I feel like touching you, I don't see where the problem is. We're not from the same woman, you don't know your father and I know mine; nothing connects us. How far back do we have to go to feel free? At what point are we foreign to each other? How many generations do we have to jump to cut the family ties?

FATIMA: The world is full of women, so why are you always squeezing and touching me? I'm not interested. You're too much my cousin for me to be interested, and, in any case, cousin or no, family or no, I don't like anybody touching me.

MATHIEU: There aren't that many women out there.

FATIMA: More than half the world, and I'm the one you come to bother.

MATHIEU: Then we need at least two words for the word woman. Maame Queuleu is a woman. She passes in front of me but I don't even see her. Even in my imagination, I only see her how she is: badly dressed, carrying rags. Why do we call Maame Queuleu and you by the same name of woman, since you don't look at all alike? You wrap up for mid-winter even though it's warm and mild out, but I see you differently. In my dreams and in life I want to look at you like I have never looked at a woman before.

FATIMA: You're thirty years old and you've never looked at a woman?

MATHIEU: I'm not thirty yet, and I've seen plenty of women in my life, starting with Maame Queuleu, whom I've seen every day since my birth. But I haven't had a good look at a woman for a while, because they don't come to the house.

FATIMA: Then go out to the bad parts of town. There are plenty of women who'll let you look if you pay them, and for a little more money they'll even let you touch. They'll do it with pleasure since you're not that ugly and you have money.

MATHIEU: But I go out, Fatima. I'm always going out. I've gone out so many times in my life: starting with church and the factory, which is very far from here; I've visited it because it's my inheritance. But I haven't been out in a while, because I don't have the time, and I don't have much money, at least not yet.

FATIMA: I don't care about saving you time or saving you money. Go away, Mathieu. My mother's coming. If she sees you with me, you can bet she'll give you a piece of her mind.

MATHIEU: Bring her on then. The back of my hand would shut her trap. She's always prying and it gets on my nerves. It's time I showed her just who I am.

Enter MATHILDE

MATHILDE: Fatima, I've been looking for you. Seeing you here now with your cousin, I find this reassuring. I'd like you two to be friends. Mathieu is a sensible boy, so poised and thoughtful, and this little savage could do with some sense. Matthie, my little Mathieu, the evening is so mild, let's take a walk in the garden and have a quiet chat.

MATHIEU: Aunt, I'd love to, since I like your company too. But I must do my work. I was telling Fatima that, even though the warm weather makes us feel lazy, sometimes we have to sacrifice for the sake of study.

MATHILDE: Mathieu, Mathieu, maybe you can help me get that through the heads of my two children. Go. I won't keep you from your studies.

He exits

> Fatima, I don't want you lingering in this garden at night. I too lingered here in my day. I lingered here one night too many and that's what gave me your brother, and I didn't even see the gift-giver's face. Fatima, there are people who jump over walls and lie in wait for women to lose their way, and afterwards you end up with a gift you never wanted. The gardens of this town are dangerous, because of the barracks; the soldiers leap garden walls to give gifts. Fatima, are you alone?

FATIMA: I am alone, but I'm waiting for someone, and it's not a soldier from the barracks. You shouldn't stay.

MATHILDE: Fatima, let me see her. I'll hide back there. I won't make any noise, but let me see her, because I've never stopped grieving, even after fifteen years.

FATIMA: Mom, look, behind the walnut tree. Don't you see the light?

MATHILDE: I see nothing.

FATIMA: Look carefully. Don't you see the edge of a white dress? She doesn't dare show herself.

MATHILDE: Fatima, I see nothing.

FATIMA: Don't you feel a bitter cold, a terrible cold?

MATHILDE: Yes, I feel it: a terrible cold.

FATIMA: That's her. That's Marie. Hide better. She's scared.

MATHILDE: Why would I scare her? I'm Mathilde. I'm her best friend.

FATIMA: She thinks I've betrayed her. Get out of here.

MATHILDE: Marie, it's me, Mathilde. Could it be dear old Mathilde that's scaring you? I'm older, but it's still me, Marie. I'm sorry I got old. You died just in time. You always were more clever than me. (*To* FATIMA) Is she still there?

FATIMA: She's there.

MATHILDE: Can you see all of her?

FATIMA: Yes, all of her. She's all there, and she's looking at you.

MATHILDE: Are you sure?

FATIMA: Yes, she's looking at you.

MATHILDE: Leave me alone, Marie. I don't want you to look at me. I don't want you remembering me, and I don't want to remember you. Why won't things get out of our head when we ask them to get out? Why don't we have a choice? You were always there, in my mind's eye, with your goody-goody angel face, with your sanctimonious sneer, while I was in the shit, especially while I was in the shit. What the fuck were you doing there? What the fuck are you doing, always near me, always between me and Adrien, always near Adrien. You had him. You clung to him, you clung to me; what the fuck are you always clinging to us for? What the fuck were you doing in my head in Algeria, you who never left your house, except to cross the street and marry that monkey you'd always had the hots for. And then you never left his house until you slipped away, until you pulled it together enough to skip out on life, until you packed it in just to avoid wallowing with us in the muck, your hands and your angel face unstained by this shitty life. (*To* FATIMA) Is she still here?

FATIMA: She's here, and she's crying.

MATHILDE: Fine, let her cry, let her cry her eyes out, buckets and buckets. Let the dead be good at least for that: crying and being ashamed before us. What's she got to complain about? She's all set. She knows where she lives, in the land of virgins and little angels. She's at peace. Nobody's coming to pester her, so she kills time by pestering others. Why do the dead, just by dying, all of a sudden turn so virtuous, so beautiful, so respectable? I'm sure she wasn't as beautiful as all that, or even as nice as I remember. Anyway, she wouldn't've stayed that way.

FATIMA: Mom, she's leaving. She's turning away, she's vanishing behind the tree.

MATHILDE: Let her vanish. May she sleep in her cotton bed, may she chant hymns with the angels, and leave us in the shit, alone, without a house, without a roof, without a land.

FATIMA: Mom, she's gone. You've scared her off.

FATIMA *exits*.

MATHILDE: What homeland do I have? Where is my land? Where is that land where I may lay my head? In Algeria, I am a foreigner, and I dream of France; in France I am even more foreign and I dream of Algiers. Is our homeland the place where we aren't? I'm sick of not being in my place, and not knowing where my place is. But homelands don't exist, nowhere do they exist. Marie, if you could die a second time, I would wish for your death. Chant your hymns, wallow away in heaven or in hell, but stay there wallowing so I may be rid of you.

She exits.

9

Hallway.
BORNY *exits through an open door*
Then, PLANTIÈRES.

PLANTIÈRES: You're leaving, Borny. You're running away.

BORNY: I'm not running away, Plantières. I forgot something in my car.

PLANTIÈRES: What did you forget? What could you possibly need from your car?

BORNY: My bag, my briefcase. I forgot my briefcase in the car.

PLANTIÈRES: And in order to fetch your briefcase from the car, you took advantage of a moment of inattention to give us the slip?

BORNY: Give you the slip? What are you talking about, give you the slip? That's not what I'm doing. I usually attach my glasses to a cord around my neck, and this time I've forgotten the cord. I get nothing without my glasses, and this discussion is too important. Plantières, if you don't mind I'm going to go find my glasses.

PLANTIÈRES: Now it's your glasses? Are you sure you know what you're looking for?

BORNY: My glasses which are in my briefcase which is in my car. Plantières, you're insulting me.

PLANTIÈRES: Not for the world, Borny. But I'll escort you to your car.

BORNY: And why are you escorting me?

PLANTIÈRES: To make sure you don't lose your way.

BORNY: You doubt me, Plantières, and that hurts. I just told you your idea is excellent, that I approve of it.

PLANTIÈRES: Your idea, you say. What is the meaning of "your"? It has a nasty ring to it. You would exclude yourself from this "your"?

BORNY: Not for the world. When the time comes, I shall applaud with both hands.

PLANTIÈRES: You'll applaud, well how about that! Where will you applaud? Will you applaud in the secrecy of your bedroom? The door bolted shut so no one can hear? Your canary the sole eyewitness? What do we care about your applause?

BORNY: Plantières, I'm gonna slug you.

PLANTIÈRES: Slug me.

BORNY: I'll do it, I swear.

PLANTIÈRES: Do it then, and stop swearing.
Coming out through the door are ADRIEN, SABLON, then several other men.

ADRIEN: What noise, what ruckus, what a fucking mess!

BORNY: Plantières insulted me.

PLANTIÈRES: Borny's skipping out.

BORNY: He's lying.

PLANTIÈRES: He's got cold feet.

SABLON: Please, gentlemen, please. No talk of discord in our group.

PLANTIÈRES: Commissioner, at the critical moment, Borny all of a sudden forgot his glasses in the car.

ADRIEN: His glasses? I didn't know you wore glasses, Borny.

BORNY: (*To* SABLON) Commissioner, please listen to me. You know I've never flinched at the moment of action. But this time, given my position, it's in everyone's interest that I not be mixed up in this, at least not directly. Rest assured, gentleman, that I am with you in spirit.

PLANTIÈRES: What good is your spirit to us? Do you think we need you in spirit? The point is to blow up the Saïfi Café.

ADRIEN: Enough with the screaming, or I'll throw you all out.

BORNY: Fair enough. Of course we have good intentions. But have you taken a close look at the punk you hired for this job? He'll blow up the café even if it's packed. I don't want my conscience splattered with blood. Adrien, what became of the days when anarchists preferred to blow themselves up along with their bomb, rather than risk wounding a child?

SABLON: Shut up already. Where do you think you are? Let's get back in the room.

PLANTIÈRES: You too, Borny.

BORNY: Plantières, I swear to God, I'm gonna slug you.

PLANTIÈRES: Go ahead and swear, it's less harmful than a slug.

SABLON: Shut up, Borny.

BORNY: Why me? Why always me?

ADRIEN: Quiet!

They enter the room. ADRIEN *shuts the door.*

10

By the compound walls, at night.
MATHIEU *and* EDOUARD

MATHIEU: What a marvelous world, and how well it's made. Even this wall seems like it was built just so I could have the pleasure of hopping over it. Edouard, look. Night is falling and this good little town is sleeping like a tired old granny. We have the town square all to ourselves. And now you tell me there are places with women, where they'll let us touch them? Here, in this town? I've lived here for over twenty-five years and never knew what you already know. My buddy Edouard, you're light in the muscle department, but that's some head on your shoulders. But stop saying the world's not worth it. Feel how this mild weather excites us. If the world was that bad, we'd be excited by the cold and the winter, and have to get pleasure through layers of clothing while shivering. But in this marvelous world, the heat of the beast hooks up with the heat of the air, the heat of the air makes us strip, and, then, Edouard, the naked beast is ready to do his business. Let's move, Edouard.

EDOUARD: Even the dinkiest little village has its whorehouse, dumbass. The girls won't vanish if we take our time. Besides, we need to wait for Aziz, who's going to take us to Rue Caire where we can meet the best girls. All I did was ask Aziz, something you could've done for twenty-five years. Your muscles may indeed be big, but you've got a tiny little brain. I wonder how you've managed for this long. Still, you're not bad-looking, and you seem to be bursting with health.

MATHIEU: As for health, little Edouard, this is true, this I've got. See how I hop this wall? I could hop it ten times before you'd manage to climb up. It's important to be strong. Who needs a big brain, what good is being clever if you're fragile? Come here, little man. I'll carry you over, and drop you on the other side without you even noticing, and neither will I, because you're light as a baby. Look at these muscles, see how toned they are. I think women will like them. Poor little Edouard, why don't you take better care of your body? How are you going to tempt women with those rickety arms and that scrawny neck? Edouard, you're my friend and I'll help you train. With a few months' work, we'll double the size of your snaky little body.

EDOUARD: I don't want to double anything. I have enough of what I have, it's plenty, I do fine with this body of mine. Besides, that body you're always working on is continually renewing itself, those cells you expend so much effort toning will leave you tomorrow with your soap and water; and after seven years go by, there'll be nothing left of who you've made of yourself today. It'll have been a waste of time spending two hours each morning training.

MATHIEU: Seven years is a very long time, and my hours of training will at least please women; because they'll like me, that's for sure. Let's move, Edouard.

EDOUARD: Aziz isn't here yet.

MATHIEU: Aziz bores me. He's sullen and mean, and even when he goes out for fun, he's so sad that, if he didn't tell me different, I'd think he didn't like women. Why does he go to the whorehouse like it's a chore?

EDOUARD: Once you've been often enough, you'll also go each time with a little less speed and a little less joy.

MATHIEU: While we're waiting, let's do some chores, to work, to work. Let's lift these rocks, let's break our backs, I love this kind of pain, I want to suffer. To the chain gang. To the chain gang!

Enter AZIZ

AZIZ: You're making fools of yourselves on top of that wall, and you're going to wake the neighborhood. Quiet. I don't want any trouble with your families.

MATHIEU: Aziz, my buddy Aziz, if you like women, why the frown?

AZIZ: I didn't say I liked women, I said I fucked them.

MATHIEU: Whatever. Let's get there, Aziz, and the world is marvelous.

AZIZ: I don't know how the world is, but I know you're going to wake your families. Come on: I see a light in one of the bedrooms, it just came on.

MATHIEU: That's Maame Queuleu's room. The old lady has insomnia. The old lady mourns her youth. She's sorry she didn't have more fun.

AZIZ: I'll take you to Rue Caire and then leave you there, because I'm not visiting the women today. I'll wait for you in the Saïfi Cafe, right next door.

EDOUARD: Come with us, Aziz. I don't want to be left alone with this moron.

AZIZ: Hurry up already, another light just came on. I'm not part of the family, and they'll fire me if they catch me corrupting you.

MATHIEU: It's your mother, Edouard, I think she's going to make sure you're in bed with your teddy bear. Get a move on, Edouard, your mommy's coming to the window.

EDOUARD: What about that other one that just lit up? Whose room is that?

MATHIEU: That's dad's room. Move out.

They exit.

11

Veranda. ADRIEN.
The big black paratrooper looms into view.

PARATROOPER: Everyone's sleeping in this house, colonel.

ADRIEN: Don't call me colonel, I'm not a soldier. Who are you? How did you get in?

PARATROOPER: This town seems asleep, boss. Has it been abandoned?

ADRIEN: How did you get in?

PARATROOPER: From the sky, obviously. We came in tonight. The army's in town, boss. Not the pavement-crawling grunts or sheltered tank-drivers, not the pencil-pushing armchair generals or KP duty shit shovelers—but the army in the charge of Heaven and Earth. I have dropped from the heavens like a snowflake in July just so you can sleep tight. Cause maybe you think these thick walls protect you? Maybe you think your money can? All of that would shatter into a thousand pieces with a single shot right between your eyes.

ADRIEN: You've been drinking, soldier. I'll speak to your officers.

PARATROOPER: Speak, boss, speak, but respect me.

ADRIEN: I respect you, my boy, but why are you harassing me? Aren't you here to bring us security?

PARATROOPER: First you've got to bring trouble, if you want security.

ADRIEN: Well then, welcome. Welcome, soldier. I'm a respectable little boss and I love the army.

PARATROOPER: You better love it, since she's the one who made you rich.

ADRIEN: And I'm the one who pays you, soldier.

PARATROOPER: Less than your servant, less than nothing. Just enough to buy smokes. But I'm the one who fattened you up, I let you count your pennies and play at politics. We soldiers are the heart and veins of this world, and you bosses are the bowels.

ADRIEN: You're very excited, my boy.

PARATROOPER: Excited, excited, excited, yes.

ADRIEN: I welcome your excitement. But know that this town is a calm little town, quiet, used to its soldiers. And your place, soldiers, is within the walls of your barracks. Be good, be calm, and the town will love you, the town will take good care of you. Get back to your barracks, now.

PARATROOPER: Where are the women?

ADRIEN: Excuse me?

PARATROOPER: Women? Dames, hens, fillies, cows, bunnies, pussies, bitches, bitches, where are you hiding them? I smell them; I smell woman here. Out of my way, boss.

ADRIEN: Calm down, my boy. Calm down.

PARATROOPER: No calm. We're here, boss. Where are the women?

ADRIEN: There's no one here but ladies.

PARATROOPER: Don't you worry, daddy, I'll turn 'em into women. Hide your bitches, the army's let the dogs out.

ADRIEN: Don't you love this country? Don't you love this land? Are you a barbarian come to pillage, or a soldier here to protect?

PARATROOPER: I love this land, boss, but I don't like its people. Who's the enemy? Are you friend or enemy? Who must I defend and who must I attack? Since I don't know who's the enemy, I'll shoot anything that moves.

I love this land, yes, but I do miss the old days. I miss the soft glow of oil lamps and the splendor of sailing ships. I'm nostalgic for the colonial age, an age of verandas and croaking toads, an age of long evenings, when everyone knew his place, stretched out in a hammock, swinging in a rocking chair or squatting under the mango tree, each in his place, at home in his place. His place was his. I miss the little piccaninnies scooting under cow paws, I miss swatting them away like pesky mosquitoes. Yes, I love this land, don't doubt it. I love France from Dunkirk to Brazzaville. I have guarded its borders. I have marched all night, weapon in hand, ears to the ground, sharp eyes turned outward. And now they tell me to put my nostalgia to sleep. They say times have changed. They tell me that borders shift like the crests of waves, but does one die for the movements of waves? They tell me a nation exists and then no longer exists, a man finds his place, then loses it. They tell me the names of towns, estates, houses, and people in houses all change in the course of a lifetime, and then everything is put back in a different order and man no longer knows his name, or where his house is, or his country, or his borders. He no longer knows what to keep. He no longer knows who's foreign. He no longer knows who's giving the orders. They tell me history drives man, but a man's life is far too short, and history, that fat old sow, once she's done chewing things over, stamps her hoof with impatience. I exist to make war, and my only peace will be death.

He disappears.

ADRIEN: How'd he get in here, by God.

IV MAGHRIB

12 ON THE EDGE OF THE BED

MATHILDE's *bedroom*
MATHILDE *and* FATIMA *in bed.*

MATHILDE: Fatima. Fatima, are you sleeping? I hear your uncle's footsteps in the hall. He's getting closer, he's by the door, he's waiting. He's here to hurt me. Under cover of night, he'll do things he's never dared do by day. Stir, Fatima. Wake up and speak to me, so he knows you're here. If he comes in, open your eyes wide, and don't stop staring at him so he knows you're awake. And if he's blinded by anger and can't see you, get up and raise the roof. Everyone thinks you're crazy: it won't bother anyone. Fatima, my dear, stop sleeping, or pretending to sleep; your uncle is pacing by the door, and I'm trembling.

You think I'm raving, Fatima, but I'm not. I swear to you I'm not. This town is full of people who die smothered by a pillow or strangled with cord, from the stab of a sadist who's climbed in through the window or a robber who's come for the pearls. And your uncle, knowing so many doctors and police officers, risks nothing. Nobody would know a thing. Mathilde, finished off like Marie, finished off. How and why could we know how and why people die in this town? At this time of night, the whole town has its eyes shut, snoring, except for the killers, except for their victims.

You're not asleep. I know how sleepers breathe. Have you ever passed through the room of a sleeper? Fatima, if you want to be disgusted by men, slip into their bedrooms, and watch and listen as they sleep. Why do they dress like gentlemen by day, when half their lives are spent sprawled out like pigs in a pen, unconscious, out of control, as senseless as a tree trunk drifting down the river, an eye spinning full speed in its socket, and when they awake, they remember nothing. This time of night is scary, when all of humanity is sweating in its sheets, a time when thousands of people belch, spit, gnash their teeth, eyes closed as they sigh, digesting, digesting, throats rasping, mouth agape towards the ceiling. They're absolutely right to lock themselves away at bedtime. Every man should bear each day the shame of the previous night, the shame of sleep's abandon. I never lock my door, because I don't sleep. I should've locked it, because I hear your uncle pacing by the door.

Fatima, if he comes in—and I think he'll come in—sit straight up and ask him how she died. Maybe surprise will force the truth out of his mouth before spite locks it shut. I'm trembling, my dear, my little girl. Before he comes in, and he will come in, hide under the bed, and when he's about to smother me with the pillow, pull hard on his feet, until he falls. Fatima, my dear, don't leave me all alone. Let a ray of light escape your eyelids, so I know you're not asleep. Because I'm trembling, Fatima. I'm trembling.

Enter ADRIEN

ADRIEN: Mathilde, are you asleep? All the better. Mathieu is leaving for the army. They finally tracked him down. It looks like my friends have given me up. Unless it's your fault. It's likely enough; there's no smoke without fire. Whatever the case, he's going to Algeria, he'll be massacred out in the boonies, they'll bring home his remains with all honors. I'll no longer have an heir. But I warn you, my dear, you'll never get the factory.

My first thought was to go to the cemetery and put a bullet in my head, like our grandfather did when his son joined the army, and like our great-grandfather did for our grandfather. It's a family tradition, and it's important to respect tradition. But I didn't do it, because, first off, my father didn't do it for me, and then it was raining and my shoes were hurting me, and then finally you would've inherited the factory and that, my dear, can't happen.

I don't like your children. You've raised them badly. Children need to be raised with a good beating and wise instruction, if not they'll shit all over you the first chance they get. They'll shit all over you, my dear, and I won't be the one to wipe you off.

Mathieu is dead. That's what it feels like: like he's already half-dead in an Algerian trench, so at this point I don't give a fuck; Why should I care about a soon-to-be dead man? I'm not the kind who'd visit his grave saying: if he were alive. . . my son's soon-to-be corpse doesn't interest me. I inherit from myself, I declare myself sole heir. Nobody else will touch my inheritance.

We must respect our traditions. The women of our families die young and often nobody knows exactly why. Your time's about to come. As Maame Queuleu says, you are still young. When we say that someone's still young, it means they're already old.

Maybe you'll follow Aunt Armelle's lead and hang yourself from a tree in the garden, maybe you'll plunge yourself into the canal, calmly, unexpectedly, after carefully folding your clothes at the water's edge, just like the sweet, the discreet, the silent Ennie. Or perhaps you'll end up smothered under a pillow, a typical end for women who get in the way. None of this has ever drawn attention, the authorities here are accommodating; it's such an old town tradition; we all have understanding friends. At least I hope so. I do believe my friends have given me up. It's your fault; you've fucked everything up since you came back. A person can't live in a town like this without friends.

You push too hard, Mathilde. One of these days you'll pay, my dear. You're already a cracked jug, soon you'll shatter into a thousand shards. You bang too hard, Mathilde, it's better not to stir things up in these quiet little towns, better not to shake up good families living quiet lives. You've travelled too much, my dear, travels trouble the head, they twist your point of view. You think you're so strong, but you're already all cracked up. If a stone falls on a pitcher, too bad for the pitcher; if a pitcher falls on a stone, too bad for the pitcher. And you're the pitcher, Mathilde. Are you in a rush to meet your maker?

I don't like you scorning my wife. That you fuck with me, that you want my inheritance, that I expect, it's in the blood, it's tradition. But I won't put up with you scorning my wife. She's as good as the other one, just as good as the other. I wavered between the two of them for a while, and then I married the eldest, out of courtesy. In the end, I also married the other; that way, there's no one left to marry. But I forbid you to scorn her, Mathilde; for that, I could kill you.

I like you best when you're sleeping: you shut your mouth, you don't stick your nose in everything, you wisely listen to what I tell you, like a sister is supposed to listen when her brother speaks. Maybe I'll sleep all day and live by night. That way we'll be the ideal sister and brother. Meanwhile sleep, Mathilde, your slumber protects you.

He exits.

FATIMA: Good God, mother, if Edouard was like that with me, I swear to you I'd give it right back to him in the jaw and flatten him, he wouldn't do it again. Why do you let guys get away with that? It's all hot air, bluff, sham, bull shit. A woman is the belt of a man's pants. If she drops them, he's left buck naked. Your brother will be left buck naked if you drop him. Why don't you want to drop him? What do you gain, aside from forgetting your children? Because you don't even look at us anymore, you're too busy fighting, and Edouard, poor Edouard, his mind is breaking down, the screws are loosening, he's can't even walk straight anymore, and you don't even notice. Don't you give a damn?

Mom, I want to go back to Algeria. I don't understand people here. I don't like this house, I don't like the garden, or the street, or any of the houses, or any of the streets. It's cold at night, it's cold by day, the cold scares me more than the war. Why do you want to stay, to fight with your brother all day? In Algeria, you didn't fight with anybody. I loved you more in Algeria than in France, you were stronger and you loved us. Did you come back just because you love to fight? Is that why, just for that? Why stay here freezing when things over there were so good? I was born there, and I want to go back. I don't want to suffer in a foreign country. Mom, are you asleep? For real?

13 I DON'T WANT TO GO THERE

In the kitchen.

MATHIEU: Aziz, help me.

AZIZ: That's what I'm doing: I work for your father and for you.

MATHIEU: Not that sort of help, Aziz. Help me, buddy.

AZIZ: How else can I help you?

MATHIEU: They want to send me to war. I've received my draft papers, and I'm supposed to join the army.

AZIZ: Everybody joins the army. You're born, you suckle, you grow, you sneak smokes, you get beaten by your father, you join the army, you work, you marry, you have children, you beat your children, you get old, you die full of wisdom. That's how it is.

MATHIEU: But they're going to send me to Algeria, Aziz. I don't want to fight, I don't want to die. How am I supposed to marry and have children, then get old and wise, if I die first.

AZIZ: That's the price you pay for your silver spoon. I didn't have a father, so I served when the time came, and since the war hadn't started yet, I served at Commercy, quietly.

MATHIEU: How is the army, Aziz?

AZIZ: It's not all that bad, buddy. You get up early, you go to bed early, you play sports, you make friends, you get leave, you don't have money problems, you don't think about anything. It's very very good.

MATHIEU: I shouldn't have to serve: I have flat feet. Why should I have to, since people with flat feet normally don't serve?

AZIZ: You have flat feet?

MATHIEU: My father has them, so I have them too. That's how it is.

AZIZ: If they've said you have to serve, it means either you don't have flat feet, or people with flat feet serve like the rest of us. It's one or the other, that's how it is.

MATHIEU: Does a war last long?

AZIZ: I believe so, very long.

MATHIEU: How long?

AZIZ: Once it gets started, no one knows when it's going to end. Your children might still be at it.

MATHIEU: If I die in war, I won't have a child.

AZIZ: Maybe you won't die. Not everyone dies in war.

MATHIEU: And wounded, Aziz? If I come back crippled?

AZIZ: Not everyone gets wounded in war. You might even come back in full bloom of health with your face bronzed by the sun.

MATHIEU: How is Algeria?

AZIZ: I've forgotten.

MATHIEU: Remember. Try harder.

AZIZ: Even if I try, I've completely forgotten.

MATHIEU: Why do you think of nothing but money, Aziz? All you do is work, work to pile up money. Stop working, Aziz; I'm talking to you.

AZIZ: Because I need money. I make money by working and, since your father pays me badly, I can't stop working.

MATHIEU: I'll tell him to pay you better. What's the war like, Aziz?

AZIZ: I don't know, I've never known, and I don't want to know.

MATHIEU: Me neither, I don't want to know about it.

AZIZ: My dear Mathieu, don't be sad. We'll go to Saïfi's place this evening, and you'll forget your sadness.

MATHIEU: I don't want to forget my sadness. And what's death like?

AZIZ: How should I know? No more need for money, no need of a bed to sleep in, no more work, no suffering, I guess. I guess it's not all that bad.

MATHIEU: I don't want to die.

AZIZ: You'll be a hero, Mathieu. The French think of themselves as 45 million heroes, why should you be the exception, my friend? You're no stupider than any other Frenchman. You'll come back and breed quickly, just so you can tell your kids about the war. And if you don't come back, we'll tell stories about you to other people's children.

MATHIEU: I don't want to suffer.

AZIZ: Wipe your face, there's Maame Queuleu, she might think you're crying.

MATHIEU: But I am crying, Aziz, I am crying.

Enter MAAME QUEULEU

MAAME QUEULEU: Are you crying, Mathieu?

MATHIEU: Don't be stupid, Maame Queuleu; I've never cried in my life and I'm not about to start up today.

He exits.

MAAME QUEULEU: I love, Aziz, when sadness rules this house. Mathilde sulks with Monsieur in the living room. Mathieu is crying and Fatima sighing and complaining about the cold; Edouard is buried in his book: all is calm, silent and sad. The house is ours.

14

A bell rings for complines in the distance.

MATHILDE: (*To the audience*) I never speak in the evening, for the simple reason that evening is a liar. Visible trembling is just a sign of a soul's peace. The calm of houses is treacherous, hiding the violence of tempers within. It's why I don't speak in the evening, for the simple reason that I myself am a liar, I have always been one, and I have every intention of continuing to be one: there are as many letters in a yea as in a nay, right? And we may freely use one or the other. But things are going badly between evening and me. Two liars cancel each other out because, when lie faces lie, truth starts to rear its ugly head. I dread truth. That's why I don't speak in the evening; anyway I try not to, because it's also true that I like to talk.

The true blot on our lives is children. They get themselves conceived without asking anyone's advice, and then they're there, fucking things up all life long. They wait quietly to profit from the happiness we've been building all our lives; they'd so love to leave us with no time to enjoy it. We should eliminate inheritance: that's what rots these small country towns. We should reinvent the reproductive system: women should bear stones: a stone never got in anyone's way, you gather it tenderly, you place it in the corner of the garden, you forget about it. Stones should bear trees, the tree would bear a bird, the bird a pond, from the ponds would emerge wolves, and the she-wolves would bear and suckle human babies. I wasn't made to be a woman. I should've been Adrien's blood brother. We'd slap each other on the shoulder, we'd bar hop and arm wrestle, we'd tell dirty stories at night, and every now and then we'd beat the shit out of each other. But I'm not really made to be a man either. Fatima's right. They're too stupid. Except she's not completely right. Men know how to be pals, when they like each other, they really like each other, they don't pull any crap. Besides, they don't pull any crap because they're stupid, they don't even think of it, they're one or two stages behind us. Because once they're friends, women happily pull crap on each other. They like each other, and because they like each other, whatever harm they can do to you, they do. That's due to the extra evolutionary stages in their heads.

Never tell anyone that you need him, or that you're fed up with him, or that you love him, because then he'll immediately think he's made it. He'll act like he's wearing the pants, pretend he's holding the reins, and show off. Never say anything at all, except in anger, because at that point we can say just about anything. But at times like this when we're not angry, unless you're a pathetic loudmouth, it's best to shut up.

Whatever happens, Adrien will come back with me. This I know. I wanted it, I'll have it. I came without, I'll go back with. But silence, no more lies. Mathilde, the evening betrays you.

V

15

The Café Saïfi

SAÏFI: عَزِيزْ فِيسَعْ، هَاتْ اصْحَابَكْ... قُلُهُمْ يخَلَّصُوا غَادِي نْبَلَّعْ الحَانُوتْ.

AZIZ: مَازَالْ صيفي. غْلَاشْ زَرْبَانْ؟

SAÏFI: I'm closing up shop. Pay me and leave.

AZIZ: Pay him.

MATHIEU: This wimp thinks of nothing but money.

AZIZ: وَا لُو بَاسْ صَيْفِي؟

SAÏFI: قُلْتِلَكْ غَادِي نْبَلَّعْ.
   Shut up. All of you shut up. I don't want to hear it. Pay me, hurry up; pay me.
   عَزِيزْ، مَاتْسَارَاشْ في هَادِ السَّاعَةْ. كَايْنْ بالزَّافْ دِيَالْ رَاسِيسْتْ
   They're going to burn down my shop. They've gone crazy. Pay me.
   عَزِيزْ، عَزِيزْ عِندَكْ تْخُرُجْ مِنْ الدَّارْ. قُلُهُمْ يخَلَّصُونِي وْرُوحْ.

AZIZ: Pay him.

MATHIEU: The world is fucked up. Every pleasure has a price. I'm sick of pleasure.

EDOUARD: Don't worry, Mathieu; it's just the post-fuck blues.

MATHIEU: Why do women throw themselves at you, Edouard? You're scrawny, you're ugly, you're weak. Women are stupid, I'll never understand anything.

EDOUARD: You'll get it, you'll get it.

SAÏFI: This guy who's not from the neighborhood has been hanging around the shop. I saw him the day before yesterday, yesterday, and today.

EDOUARD: Maybe he was here for the whores.

SAÏFI: No, he wasn't here for the whores.

MATHIEU: He's visiting the neighborhood, he's taking a stroll. Are you scared of people taking strolls in your neighborhood?

SAÏFI: People don't take strolls in this neighborhood. I didn't say I was scared.
اصْحَا بَكْ كَايِنْ يِزْعَقُوا عْلَيْ . مَا نِبْغِيشْ نْعَاوِدْ نْشُوفْهُمْ .

MATHIEU: Stop saying all that shit in Arabic.

AZIZ: كَانْ نْعَاهْدَكْ مَا نْعَاوِدْشْ نْجِيبْهُمْ .

SAÏFI: (*To* MATHIEU) Pay me.

MATHIEU: Why are you asking me, Saïfi? We're three here: the little wimp, the Arab, and me. Why am I always supposed to pay?

AZIZ: I'm not the Arab.

SAÏFI: أَ سْكُتْ عَزِيزْ

EDOUARD: Me neither, I'm not paying.

AZIZ: I'm the one who brought you here.

EDOUARD: And I'm the one who got you out of the house, Mathieu. If not for me, you'd still be clinging to your stepmother's skirts.

SAÏFI: Get the fuck out, get the fuck out, and don't pay me.

MATHIEU: If you're not an Arab, then what are you? A Frenchman? A servant? What should I call you?

AZIZ: A wimp, I'm a wimp. Aziz, they only remember his name to ask him for money. I act like a wimp in a house that's not mine, minding a garden, washing dishes that aren't mine. And with the money I make, I pay taxes to France, so they can make war on the Front, and I pay taxes to the Front, so they can make war with France. And who is there to defend Aziz? Nobody. Who makes war on Aziz? Everybody.

SAÏFI: Don't talk like that, Aziz.

AZIZ: The Front says I'm Arab, my boss says I'm a servant, the military says I'm French, and I say I'm a wimp. Cause I could give a fuck about Arabs, Frenchmen, bosses and servants, I don't give a fuck about Algeria, and I don't give a fuck about France, I say fuck this whole business of what side I should be on or where I'm at; I'm not for or against anything. And if they tell me I'm against it, because I'm not for it, well so it goes, I'm against everything. I'm a true wimp.

MATHIEU: He's drunk.

EDOUARD: It's Ramadan that's set him off.

SAÏFI: .. إِنْتَ غَيْرْ تْزَايْرِي عَزِيز

AZIZ: .. رَانِي مَا عْرِفْتْ حَاجَهْ صَيْفِي ، وَاللهِ مَا عْرِفْتْ حَاجَهْ

EDOUARD: Let's split.

They support AZIZ *and head off.*
Exit SAÏFI. *The lights go out.*

16

The garden.
Enter ADRIEN, PLANTIÈRES, BORNY

ADRIEN: Borny, don't make so much noise.

BORNY: Plantières is glued so tight to my ass he's making me stumble.

PLANTIÈRES: I'm scared you might just vanish into the night.

BORNY: Plantières, I'm going to, I'm going to. . ..

PLANTIÈRES: Do it, then.

ADRIEN: Quiet. Where's Sablon? What's happened to him? When did he leave us?

BORNY: See, Plantières: Sablon's the one who skipped off. Ah-hah. You're glued to my ass, and meanwhile, Sablon disappears. He's gone to his country house, and here we are: all alone, feet to the fire, on the hot seat, baking on the frontline. Ah-hah, Plantières. You're a sharp one.

ADRIEN: Shut up, there's the girl.

They hide in the bushes.
Enter FATIMA, *followed by* MATHILDE

MATHILDE: Stop your nonsense, Fatima. Don't think I believed you even for a moment. Nonsense, horse shit, sanctimonious mumbo-jumbo. The idea: that people still come back to haunt these days. It was fine for hysterical little country peasants, long, long ago. But nowadays, it's grotesque. Even the Holy Virgin wouldn't dare. And you think I believed you? Watch out, Fatima; your uncle is waiting for the first sign of madness to get you.

ADRIEN: My little sister's a clever one.

FATIMA: There she is: the cold, the light behind the walnut tree. Marie.

Explosion of the Saïfi Cafe, in the distance.

PLANTIÈRES: That's the Saïfi café.

BORNY: We're in trouble now.

PLANTIÈRES: Shut up, Borny.

MARIE *appears*

ADRIEN: And look at the crazy girl, look at the crazy girl.

FATIMA: Marie, Marie, show yourself to the others too, because they don't believe me.

MARIE: And why should I show myself to them, you little fool?

FATIMA: Because, because. . .

MARIE: Shut up. I know them all too well; Borny, Plantières, those country bumpkins, those red-neck sons of bitches, that band of flunkeys that thinks it's got class. Don't you think I've had my fill of those upstarts?

FATIMA: To mom, at least; at least to her.

MARIE: Out of the question. She's an idiot.

FATIMA: Then to my uncle, so he doesn't hurt me.

MARIE: He'll hurt you, all right. He did it to me, he'll do it to you. Wealth doesn't change a man. Adrien there, who's hiding in the bushes behind you, crawled out of the mire, and he still has slimy feet. Who do you think his grandfather was? A miner, you little fool, a miner deep in the pits, blackened even in his wedding bed. And his father? A miner too, and just because he got rich doesn't mean he wasn't filthy until the end of his life. Shame on me for misallying myself with this family. I won't forgive myself for it. I will never forgive myself. We were the true bosses of this town; nobody had dirty hands at the Rozerieulles. But all those men in the bushes, they stink of belches and new wealth. And you're no better.

PLANTIÈRES: Nothing's happening.

ADRIEN: Look at the girl. Look at how she's shaking.

MARIE: Tell your mother she's an idiot. That idiot took the smallest part of the inheritance, she chose it herself. She picked this ridiculous house over the factory. Given that she's a commoner, she could at least have been rich. Now she's nothing at all. I'm ashamed for her. I, at least, would've kept the dignity of my class, even rich, I would've kept it.

FATIMA: Madame, madame, how did you die?

PLANTIÈRES: The girl is crazy, there's no doubt about that. But where is Sablon, to witness it?

MARIE: My poor girl, do you know how much my dignity suffered with your uncle? The first time he brought me to his parents' house, his mother had made some kind of cake in my honor, some kind of workman's cake, with apples and some kind of coarse flour, and of course margarine or pig's grease. But I was ready for anything, to avoid making a face, to pretend to swallow it. But do you know what she did? To this day, I'm still ashamed. This shame keeps me from finding peace.

FATIMA: How did you die?

MARIE: Her cake, her filthy cake, she brought it out to me, you'll never guess, she brought it out to me, me, on newspaper. I wasn't asking for porcelain, I wasn't expecting crystal, I knew where I was. But newspaper! This I cannot forgive, this I will never forgive.

MATHILDE: (*To* FATIMA) Stop pretending, stop faking a trance. What are you reading these days that's got you so crazy?

Enter SABLON, *supporting* MATHIEU *and* EDOUARD.

SABLON: Serpenoise, Serpenoise, look who I found in the headlights, staggering, bloodied, drunk, coming out of the Saïfi Cafe which had just blown up.

ADRIEN *approaches* MATHIEU *and slaps him.*

MATHIEU: Why should I let you slap me when I'm bleeding all over?

ADRIEN: (*Hitting* MATHIEU *again*) Here's one more to cancel out the first. That's from an ancient Biblical law.

FATIMA: Marie, how did you die? My mother wants to know.

MARIE: I've got to go, I'm in a rush, you think I have nothing better to do?

She vanishes.
Enter MARTHE

MARTHE: A ghost. It seems like there is a ghost here.

MATHILDE: This woman is still dead drunk.

ADRIEN: Sablon, did you see the crazy girl?

MATHILDE: My daughter is having a bit of a nervous breakdown, that's all. This rotten town would break down a mountain.

MARTHE: No, I'm sure it's a ghost. But only an innocent child has the eyes to see it. It's like that at La Salette, Rue du Bac, at the Mountain of Tepeyac, everywhere. Mama Rosa, Mama Rosa, there's a saint in my garden.

EDOUARD *and* FATIMA *exit.*

SABLON: As for your servant, Adrien. . .

ADRIEN: Yeah?

SABLON: Dead. Completely dead.

ADRIEN: Poor Aziz.

SABLON: What was your son doing at the Saïfi Café?

PLANTIÈRES: If we'd only known, my poor Adrien. Your own boy. With our own hands. But what was he doing there?

BORNY: If we'd only known. . .

ADRIEN: But I knew, my friends, I knew.

They exit

17 A LIMITED DOSE OF RELATIVITY

EDOUARD: *(To the audience)* If we give the slightest bit of credit to the very ancient scholars, if they weren't too far off base; if we understand at least in part the theories of the modern scientists, which are much more complicated; in short, if I believe that the scholarly and scientific conclusions are exact, or more or less exact, that they contain at least a little truth, and if I believe in it without entirely grasping the reasoning, I arrive at the following conclusion: if the world is truly round, if its circumference actually is twenty-four thousand nine hundred and two miles, if it really rotates in twenty-three hours and fifty-six minutes as one supposes, then, at this moment, I'm moving west to east at a speed of just over one thousand miles per hour. But it seems like my feet are planted firmly on the ground. These days one supposes, you suppose, and I suppose that the Earth completes one revolution around the Sun in three hundred sixty-five point two-five days; that its orbital circumference is five hundred eighty three million ninety-one thousand miles, and its speed of revolution one million five-hundred ninety six thousand four hundred fifteen miles per hour, which we combine with the preceding. I could therefore be moving, at this very moment, without any effort, at a speed of one million five-hundred ninety-seven thousand four hundred fifty-one miles per hour. I tend to believe it. I have no proof, aside from my firm faith in the ancients. I may not entirely understand them, but I have faith in them, and in the moderns as well. And so, unless I've overlooked a rule, unless some law has escaped me, unless two pages have stuck together and slipped past my nose, if all of this is true, and I were to jump in the air, and the Earth remain on its course through space, if I jump in the air, and remain aloft if only for two seconds, then I should end up, in descent, eight-hundred sixty-eight miles away in space, the Earth hurtling away from me at tremendous speed, she'll have escaped me, and I shall have escaped the earth. There's no reason it won't work, the calculations are accurate, the scholars right. The only thing that concerns me is that, as far as I know, no one has ever done this before. Clearly everyone else is too attached to the Earth, clearly no one wants to end up God knows where in space, clearly this planet's inhabitants cling to their planet with their hands, their toenails, their teeth, never letting go, so it doesn't let them go. They think their union with their planet is unbreakable, like leeches clearly believe it's the skin that holds them tight, whereas if they were to loosen their clutches, each would fly off into space, each go its separate way. I'd like the Earth to speed up. I find it a little sluggish, a little slow, without vigor. But it's not bad for a start; when I end up millions of miles from here, aloft, things will already be better. I've been secretly letting out the ropes. I don't want to set a bad example. It would be catastrophic if the planet were emptied, and even more catastrophic if space were populated. Anyway, I'm trying, I have nothing to lose. Two seconds aloft, and all will be well. I think this'll work. I believe in the scholars, ancient and modern. I have faith in them. I hope I haven't overlooked anything. Time to find out.

He gets up to speed, jumps, and vanishes into space.

18 AL-'ÎD AÇ-ÇAGHÎR

MATHILDE: You're putting on shoes, Adrien?

ADRIEN: You got me into fights with everybody. I've lost my friends, my son is practically dead, there's nothing left for me in this town.

MATHILDE: It's good to get into fights with friends; You should do that every seven years. You can't spend your life with prep school pals. And where are you going?

ADRIEN: To Algeria.

MATHILDE: To Algeria? You're crazy.

ADRIEN: That's where you went, so why can't I? Where should I go? I know about nowhere, aside from here. I've never left. I even did my military service down the street because of my foot problems, and I came home every night.

MATHILDE: There is Andorra, Monaco, Geneva, all of those rich folks paradises, the only places in the world where life's worth living. The rich stay among the rich, wars never get that far, there are no children, or else they're kept out of sight by nurses, everyone is sterile, old, and satisfied, nobody bothers anybody. Why does everyone want to be young? It's stupid.

ADRIEN: That sort of life must be very expensive. The factory's not doing so well, I don't think I'll get a very good price for it. Because of you, I've neglected it; you owe me damages, Mathilde. Compensate me for it, and for the money I poured into this house, and then I'll go to Tahiti.

MATHILDE: You're dreaming, Adrien. Not a penny. It's looks like you're Algeria bound. It's very mild down there.

ADRIEN: Why'd you leave then, if it was so mild? Just to bug me?

MATHILDE: I was bored down there. Mildness bores me. The mildness there is not of this world.

ADRIEN: Wasn't there a war going on, or something like that?

MATHILDE: What are you talking to me about war for? I'm telling you something important.

Enter MAAME QUEULEU

MAAME QUEULEU: Madame, Madame, your daughter Fatima has just fainted. She's collapsed to the ground like a tree uprooted by a typhoon, she's moaning and writhing, she won't let us touch her.

ADRIEN: Loosen her shirt collar; pull off those ridiculous layers of clothing. Anyone would faint, wrapped up like that in the middle of summer.

MAAME QUEULEU: She refuses, Monsieur, she says she's cold; she's shivering and chattering her teeth and she refuses.

MATHILDE: Force her.

Exit MAAME QUEULEU

ADRIEN: So Mathilde, you were bored in Algeria?

MATHILDE: Yes, I was bored.

ADRIEN: Missed me?

MATHILDE: I was bored, Adrien.

ADRIEN: Me too. I was bored too.

MATHILDE: But you stayed here. Why would you be bored?

ADRIEN: I was bored here.

MATHILDE: You had your son.

ADRIEN: So what? I was bored here, with my son.

Enter MAAME QUEULEU

MAAME QUEULEU: Madame, Madame, what misfortune!

MATHILDE: What now?

MAAME QUEULEU: Your daughter was pregnant, Madame, and she's giving birth. What should I do? What should I do?

MATHILDE: What do you think? Deliver it, pull it out, cut the cord. You know how to do all that, don't you?

MAAME QUEULEU *exits*.

ADRIEN: How about that? Acts all childish, but she gets around.

MATHILDE: No need to get around, Adrien.

ADRIEN: You'd know something about that, Mathilde.

MATHILDE: Fuck off. I know it's shaky, but I still have a leg to stand on. Adrien, you can't leave. You have your woman, your wife, your concubine. Poor Marthe can't manage all alone. And besides, I'm pretty sure she loves you, old friend. It's not that easy to get rid of a woman who loves you.

ADRIEN: Maame Queuleu will take care of her. And besides I don't give a fuck. I'm not going to spend my life coddling a drunkard.

MATHILDE: Poor Marthe. Men are scum.

ADRIEN: Meanwhile, your daughter—what's her name again? Caroline?—she's going to inherit your house. Your daughter's a shark.

MATHILDE: Women deal better with misfortune, that's all.

ADRIEN: With the misfortune of others, yes; they blossom with the misfortune of others. For that matter, there you are, Mathilde, my sister, looking so pretty.

MATHILDE: Anyway, she won't get anything. I'm selling this damnable hovel and leaving.

ADRIEN: Where are you going, Mathilde, my sister?

MATHILDE: Why should you care, Adrien, my brother? Why should you care? Hey Adrien?

ADRIEN: Yes?

MATHILDE: Am I really as pretty as you say? Still pretty, at least, still a little bit pretty?

ADRIEN: Yes, you are Mathilde, absolutely.

Enter MAAME QUEULEU

MATHILDE: What now, Maame Queuleu? The look on your face could wither leaves on trees.

MAAME QUEULEU: Oh, Madame, Monsieur.

ADRIEN: What is it? It didn't come out? You didn't manage? Should I call a doctor?

MAAME QUEULEU: No need, Monsieur. To the contrary, everything went well.

ADRIEN: So?

MATHILDE: It's dead.

MAAME QUEULEU: Oh no, Madame, far from it.

MATHILDE: What do you mean, far from it? It's alive, then?

MAAME QUEULEU: They are alive, Madame, they are alive; there are two of them. And, just before she passed out, she baptized them with two strange names.

ADRIEN: What names? What names?

MAAME QUEULEU: Remus, I think; and Romulus, the second.

MATHILDE: Adrien, you're a pain in my ass, all it takes is for me to decide to take off, to leave this town, to sell out and clear out, for you to do the exact same thing. I may be the eldest, but I've had enough of your imitating my every move.

ADRIEN: I'm sorry, Mathilde, but I've already got my shoes on, while your bags aren't even packed, and I told you I was leaving before you even brought it up. Me imitate you? I'm not crazy. I've always been a good boy. I've never approved of the way you live your life. I've always been on the side of good manners. I've always been on dad's side.

MATHILDE: On dad's side, against me. You aped him like a little dog. You cheered him on, snickering, and watched me eat on my knees.

ADRIEN: I wasn't snickering, Mathilde, I swear to you. It was a grimace of pain.

MATHILDE: And now that our father is dead, you want to imitate me. Out of the question. I'm not your dad.

ADRIEN: I want to sell out and leave. I will sell out and leave.

MATHILDE: So do I. There's no reason I can't do it too.

ADRIEN: You'll pull a good sum from this house, my dear sister.

MATHILDE: And you from your factory, my dear Adrien.

ADRIEN: Not all that much.

MATHILDE: Me neither, not all that much.

ADRIEN: You've already started cooking the books.

MATHILDE: I'm not cooking any books. I'm straight. I always have been.

ADRIEN: Maame Queuleu, were you listening through the door?

MATHILDE: What's with you, rooted there like a tree stump?

ADRIEN: Speak, or get out.

MATHILDE: Speak, Maame Queuleu. What is it now?

MAAME QUEULEU: It's that. . ..

MATHILDE: They're deformed? They're blind? They're disfigured? They're stuck together?

MAAME QUEULEU: Oh no, Madame, to the contrary.

MATHILDE: Well-formed, then?

MAAME QUEULEU: Magnificient, alas, Madame. Big, strong bawlers, with bright eyes. Splendid, alas.

MATHILDE: So what are you complaining about?

MAAME QUEULEU: I'm not complaining, Madame, I'm not complaining for me. It's you I pity.

MATHILDE: What about me? Be so kind as to tell me what else could happen to me?

ADRIEN: Speak up already, Maame Queuleu, or I'll hit you.

MAAME QUEULEU: It's that, Monsieur, they are. . ..

MATHILDE: Yes?

ADRIEN: Well?

MAAME QUEULEU: They are, they are. . .

ADRIEN: Spit it out, for God's sake.

MAAME QUEULEU: Black, Monsieur; they're all black, with frizzy hair.

She exits crying.

MATHILDE: Hurry up, Adrien, in God's name, hurry up. Do you need hours to tie your shoes?

ADRIEN: And your bags, Mathilde?

MATHILDE: They're ready, my poor old friend. I never unpacked them.

ADRIEN: I'm coming, I'm coming, but why are we in such a rush, my little sister?

MATHILDE: Because I don't want to watch my daughter's children grow up. Those two will fuck this town to hell, and they'll do it fast.

ADRIEN: I thought you came back to fuck it up yourself.

MATHILDE: Too late for me, old friend. I'll settle for being a pain in your ass.

ADRIEN: Don't start, Mathilde, don't start.

MATHILDE: You call that starting, my Adrien?

They exit.

END OF PLAY

TRANSLATION FROM THE ARABIC

I, 1

AZIZ: It looks like we're in for an ugly day.

MATHILDE: And why should this be an ugly day?

AZIZ: Because if the sister is as stupid as the brother, that's what we'll get.

MATHILDE: The sister is not as stupid as the brother.

AZIZ: How would you know?

MATHILDE: I'm the sister.

V-15

SAÏFI: Aziz, hurry up, and take your pals with you. Tell them to pay me so I can close up shop.

AZIZ: It's not time, Saïfi; why are you in such a rush?

What's wrong, Saïfi?

SAÏFI: I've got to close up. I'm telling you

> Aziz, don't linger in the street right now. There are bands of fascists out.
>
> Aziz, Aziz, don't leave your house anymore. Tell them to pay me and leave.
>
> Your friends piss me off, Aziz, I don't want to see them here again.

AZIZ: I won't bring them here any more, I promise you.

SAÏFI: Shut up, Aziz.

SAÏFI: You're Algerian, Aziz, that's all there is to it.

AZIZ: I don't know, Saïfi, I just don't know.

The five daily prayers in the Islamic religion are, according to the hour of the day, sobh (dawn), zohr (Towards midday), 'acr (the afternoon), magrib (the evening) and 'icha (at night)

AL-'ÎD AÇ-ÇAGHÎR is the name of the feast that marks the end of Ramadan.

The office of social action (OAS) was the title used for the collectors of funds, in France, for the benefit of the OAS.

A HUNDRED-YEAR HISTORY
OF THE SERPENOISE FAMILY
(APPENDIX TO *BACK TO THE DESERT*)

Translated by Amin Erfani

César Serpenoise was born in 1867, the eighth child in a family of miners, in a working-class neighborhood where everything—its houses, its businesses, its churches, its streets, its doors, its beds, its tableware— belonged to Rozérieulles Steelworks. A few months before César's birth, the day his eldest son started his military service, his father killed himself with a bullet in the head. His body was found lying over an anonymous grave in the neighborhood cemetery.

At fourteen, César joins his brothers at the deep end of the mine. After some time and because of his fragile health, he is transferred to work in the open air. A foreman first notices his hard work and his sharp mind: he speaks to the neighborhood priest who, in the evenings, teaches him counting and Latin.

Named accountant at eighteen, he takes the ingenious initiative of reorganizing the folder classification system and, six years later, becomes head accountant at Rozérieulles Steelworks.

The old Rozérieulles liked his workmen, and his workmen liked him; he knew hundreds and hundreds of his workmen's names, he shook their hands and knew how many children they had. The workmen cheered at the Rozérieulles family's weddings and baptisms and cried at their burials. That is why, despite technical problems with extractions, the family board of directors never laid off workers. Most importantly, by the end of the century, an extreme and inexplicable weariness had suddenly taken over the entire family, from the patriarch to the youngest. Nobody thought about innovating: they conducted business the way an old man makes dinner. After a few years, Rozérieulles Steelworks, while thriving beforehand, found itself in a deplorable situation. In 1900, the old Rozérieulles gives César Serpenoise the title of general manager, and dies. The rest of the family, seeing their ambition die with their father, give away their power and leave decisions to César. César buys a large house in the town's upper-class neighborhood.

In 1908, the Rozérieulles family sells all their stocks and step back: César buys a majority of them. He lays off, he reorganizes, he invests. From then on, Rozérieulles Steelworks is called Serpenoise Steelworks.

In the same year, César quietly marries some obscure laundry lady whom he keeps locked up in his house: three months later she gives birth to Mathilde. The same hour, in another upper-class home inside the same neighborhood, Marie Rozérieulles is born.

In 1910, the sequestered laundry lady gives birth to Adrien and dies soon after, without any doctor being summoned at her bed, except to pronounce her dead.

1911: César Serpenoise is elected town mayor. He is forty-four.

1916: Birth of Marthe Rozérieulles.

César proving himself as good a manager of the town as of his factory, in 1930, the town council decides to name the town's main street after him.

Mathilde turned into a somber teenager, withdrawn and almost mute. His brother, who was noisy and violent, entertained himself for many years by provoking her, then grew weary of her lack of response, and they lived together without seeing each other, except during mealtime when they stared at each other in silence.

In the fall of the year 1930, one evening, Mathilde took a walk in the garden where she used to meet Marie Rozérieulles and secretly chat. That evening, Marie did not show up. When the night was complete, Mathilde was taken over by an inexplicable torpor that made her dizzy. Eyes half-closed, she approached the tree, laid down, and immediately fell into a deep sleep. His brother found her, in the morning, sleeping; he alerted the servant who put her to bed and attended to her high fever over a few days.

After months passed, her belly grew until César realized the scale of the scandal that loomed over the house. He locked up his daughter inside her room under Maame Queuleu's supervision. Two months early, Édouard came out of his mother's belly, and Maame Queuleu took care of everything.

Mathilde was severely punished: for a year, her father forced her to eat on her knees at the family table. Her brother kept staring at him during the meal, but Mathilde did not lay eyes on him anymore.

Worried she no longer saw her friend, Marie tried to enter the Serpenoise house, to no effect as she was obstinately met with opposition. So she found other means to get close to her friend: laboriously, tirelessly, without precaution, she courted Adrien who, stunned by such vigor, finally married her a few months later. Marie was then granted access to her friend's bedroom and her secrets. The following year, Marie gave birth to Mathieu.

In 1933, Mathilde managed to escape her room through the window in order to take a walk in the garden. She fell asleep again and, soon after, realizing she was pregnant one more time, she plotted to escape the town with Marie's help. She stole money from her father's safe and took a boat to Algeria where Fatima was born the following year.

The year of the Liberation, César, in agony, summoned both his children in order to divide his inheritance: Mathilde returned with Édouard and Fatima. César divided his fortune into two parts, the house on the one hand and the factory on the other. Against all expectations, he left the choice to Mathilde. Also against all expectations, Mathilde chose the house, and as soon as César died she demanded the eviction of her brother and nephew.

Already cursed with a bad reputation, Mathilde was accused of having slept with the Germans. Her head was shaved and she was forced to escape again to Algeria, with her children, abandoning the house to Adrien in exchange for a small rent. The same year, Marie Serpenoise mysteriously died in her bed.

In November 1960, Adrien Serpenoise received a telegram from his sister announcing her return a week from then.

The action of the play takes place here: BACK TO THE DESERT.

In 1961, following Mathilde and Adrien's departure, Mathieu was summoned to Algeria as part of the last batch called for duty. After a ferocious bender in a brothel, he wanted to get behind the wheel of the Jeep that brought him and his fellow soldiers to the garrison and, since he did not know how to drive, he crashed into a ravine and died with his buddies in the car set on fire.

Fatima traveled France on foot, traveled the Mediterranean Sea on a small boat, traveled Algeria with her bare feet, went deep into the desert where she led an ascetic life. She got so thin she resembled a cactus and dried out. Her skin, her flesh, and her bones dried out beyond any measure, were reduced to powder and turned into sand that the wind carried all the way to the borders of Mali.

As for Édouard, of course, no one ever saw him again.

Mathilde and Adrien sold everything, the house and the factory, with the help of an accountant. They traveled through large European cities but disliked them all. They went to Rio de Janeiro, the Bahamas, Las Vegas. They finally settled in a small town in Arizona, which was founded, built, organized, and managed by elderly people. They encountered difficulties getting admission, but lied about their age. After some time, Adrien had already taken over the town management and both of them spent long evenings by the pool, mocking the incurable old age of their peers.

One overly humid evening in 1967, while laughing too loudly, Adrien suffocated and died on his deckchair. Mathilde stared at him for a long time until her eyes started to close out of sleepiness. She then got up, slowly went deep into the sweltering night, and laid down under a palm tree.

Between her half-closed eyelids, in the silence of the red sky, she saw a cloud of paratroopers, very high up, slowly descending. The large white parachutes were getting closer, but before they came low enough for her to perceive the men hanging from them, her eyes closed and she stopped breathing.

Bernard-Marie Koltès
In *Le Républicain Lorrain*, October 27, 1988
(The author entrusted this text to Mr. Genson)

ROBERTO ZUCCO

Translated by Anna G. R. Miller

After the second prayer, you will see the solar disk spread out and you will see hanging from it the phallus, the origin of the wind; and if you turn your face toward the East, it will move there, and if you turn your face toward the West, it will follow you.

                Liturgy of Mithra, part of the Great Magical Papyrus of Paris.
                Quoted by Carl Jung in his last interview with the B.B.C.

CHARACTERS

ROBERTO ZUCCO
HIS MOTHER

THE YOUNG GIRL
HER SISTER
HER BROTHER
HER FATHER
HER MOTHER

THE OLD MAN
THE ELEGANT LADY

THE HULK
THE IMPATIENT PIMP
THE PANIC-STRICKEN WHORE
THE MELANCHOLY DETECTIVE
A DETECTIVE
A POLICE CHIEF
FIRST GUARD
SECOND GUARD
FIRST POLICEMAN
SECOND POLICEMAN

MEN. WOMEN. WHORES. PIMPS. VOICES OF PRISONERS AND GUARDS.

I. THE ESCAPE.

The ring road of a prison, at the base of the rooftops.
The rooftops of the prison, up to their peak.
At the time when guards, due to the silence and fatigue of staring into the night, are sometimes prone to hallucinations.

FIRST GUARD: Did you hear something?

SECOND GUARD: No, nothing at all.

FIRST GUARD: You never hear anything.

SECOND GUARD: Did you hear something?

FIRST GUARD: No, but I feel like I'm hearing something.

SECOND GUARD: Did you or didn't you hear?

FIRST GUARD: I didn't hear with my ears, but I had the idea of hearing something.

SECOND GUARD: The idea? Without your ears?

FIRST GUARD: You never have any ideas, that's why you never hear anything and never see anything.

SECOND GUARD: I don't hear anything because there's nothing to hear and I don't see anything because there's nothing to see. Our presence here is useless, that's why we always end up arguing with each other. It's completely useless; the guns, the silent sirens, our eyes open when at this hour everyone has their eyes shut. I think it's useless to have our eyes open not focused on anything, and our ears ready not to miss anything, when at this hour our ears should be listening to the sound of our inner world and our eyes contemplating our inner landscapes. Do you believe in the inner world?

FIRST GUARD: I believe it isn't useless, we're here to stop escapes.

SECOND GUARD: But there are never escapes here. It's impossible. The prison's too modern. Even a really small prisoner couldn't escape. Even a prisoner as small as a rat. If he got through the big gates, then, after that, there are gates made of the thinnest bars, like a colander, and even thinner, like a sieve. You'd have to be liquid to be able to get through. And a hand that's stabbed, an arm that's strangled can't be made of liquid. They must, conversely, be heavy and massive. How do you imagine someone can think of stabbing or strangling, just think about it at first, and then actually do it?

FIRST GUARD: Pure vice.

SECOND GUARD: Well, I've been a guard for six whole years, and I've always looked at the murderers, looking for what makes them different from me, a prison guard, incapable of stabbing or strangling, incapable of even thinking of it. I've thought, I've searched, I've even looked at them in the shower, because I've been told the murderous instinct lives in the genitals. I've seen more than six hundred, and they have nothing in common; there are big ones, there are little ones, there are thin ones, there are some really small ones, there are round ones, there are pointy ones, there are huge ones, there's nothing to the idea.

FIRST GUARD: Pure vice, I tell you. Don't you see something?

ZUCCO *appears, walking on the ridge of the rooftop.*

SECOND GUARD: No, nothing at all.

FIRST GUARD: Me neither, but I think I see something.

SECOND GUARD: I see a guy walking on the roof. It must be sleep deprivation.

FIRST GUARD: What would a man do on the roof? You're right. We should turn our eyes toward our inner world from time to time.

SECOND GUARD: I'd even say it could be Roberto Zucco, the one who was locked up this afternoon for murdering his father. An enraged beast, a savage animal.

FIRST GUARD: Roberto Zucco. Never heard of him.

SECOND GUARD: But do you see something, there, or am I the only one who sees it?

ZUCCO *has continued to advance, calmly, on the rooftop.*

FIRST GUARD: I think I see something. But what is it?

ZUCCO *starts to disappear behind a chimney.*

SECOND GUARD: It's a prisoner escaping.

ZUCCO *has disappeared.*

FIRST GUARD: Fuck, you're right: it's an escape.

Gunshots, searchlights, sirens.

II. MURDER OF THE MOTHER.

ZUCCO'S MOTHER, *wearing nightclothes in front of the closed door.*

THE MOTHER: Roberto, I have my hand on the phone, I'm picking it up and calling the police.

ZUCCO: Open the door.

THE MOTHER: Never.

ZUCCO: If I hit the door, it falls, you know that, don't play dumb.

THE MOTHER: O.K., do it, maniac, lunatic, do it and you'll wake up the neighbors. You were safer in prison, because if they see you they'll lynch you: people here will never accept someone who killed his father. Even the neighborhood dogs will look at you sideways.

ZUCCO *bangs on the door.*

THE MOTHER: How did you escape? What kind of prison is that?

ZUCCO: No one will keep me in prison for more than a few hours. Never. So open up; you'd make a slug impatient. Open, or I'll demolish this dump.

THE MOTHER: What did you come here to do? Where does this need to come back come from? I never want to see you again. You're not my son anymore. You're no more to me than a fly on shit.

ZUCCO *breaks down the door.*

THE MOTHER: Roberto, stay away from me.

ZUCCO: I've come to get my fatigues.

THE MOTHER: Your what?

ZUCCO: My fatigues: my khaki shirt and my combat pants.

THE MOTHER: That shitty military clothing. What do you need that shitty military clothing for? You're crazy, Roberto. We should have known that when you were in the cradle and thrown you in the trash.

ZUCCO: Move, hurry up, bring them to me now.

THE MOTHER: I'll give you money. It's money you want. You'll buy all the clothes you want.

ZUCCO: I don't want money. It's my fatigues I want.

THE MOTHER: I don't want to, I don't want to. I'm going to call the neighbors.

ZUCCO: I want my fatigues.

THE MOTHER: Don't shout, Roberto, don't shout, you scare me; don't shout, you'll wake up the neighbors. I can't give them to you, it's impossible; they're dirty, they're disgusting, you can't wear them like that. Give me time to wash them, dry them, iron them.

ZUCCO: I'll wash them myself. I'll go to the laundromat.

THE MOTHER: You're going off the rails, my poor boy. You're completely crazy.

ZUCCO: It's my favorite place in the world. It's calm, it's tranquil, and there are women.

THE MOTHER: I don't give a shit. I don't want to give them to you. Don't get close to me, Roberto. I'm still mourning your father, are you going to kill me too?

ZUCCO: Don't be scared of me, Mama. I've always been gentle and nice with you. Why would you be scared of me? Why won't you give me my fatigues? I need them, Mama, I need them.

THE MOTHER: Don't be nice to me, Roberto. How can you expect me to forget that you killed your father, that you threw him out the window like a cigarette butt? And now, you're being nice to me. I don't want to forget that you killed your father, and your sweetness would make me forget everything, Roberto.

ZUCCO: Forget, Mama. Give me my fatigues, my khaki shirt and my combat pants; even dirty, even crumpled, give them to me. And then I'll leave, I promise.

THE MOTHER: Is it me, Roberto, is it me who gave birth to you? Is it from me that you came out? If I hadn't given birth to you here, if I hadn't seen you leaving my body, and followed your eyes until you were placed in your cradle, my eyes locked on you, not dropping you, and monitoring each change of your body so closely that I didn't see changes happen and I see you there, the same person as the one who came out of me in this bed, I'd believe it wasn't my son I had before me. But I recognize you, Roberto. I recognize the form of your body, your size, the color of your hair, the color of your eyes, the shape of your hands, these big strong hands that never did anything but caress your mother's neck, and squeeze your father's, whom you killed. Why has this child, so smart for twenty-four years, become crazy so quickly? How did you go off the rails, Roberto? Who put a tree trunk across the straight path to make you fall into the abyss? Roberto, Roberto, a car that's crashed at the bottom of a ravine, we don't repair it. A train that's gone off the rails, we don't try to put it back on its rails. We abandon it, we forget it. I'm forgetting you, Roberto, I've forgotten you.

ZUCCO: Before you forget me, tell me where my fatigues are.

THE MOTHER: They're there, in the basket. They're dirty and all crumpled. (ZUCCO *takes out the fatigues*.) And now get out of here, you promised me.

ZUCCO: Yes, I promised.

He approaches her, caresses her, embraces her, grabs her; she groans. He drops her and she falls, strangled.

ZUCCO *undresses, puts on his fatigues, and leaves.*

III. UNDER THE TABLE.

In the kitchen.
A table, covered with a floor-length tablecloth.
Enter the SISTER *of the* YOUNG GIRL.
She goes toward the window, and opens it slightly.

THE SISTER: Come in, be quiet, take off your shoes; sit down there and shut up. (*The* YOUNG GIRL *begins to step through the window.*) So, at an hour of the night like this, I find you crouched down at the foot of a wall. Your brother's looking all over town for you in the car and I can tell you that, when he finds you, you're going to get your ass kicked, because he's gotten himself all worked up. Your mother was looking out the window for hours, coming up with all sorts of ideas for what happened to you, from a gang rape by a bunch of thugs to finding your chopped up corpse in a forest, not to mention the sadist who would've kept you cornered in the cave, she thought of everything. And your father's already so sure he's never going to see you again that he's gotten shit-faced drunk and is snoring on the couch in despair. I run around the neighborhood like a crazy woman and I find you there, just sitting against a wall. Even though all you would've had to do to reassure us was to cross the courtyard. All you will have gained is getting your ass kicked by your brother and I hope he kicks you until you bleed. (*Pause.*) But I see you've decided not to talk to me. You've decided to give me the silent treatment. Silence. Silence. Things are going on around me but I keep my mouth shut. Lips sealed. We'll see if your lips stay sealed when your brother kicks your ass. When will you open your mouth to tell me why, especially when you had a midnight curfew, why did you come home so late? Because, if you don't open your mouth, I'm going to start to panic, I'm going to come up with all sorts of scenarios too. My little sparrow, talk to your sister, I can listen to anything, and I'll protect you, I promise, against your brother's anger. (*Pause.*) You must have had a typical young girl experience, you met a guy and he was stupid like all guys, he did something he shouldn't have, did he push you? I know about that, my finch, I was once a young girl too, I went to parties where the guys were idiots. What does that matter, what could that do? You're going to get kissed a thousand times by idiots, whether or not you like it; and you're going to get your ass grabbed, my dear, whether or not you want it. Because guys are idiots and the only thing they know how to do is grab young girls' asses. They love that. I have no idea what kind of pleasure they get from it; in fact, I really think they get no pleasure from it. It's in their tradition. There's nothing they can do about it. They have idiocy in their genes. But there's no reason to make a big deal of it. The important thing is that you didn't let anyone steal what must not be stolen from you before its time. But I know you'll wait for your time, that we'll choose, all together—your mother, your father, your brother, even me, and you too of course—the person to whom you'll give it. Or maybe someone's been violent with you, and that, who would dare to do, to a young girl like you, so pure, so virginal? Tell me no one hurt you. Tell me, tell me no one stole it from you, that which must not be stolen. Answer. Answer or I'm going to get mad. (*Noise.*) Hurry, hide under the table. I think it's your brother coming home.

The YOUNG GIRL *disappears under the table.*

Enter the FATHER, *in his pajamas, half asleep. He goes across the kitchen, disappears for a few seconds, walks back across the kitchen and goes back to his room.*

You're a young girl, you're a little virgin, you're the little virgin of your sister, your brother, your father, and your mother. Don't tell me that horrible thing. Shut up. I'm going crazy. You're lost and all of us, lost with you.

Enter the BROTHER, *with a crash. The* SISTER *bolts toward him.*

THE SISTER: Don't shout, don't get worked up. She's not here but she's been found. She's been found but she's not here. Calm down, or I'm going to go crazy. I don't want all the bad things in the world to happen at the same time and, if you shout, I'm going to kill myself.

THE BROTHER: Where is she? Where is she?

THE SISTER: She's at a friend's house. She's asleep at a friend's house, in her friend's bed, warm, safe, nothing can harm her, nothing. A terrible misfortune is happening to us. Don't shout, please, because, after, you could regret it and cry.

THE BROTHER: Nothing could make me cry, except a terrible misfortune that could have happened to my little sister. But I kept such a close eye on her, and it's only tonight that she got away from me. It's only a few hours that she got away from me after years and years of me keeping a close eye on her. Misfortune takes longer than that to strike someone.

THE SISTER: Misfortune doesn't ask for time. It comes when it wants, it transforms everything in an instant. In an instant it destroys a precious object you've guarded for years. (*She picks up an object and lets it drop to the ground.*) And we can't pick up the pieces. Even shouting, we couldn't put the pieces back together.

Enter the FATHER. *He crosses the kitchen like the first time and disappears.*

THE BROTHER: Help me, my sister, help me. You're stronger than me. I can't handle misfortunes.

THE SISTER: No one can handle misfortune.

THE BROTHER: Share it with me.

THE SISTER: I'm already overwhelmed.

THE BROTHER: I'm going to have a drink. (*He leaves.*)

The FATHER *comes back.*

THE FATHER: Are you crying, my daughter? I thought I heard someone crying. (*The* SISTER *stands.*)

THE SISTER: No, I'm humming. (*She leaves.*)

THE FATHER: You're quite right. That keeps misfortune at bay. (*He leaves.*)

A moment later, the YOUNG GIRL *exits from under the table, goes toward the window, opens it partially, and lets* ZUCCO *in.*

THE YOUNG GIRL: Take off your shoes. What's your name?

ZUCCO: Call me whatever you want. And you?

THE YOUNG GIRL: I don't have a name anymore. People always call me names of little animals, chicky, finch, sparrow, lark, starling, dove, nightingale. I'd prefer it if people called me rat, rattlesnake, or piglet. What kind of work do you do?

ZUCCO: In life?

THE YOUNG GIRL: Yes, in life: your job, your occupation, how you earn money and all those things people do?

ZUCCO: I don't do what most people do.

THE YOUNG GIRL: So, tell me what you do.

ZUCCO: I'm a secret agent. You know what that is, a secret agent?

THE YOUNG GIRL: I know what a secret is.

ZUCCO: An agent, besides being secret, travels, he goes all over the world, he has weapons.

THE YOUNG GIRL: Do you have a weapon?

ZUCCO: Of course.

THE YOUNG GIRL: Show me.

ZUCCO: No.

THE YOUNG GIRL: So, you don't have a weapon.

ZUCCO: Look. (*He takes out a knife.*)

THE YOUNG GIRL: That's not a weapon.

ZUCCO: You can kill with this just as well as with any other weapon.

THE YOUNG GIRL: Besides killing, what else does a secret agent do?

ZUCCO: He travels, he goes to Africa. Do you know Africa?

THE YOUNG GIRL: Very well.

ZUCCO: I know places, in Africa, mountains so high that it snows all the time. No one knows that it snows in Africa. That's what I like most in the world: snow in Africa that falls on frozen lakes.

THE YOUNG GIRL: I'd like to go see the snow in Africa. I'd like to go ice-skating on the frozen lakes.

ZUCCO: There are also white rhinoceros that cross the lake, under the snow.

THE YOUNG GIRL: What's your name? Tell me your name.

ZUCCO: Never will I say my name.

THE YOUNG GIRL: Why? I want to know your name.

ZUCCO: It's a secret.

THE YOUNG GIRL: I know how to keep secrets. Tell me your name.

ZUCCO: I've forgotten it.

THE YOUNG GIRL: Liar.

ZUCCO: Andreas.

THE YOUNG GIRL: No.

ZUCCO: Angelo.

THE YOUNG GIRL: Don't make fun of me or I'll scream. It's none of those names.

ZUCCO: And how do you know, since you don't know it?

THE YOUNG GIRL: Impossible. I'd recognize it immediately.

ZUCCO: I can't tell it.

THE YOUNG GIRL: Even if you can't tell it, tell it to me anyway.

ZUCCO: Impossible. Something bad could happen to me.

THE YOUNG GIRL: That doesn't matter. Tell me anyway.

ZUCCO: If I told you, I'd die.

THE YOUNG GIRL: Even if you have to die, tell me anyway.

ZUCCO: Roberto.

THE YOUNG GIRL: Roberto what?

ZUCCO: That's all you get.

THE YOUNG GIRL: Roberto what? If you don't tell me, I'll scream, and my brother, who's really angry, will kill you.

ZUCCO: You told me you knew what a secret was. Do you really know?

THE YOUNG GIRL: It's the only thing I know perfectly. Tell me your name, tell me your name.

ZUCCO: Zucco.

THE YOUNG GIRL: Roberto Zucco. I'll never forget that name. Hide under the table; people are coming.

The MOTHER *enters.*

THE MOTHER: Are you talking to yourself, my nightingale?

THE YOUNG GIRL: No. I'm humming to keep misfortune at bay.

THE MOTHER: Good idea. (*Seeing the broken object.*) Good. I've wanted that trash gone for a long time.

She leaves.

The YOUNG GIRL *joins* ZUCCO *under the table.*

VOICE OF THE YOUNG GIRL: You, my dear, you've taken my virginity, you're going to keep it. Now, there will never be anyone else who can take it from me. You'll have it until the end of your days, you'll have it even when you'll have forgotten me or you're dead. You're marked by me like by a scar after a fight. No chance I'll forget it, since I don't have another to give anyone; over, it's done, for the rest of my life. It's been given away and it's you who has it.

IV. THE MELANCHOLY OF THE DETECTIVE.

The foyer of a brothel in Little Chicago.

THE DETECTIVE: I'm sad, Madam. My heart feels very heavy and I don't know why. I'm often sad, but, this time, there's something wrong. Normally, when I feel this way, like I want to cry or die, I look for the reason behind the feeling. I go through everything that's happened during the day, the night, and the day before. And I always end up finding an unimportant event that, at the time, didn't make an impression on me, but that, like a little shit of a germ, lodged itself in my heart and makes it twist in all directions. So, once I've identified which unimportant event it is that's making me suffer so much, I laugh about it, the germ is squished like a louse by a fingernail, and everything's ok. But today I looked; I went back three days, once in one direction and another in the other, and now here I am back in the same place, without knowing where the bad feeling is coming from, still just as sad and my heart just as heavy.

THE MADAM: You deal with too many dead bodies and pimps' stories, detective.

THE DETECTIVE: There aren't that many dead bodies. But pimps, yes, there are far too many. It would be better to have more dead bodies and fewer pimps.

THE MADAM: Me, I prefer the pimps; they guarantee my livelihood and they're pretty lively themselves.

THE DETECTIVE: I have to go, Madam. Goodbye.

ZUCCO *exits from one of the rooms, locks his door.*

THE MADAM: You should never say goodbye, detective.

The DETECTIVE *leaves, followed by* ZUCCO.

After a few moments, a WHORE, *in a panic, enters.*

THE WHORE: Madam, Madam, diabolical forces are coming through Little Chicago. The whole neighborhood's upset, the whores aren't working anymore, the pimps mouths are hanging open, the johns fled, everything's stopped, everything's petrified. Madam, you had the devil in your house. That boy who arrived recently, who never opens his mouth, who never answers the ladies' questions, makes you wonder if he has a voice and a sex; that boy who, on the other hand, looks so gentle; that pretty boy, really, and we've talked about it a lot, between us ladies, —there he is, the guy who's leaving behind the detective. We've been watching him closely, all of us, the ladies, we laugh, we make up stories. He's walking behind the detective who looks buried deep in thought; he's walking behind him like his shadow; and the shadow's disappearing like it's noon, he's getting closer and closer to the the detective's hunched back, and quickly, he's taking a long knife out from his jacket pocket, and he's stabbing it in the the poor man's back. The detective's stopping. He's not turning around. He's slowly swaying his head from side to side, as if he were finding the solution to the deep thought in which he was buried. Now his whole body's swaying, and he's collapsing on the ground. Neither the killer nor his victim ever looked at each other. The boy was staring at the detective's revolver; he's bending over, taking it, putting it in his pocket, and leaving, peacefully, with the peacefulness of the devil, Madam. Because no one moved, everyone, frozen, watched him leave. He disappeared into the crowd. It was the devil you had under your roof, Madam.

THE MADAM: In any case, with the detective's murder, this boy, he's done for.

V. THE BIG BROTHER.

The kitchen.

The YOUNG GIRL *is against the wall, terrified.*

THE BROTHER: Don't be scared of me, chicky. I won't hurt you. Your sister's an idiot. Why does she think I would've beaten you? You're a woman now; I've never beaten a woman. I like women a lot; they're what I like best. It's much better than a younger sister. It's a pain in the ass, a younger sister. You always have to look after her, keep an eye on her. To protect what? Her virginity? How long do you have to look after a sister's virginity? All the time I spent looking after you is wasted time. I regret all that time. I regret each day, each hour lost keeping an eye on you. It would be better to deflower girls as soon as they get their period, that way big brothers could have some peace, they wouldn't have anything left to look after, and they could do other things with their time. Personally, I'm very happy you got yourself laid; because now, I can have some peace. You'll go along your own path, I'll go along mine, I won't drag you behind me anymore like a ball and chain. Come have a drink with me instead. You're going to have to learn, now, not to lower your eyes, not to blush, to dare to look at boys. All of that, it's over. Be sassy. Raise your head, look at guys, stare at them. They love that. Being modest for even one second longer is worthless now. Have fun, my dear, and do it right now. Turn yourself loose, go hang out in Little Chicago with the whores, become a whore: you'll make some cash and you won't be anyone's responsibility anymore. And maybe I'll recognize you in the bars where they go to pick up johns, I'll wave hello, we'll be the big brother and little sister of the bar; it's less of a pain in the ass and we'll have a lot more fun. Don't waste any more of your time looking down and keeping your legs closed, chicky, that's useless now. Anyway, now, marriage, that's out of the question. It was worth it to look after you for marriage, it was worth it for you to look down timidly until your marriage day, but now marriage is out of the question, so everything else is out of the question as well. In one fell swoop, like that, everything is out of the question: marriage, family, your father, your mother, your sister; and me, I don't give a shit. Your father's snoring in despair, and your mother's crying; it's better to leave them snoring and crying and leave the house. You can have kids: we don't give a shit. You can not have any, we don't give a shit either way. You can do whatever you want. I'm done with looking after you, and you're done with being a little girl. You don't have an age anymore; you could be fifteen or fifty, it's all the same. You're a woman and no one gives a shit.

VI. SUBWAY.

Beneath a small sign reading: "Wanted," with, in the center, a picture of ZUCCO, *unnamed; sitting side by side on the subway station bench, after closing time, an* OLD MAN *and* ZUCCO.

THE OLD MAN: I'm an old man and I've let myself stay out later than reasonable. I was so glad to have caught the last train when suddenly, at an intersection in this maze of corridors and escalators, I couldn't recognize my stop, which I use so regularly I thought I knew it as well as my kitchen. But I didn't know it hid, behind the straightforward route I use every day, a dark world of tunnels, of unknown directions I would've preferred not to know but my stupid absent-mindedness forced me to know. And then suddenly the lights turn off and leave only these little white sidelights whose very existence escaped me. So I walk, straight ahead, in an unknown world, as fast as possible, which doesn't mean a lot for an old man like me. And when at the end of the station's endless escalators I think I see an exit, bam, a giant wire gate blocks access to it. So here I am, in quite a curious situation for a man of my age, punished by my absent-mindedness and the slowness of my gait, waiting for I don't know what and I don't really want to know what, because such novelties are truly difficult to swallow at my age. Without a doubt dawn, yes, without a doubt that's what I'm waiting for at this stop that was as familiar to me as my kitchen, and that scares me now. Without a doubt I'm waiting for the normal lights to turn back on and for the first train to come. But I'm deeply worried because I don't know how I'll perceive the light of day after an adventure this bizarre, this stop will never look the same to me, I won't be able to ignore the existence of these little white sidelights that didn't exist before; and what's more, a night without sleep, I don't know how that changes life, I've never done it before, everything must be shifted forward, days and nights must no longer alternate like they did before. I'm deeply worried about all of this. But you, young man, whose legs seem very agile to me, and whose mind seems very clear, yes, I can see your clear gaze is neither blurred nor foolish like that of an old man like me, it's impossible to believe you let yourself get tricked by these corridors and these closed wire gates; no, even a closed gate, a young man with a clear mind like you could get through it like a drop of water through a colander. Do you work nights here? Tell me about yourself, that'll reassure me.

ZUCCO: I'm a normal, reasonable young man, mister. I've never stood out. Would I have stood out to you if I hadn't been sitting next to you? I've always thought the best way to live peacefully was to be as transparent as a pane of glass, like a chameleon on a stone, to go through walls, to have neither color nor scent; so that people's gaze goes through you and sees the people behind you, as if you weren't there. It's a tough job being transparent; it's a profession; it's an old, very old dream to be invisible. I'm no hero. Heroes are criminals. There are no heroes whose clothes aren't soaked in blood, and blood's the only thing in the world that cannot go unnoticed. It's the most visible thing in the world. When everything's destroyed, and only the thin fog of the end of the world covers the ground, there will always be the blood-soaked clothes of heroes. I was a student, I was a good student. You never go back after getting used to being a good student. I'm enrolled at the university. In the classrooms of the Sorbonne, my seat's reserved, with other good students among whom I don't stand out. I swear, you have to be a good student, discrete and invisible, to be at the Sorbonne. It's not one of those community colleges where thugs and people who see themselves as heroes go. The halls of my university are silent and walked by shadows whose steps you can't even hear. Starting tomorrow I'll go back for my linguistics class. It's the day, tomorrow, of my linguistics class. I'll be there, invisible among the invisibles, silent and attentive in the thick fog of ordinary life. Nothing could change the course of things, mister. I'm like a train that calmly passes a meadow and that nothing could make go off the rails. I'm like a hippopotamus who's stuck in the sludge and who moves very slowly and whom nothing could deter from the path or rhythm it's decided to take.

THE OLD MAN: We can always go off the rails, young man, yes, now I know anyone can go off the rails, at any time. Even I, an old man, I who believed I knew the world and life as well as my kitchen, bam, here I am outside the world, at this hour that isn't one, in this strange light, with above all the worry about what will happen when the normal lights come back on, and the first train comes, and normal people like I used to be invade this station; and after this first night without sleep, I'll have to leave, walk through the gate that's finally open, see the day when I haven't seen the night. And now I know nothing about what will happen, about the way I'll see the world and how the world will see me or not see me. Because I won't know what's day and what's night anymore, I won't know what to do anymore, I'll go round and round my kitchen looking for the time and all of that makes me really scared, young man.

ZUCCO: There are things to be scared of, you're right.

THE OLD MAN: You stutter, very slightly; I really like that. That reassures me. Help me, at the hour when sound will invade this place. Help me, accompany the lost old man that I am, to the exit; and beyond, maybe.

The station lights turn back on.
ZUCCO *helps the* OLD MAN *stand and accompanies him.*
The first train comes.

VII. TWO SISTERS.

In the kitchen.
The YOUNG GIRL, *with a bag.*
Enter her SISTER.

THE SISTER: I forbid you to leave.

THE YOUNG GIRL: You can't forbid me to do anything. I'm older than you now.

THE SISTER: What're you talking about? You're a little sparrow perched on a branch. And me, I'm your big sister.

THE YOUNG GIRL: You're still a virgin, you don't know anything about life, you've looked out for yourself, and you've protected yourself well. I'm old, I'm raped, I'm lost, and I make my own decisions.

THE SISTER: Aren't you my little sister, who used to tell me everything?

THE YOUNG GIRL: Aren't you a spinster, who knows absolutely nothing about nothing, and who ought to keep her mouth shut considering my experience?

THE SISTER: What experience are you talking about? The experience of misfortune is worthless. It's better to be forgotten just as fast as possible. Only the experience of happiness has value. You'll always remember beautiful, peaceful evenings spent with your parents, your brother, and your sister; until you're old, you'll remember that. Whereas the misfortune that's struck us, you'll quickly forget it, my starling, under the watchful eyes of your sister, your brother, and your parents.

THE YOUNG GIRL: It's my parents, my brother, and my sister I'll forget and am already forgetting; not the misfortune.

THE SISTER: Your brother will protect you, my little swift; he'll love you more than anyone has ever loved you, because he's always loved you like he loved no one else. He'll be all the men you'll ever need.

THE YOUNG GIRL: I don't want to be loved.

THE SISTER: Don't say that. It's the only thing in this world that's worth something.

THE YOUNG GIRL: How dare you say that? You've never had a man. You've never been loved. You've stayed single all of your life, and you've been miserable.

THE SISTER: I've never been miserable, except because of your misfortune.

THE YOUNG GIRL: No, I know you've been miserable. I've caught you crying behind the curtains many times.

THE SISTER: I cry for no reason, at scheduled times, so it's done in advance, and now, you'll never see me cry again; I've cried a lot in advance. Why do you want to leave?

THE YOUNG GIRL: I want to find him.

THE SISTER: You won't find him.

THE YOUNG GIRL: I'll find him.

THE SISTER: Impossible. You know your brother's tried for days on end, to get vengeance for you.

THE YOUNG GIRL: But me, I don't want vengeance, so I'll find him.

THE SISTER: And what are you going to do, once you've found him?

THE YOUNG GIRL: I'll tell him something.

THE SISTER: What?

THE YOUNG GIRL: Something.

THE SISTER: Where do you think you'll find him?

THE YOUNG GIRL: In Little Chicago.

THE SISTER: Why do you want to lose yourself, my innocent dove? No, don't abandon me, don't leave me all alone. I don't want to be left alone with your brother and your parents. I don't want to be left alone in this house. Without you, my life will be worth nothing, nothing will make sense. Don't abandon me, I'm begging you, don't abandon me. I hate your brother, and your parents, and this house; you're the only one I love, my dove, my dove; you're my entire life.

The FATHER *enters, furious.*

THE FATHER: Your mother's hidden the beer. I'm going to hit her the way I used to. Why'd I stop one day? My arms were tired, but I should've forced myself, exercised, had somebody else do it. I should've kept it up: hit her every day, at scheduled times. But here we are, I was negligent, and now, she's hiding the beer from me, and I'm sure you're helping her. (*He looks under the table.*) There were five bottles left. I'll hit you each five times if I don't find them.

He leaves.

THE SISTER: My turtledove in Little Chicago! How miserable you must be, and how miserable you will be.

Enter the MOTHER.

THE MOTHER: Your father is drunk again. He guzzled down one after another. What are you doing, you two, being so complacent with this crazy old man? You're letting me fight all alone against this drunk. You don't give a shit, you just let him spend all our money on alcohol. You're two silly girls who just chit chat, chit chat, you're only interested in each others' silly, idiotic stories, and you're leaving me alone with this lush. What's that bag?

THE SISTER: She's going to her friend's house, to spend the night there.

THE MOTHER: Her friend, her friend… Who is this friend? What's going on between you girls? Why does she need to spend the night at her friend's house? Are the beds better than here? The darkness of night, is it darker there than here? If you were still little and I had the strength, I'd hit you both.

She leaves.

THE SISTER: I don't want you to be miserable.

THE YOUNG GIRL: I'm miserable and I'm happy. I've suffered a lot, but I've gotten a lot of pleasure from that suffering.

THE SISTER: And me, I'll die if you abandon me.

The YOUNG GIRL *takes her bag and leaves.*

VIII. RIGHT BEFORE DYING.

A seedy bar. A phone booth.

ZUCCO *is thrown through the window, in a big crash of broken glass. Screams from inside. Gathering at the door.*

ZUCCO: "Thus was I created like an athlete.
   Today your great anger completes me.
   O sea, and I am tall on my divine pedestal
   With all your greatness gnawing at my feet in vain.
   Naked, strong, forehead plunged in an abyss of fog."

A WHORE: We're freezing to death. This guy's going to catch his death of cold.

A MAN: Don't worry about him. He's sweating, he must be nice and warm on the inside.

ZUCCO: "Enveloped in sound and hail and foam
   And nights and winds that collide against each other,
   I raise my two arms up toward the dark ether."

A MAN: He's drunk, that guy.

A MAN: Impossible. He didn't drink anything.

A WHORE: He's crazy, that's all. Just leave him alone.

THE HULK: Leave him alone? He's been annoying us for hours and we're supposed to leave him alone? Let him pick a fight with me one more time and I'll crush him.

A WHORE: (*Approaching* ZUCCO *to help him get back up.*) Stop picking fights, kid, stop picking fights. Your pretty face is already really messed up. Do you want the girls not to look at you anymore? It's fragile, a baby's face. You think you'll have it your whole life and then all of a sudden, it's all screwed up by some big asshole whose own face's got nothing to lose. You, you've got a lot to lose, baby. A broken face and your whole life goes to shit as if it'd been cut short. You don't think about it before, but I swear you'll think about it after. Don't look at me like that or I'm going to cry; you're one of those ones who makes you want to cry just looking at them.

ZUCCO *goes up to the* HULK *and punches him.*

A WHORE: They're not going to start again.

THE HULK: Don't pick a fight with me, little guy, don't pick a fight with me.

ZUCCO *punches him again.*

The HULK *hits back. They fight.*

A WHORE: I'm calling the cops. He's going to kill him.

A MAN: No way we're calling the cops.

A MAN: In any case, he's already down for the count.

ZUCCO *gets back up and follows the* HULK, *who was leaving. He grabs onto him and hits him in the face.*

A WHORE: Don't hit him back, leave him alone, he already can't stand up.

ZUCCO: Fight, you coward, chicken, with no balls!

The HULK *sends him flying in the air.*

THE HULK: One more time, and I'll crush you like a mosquito.

ZUCCO *gets back up, picks a fight again.*

A WHORE: (*To the* HULK) Don't touch him, don't touch him, don't hurt him.

The HULK *knocks* ZUCCO *senseless with one punch.*

A MAN: He demolished him, that guy.

A WHORE: It was easy. He's right to say you're cowards.

THE HULK: A man should never let the same dog bite him twice.

They go back into the bar.

ZUCCO *gets back up, goes to the telephone booth. He picks up the phone, dials a number, waits.*

ZUCCO: I want to leave. I have to leave right now. It's too hot, in this fucking town. I want to go to Africa, where it snows. I have to leave because I'm going to die. Anyway, no one cares about anyone else. No one. Men need women and women need men. But love, there's none of that. With women, for me, it's out of sheer pity that I do it. I'd like to be reborn a dog, to be less miserable. A stray dog, forager of the trash; no one would notice me. I'd like to be a yellow dog, munched on by mites, that people would pass by without noticing. I'd like to be a forager of trash for eternity. I believe they're no words, there's nothing to say. We have to stop teaching words. We have to close the schools and expand the cemeteries. Anyway, a year, a hundred years, it's all the same; sooner or later, we all have to die, all of us. And that, that makes the birds sing, that makes the birds laugh.

A WHORE: (*At the door of the bar.*) I told you he was nuts. He's talking on a broken phone.

ZUCCO *drops the receiver, sits down against the booth.*

The HULK *approaches* ZUCCO.

THE HULK: What are you thinking about, little guy?

ZUCCO: I'm dreaming about the immortality of the crab, the slug, and the June bug.

THE HULK: You know, I don't like fighting much myself. But you were so in my face, little guy, I couldn't put up with doing nothing. Why were you so determined to fight? It's as if you want to die.

ZUCCO: I don't want to die. I'm going to die.

THE HULK: Like everyone else, little guy.

ZUCCO: That's not a reason.

THE HULK: Maybe not.

ZUCCO: The problem, with beer, it's that you don't buy it; you only borrow it. I have to take a leak.

THE HULK: Go ahead, before it's too late.

ZUCCO: Is it true even dogs will look at me sideways?

THE HULK: Dogs never look at anyone sideways. Dogs are the only beings you can trust. They'll love you or they won't love you, but they'll never judge you. And when everyone's walked out on you, little guy, there will always be a dog hanging around who will lick the soles of your feet.

ZUCCO: "Morte villana, di pietà nemica,
di dolor madre antica,
giudicio incontastabile gravoso,
di te blasmar la lingua s'affatica."

THE HULK: You have to go take a leak.

ZUCCO: It's too late.

Dawn rises.
ZUCCO *falls asleep.*

IX. DELILA.

A police station. A DETECTIVE; *a police* CHIEF.
Enter the YOUNG GIRL, *followed by her* BROTHER.
He stays in the shadow of the door.
The YOUNG GIRL *approaches the picture of* ZUCCO *and points at it.*

THE YOUNG GIRL: I know him.

THE CHIEF: What do you know?

THE YOUNG GIRL: This guy. I know him really well.

THE DETECTIVE: Who is he?

THE YOUNG GIRL: A secret agent. A friend.

THE DETECTIVE: Who's that guy, behind you?

THE YOUNG GIRL: My brother. He came with me. He's the one who told me to come see you because I recognized this picture on the street.

THE DETECTIVE: Do you know we're looking for him?

THE YOUNG GIRL: Yes; me too, I'm looking for him.

THE DETECTIVE: He's a friend, you say?

THE YOUNG GIRL: A friend, yes, a friend.

THE DETECTIVE: A cop killer. You'll be arrested and charged for being an accomplice, concealing weapons, and abetting a criminal.

THE YOUNG GIRL: It's my brother who told me to come tell you I knew him. I'm not hiding anything, I'm not denouncing anyone, I know him, that's all.

THE DETECTIVE: Tell your brother to leave.

THE CHIEF: Didn't you hear? You, get out of here.

The BROTHER *leaves.*

THE DETECTIVE: What do you know about him?

THE YOUNG GIRL: Everything.

THE DETECTIVE: French? Foreigner?

THE YOUNG GIRL: He had a very light, very pretty foreign accent.

THE CHIEF: Germanic?

THE YOUNG GIRL: I don't know what Germanic means.

THE DETECTIVE: So, he told you he was a secret agent. That's strange. In theory, a secret agent has to stay secret.

THE YOUNG GIRL: I told him I'd keep the secret no matter what.

THE CHIEF: Bravo. If all secrets were kept like that, our work would be easy.

THE YOUNG GIRL: He told me he was going on a mission to Africa, in the mountains, where it snows all the time.

THE DETECTIVE: A German agent in Kenya.

THE CHIEF: The police's theories weren't so wrong, after all.

THE DETECTIVE: They were right, Chief. (*To the* YOUNG GIRL) His name, now. Do you know it? You must know it since he was your friend.

THE YOUNG GIRL: Yes, I know it.

THE CHIEF: Say it.

THE YOUNG GIRL: I know it, very well.

THE CHIEF: You're trying to get a rise out of us, little girl. Do you want to be slapped?

THE YOUNG GIRL: I don't want to be slapped. I know it, but I can't seem to say it.

THE DETECTIVE: What do you mean, you can't seem to say it?

THE YOUNG GIRL: I have it on the tip of my tongue.

THE CHIEF: On the tip of my tongue, on the tip of my tongue. Do you want to be slapped, and punched, and have us pull your hair? We have rooms specifically for that here, you know.

THE YOUNG GIRL: No, no, it's on the tip of my tongue; it'll come.

THE DETECTIVE: His first name, at least. You must remember his first name, you must've whispered that in his ear.

THE CHIEF: A first name, a first name. Any one, or I'll drag you into the torture room.

THE YOUNG GIRL: Andreas.

THE DETECTIVE: (*To the* CHIEF) Write that down: Andreas. (*To the* YOUNG GIRL) You're sure?

THE YOUNG GIRL: No.

THE CHIEF: I'm going to kill her.

THE DETECTIVE: Let's have that fucking name, or I'll punch you in the face. Hurry up, or you'll remember this.

THE YOUNG GIRL: Angelo.

THE DETECTIVE: A Spaniard.

THE CHIEF: Or an Italian, a Brazilian, a Portuguese, a Mexican: I've even met a man from Berlin whose name was Julio.

THE DETECTIVE: You really know a thing or two, Chief. (*To the* YOUNG GIRL) I'm losing my patience.

THE YOUNG GIRL: I feel it, on the edge of my lips.

THE CHIEF: Do you want a slap on the lips, to help it out?

THE YOUNG GIRL: Angelo, Angelo, Dolce, or something like that.

THE DETECTIVE: Dolce? Like Sweet?

THE YOUNG GIRL: Sweet, yes. He told me his name was like a foreign name that meant sweet, or sweetened. (*She starts to cry.*) He was so sweet, so nice.

THE DETECTIVE: There are lots of words that mean sweetened, I suppose.

THE CHIEF: Azucarado, zuccherato, sweetened, gezuckert, ocukrzony.

THE DETECTIVE: I know all that, Chief.

THE YOUNG GIRL: Zucco. Zucco. Roberto Zucco.

THE DETECTIVE: Are you sure?

THE YOUNG GIRL: Sure. I'm sure.

THE CHIEF: Zucco. With a Z?

THE YOUNG GIRL: With a Z, yes. Roberto. With a Z.

THE DETECTIVE: Go take her deposition.

THE YOUNG GIRL: And my brother?

THE CHIEF: Your brother? What brother? What do you need a brother for? We're here.

They leave.

X. THE HOSTAGE.

In the middle of a park.
An elegant LADY *is sitting on a bench.*
Enter ZUCCO.

THE LADY: Sit down next to me. Talk to me. I'm bored. We'll talk. I really hate parks. You look shy. Do I intimidate you?

ZUCCO: I'm not shy.

THE LADY: But, your hands are shaking like a little boy in front of his first girlfriend. You have a good-looking face. You're a good-looking kid. Do you like women? You're almost too good-looking to like women.

ZUCCO: I like women, yeah, a lot.

THE LADY: You must like those eighteen-year-old girls.

ZUCCO: I like all women.

THE LADY: That's very good. Have you ever been harsh with a woman?

ZUCCO: Never.

THE LADY: But the desire? You must've had the desire to be violent with a woman, right? That desire, all men have had it once; all of them.

ZUCCO: Not me. I'm gentle and peaceful.

THE LADY: You're a funny kind of guy.

ZUCCO: Did you take a cab here?

THE LADY: Oh, no. I hate cab drivers.

ZUCCO: So you drove here.

THE LADY: Of course. I didn't walk here; I live on the other side of town.

ZUCCO: What kind of car?

THE LADY: Maybe you were thinking I had a Porsche? No, I have a pathetic little car. My husband's stingy.

ZUCCO: What kind?

THE LADY: Mercedes.

ZUCCO: Which one?

THE LADY: 280 SE.

ZUCCO: That's not a pathetic little car.

THE LADY: Maybe not. But my husband's still stingy.

ZUCCO: Who's that guy? Does he always look at you?

THE LADY: It's my son.

ZUCCO: Your son? He's big.

THE LADY: Fourteen years old, not one year older. I'm not an old hag.

ZUCCO: He looks older than that. Does he play sports?

THE LADY: He does nothing but play sports. I pay for him to go to all the clubs, all the tennis courts, hockey rinks, golf tees, and with that, he finds a way to insist I accompany him to practice. He's a little brat.

ZUCCO: He looks strong for his age. Give me the keys to your car.

THE LADY: Of course, of course. Maybe you want the car also.

ZUCCO: Yes, I want the car.

THE LADY: Take it.

ZUCCO: Give me the keys.

THE LADY: You're annoying me.

ZUCCO: Give me the keys. (*He takes out the gun, lays it across his lap.*)

THE LADY: You're crazy. You shouldn't play with things like that.

ZUCCO: Call your son.

THE LADY: Absolutely not.

ZUCCO: (*Threatening her with the gun*) Call your son.

THE LADY: You're nuts. (*Screaming to her son*) Get out of here. Go home. Get home on your own.

The son approaches, the LADY *stands,* ZUCCO *puts the gun to her throat.*

THE LADY: Fire then, idiot. I won't give you the keys, if only because you take me for an idiot. My husband takes me for an idiot, my son takes me for an idiot, the maid takes me for an idiot—you can fire, that would make one less idiot. But I won't give you the keys. Too bad for you, because it's a superb car, leather interior and walnut dashboard. Too bad for you. Stop making a scene. Look: those idiots are going to get closer, they're going to start talking, they're going to call the police. Look: they're already licking their chops. They love that. I can't stand their chattering. So, fire. I don't want to hear them, I don't want to hear them.

ZUCCO: (*To the* CHILD) Don't come any closer.

A MAN: Look how he's trembling.

ZUCCO: Don't get any closer, goddammit. Get down on the ground.

A WOMAN: He's scared of the child.

ZUCCO: And now, hands by your sides. Come closer.

A WOMAN: But how can he want him to crawl with his hands by his sides?

A MAN: It's possible, it's possible. I could do it.

ZUCCO: Slowly. Hands on your back. Don't raise your head. Stop. (*The* CHILD *moves slightly.*) Don't move at all, or I'll kill your mother.

A MAN: He'd do it.

A WOMAN: Of course. He's going to do it. Poor kid.

ZUCCO: Do you swear you won't move?

THE CHILD: I swear.

ZUCCO: Make sure your head's on the ground. Turn slowly so your head's on the other side. Turn, I don't want you to be able to see us.

THE CHILD: But why are you scared of me? I can't do anything. I'm a child. I don't want my mother to get killed. There's no reason to be scared of me: you're much stronger than me.

ZUCCO: Yes, I'm much stronger than you.

THE CHILD: So, why are you scared of me? What could I do to you? I'm so small.

ZUCCO: You're not that small, and I'm not scared.

THE CHILD: Yes, you are. You're trembling, you're trembling. I can hear that you're trembling.

A MAN: The cops are here.

A WOMAN: Now he's going to have reasons to tremble.

A MAN: We're going to laugh. We're going to laugh.

ZUCCO: (*To the* CHILD) Shut your eyes.

THE CHILD: They're closed. They're closed. Good God, you're a real chicken.

ZUCCO: Shut your mouth, too.

THE CHILD: I'll shut everything, okay. But you're a chicken. It's a woman you're scaring. It's a woman you're threatening with your gun.

ZUCCO: What kind of car does your mother have?

THE CHILD: It might be a Porsche.

ZUCCO: Shut up. Shut the fuck up. Shut your mouth. Shut your eyes. Act dead.

THE CHILD: I don't know how to act dead.

ZUCCO: You're going to know it soon. I'm going to kill your mother and then you'll see how to play dead.

A WOMAN: Poor kid.

THE CHILD: I'm playing dead, I'm playing dead.

A MAN: The cops aren't getting any closer.

A WOMAN: They're scared.

A MAN: No. It's strategy. They know what they're doing. They have methods we don't know about. But they know what they're doing, believe you me. The guy's a goner.

A MAN: The woman too, undoubtedly.

A MAN: You can't make an omelet without breaking some eggs.

A WOMAN: But let him not hurt the kid, above all not the kid, God almighty.

ZUCCO *gets closer to the* CHILD *by pushing the* LADY, *still with the gun on her neck. Then, he puts his foot on the* CHILD*'s head.*

A WOMAN: My God, children see horrible things nowadays.

A MAN: We too saw horrible things when we were kids.

THE WOMAN: Because you were threatened by a crazy man, you too?

THE MAN: And the war, lady, have you forgotten the war?

THE WOMAN: Oh really? Because the Germans put their foot on your head and threatened your mother?

THE MAN: Worse than that, lady, worse than that.

A WOMAN: In any case, here you are alive, old, and fat.

A MAN: You're rude, lady.

A WOMAN: I'm only thinking of the child, I'm only thinking of the child.

A MAN: Stop with your child. It's the woman who's got the gun to her throat.

A WOMAN: Yes, but it's the child who will suffer.

A WOMAN: Tell me, sir, is that what you call special police tactics? Talk about tactics. They're staying on the other side. They're scared.

A MAN: I said it was a strategy.

A MAN: Strategy my ass!

THE COPS: (*From afar*) Drop your weapon.

A WOMAN: Bravo.

A WOMAN: We're saved.

A MAN: Brilliant strategy.

A MAN: They're getting ready to strike, I'm telling you.

A WOMAN: I can only see that one over there getting ready to strike.

A MAN: Besides, the strike's already practically over.

A WOMAN: Poor kid.

A MAN: Lady, I'm going to slap you if you keep talking about the kid.

A MAN: Do you really think now is the time to argue? A little dignity. We're witnessing a drama. We're facing death.

THE COPS: (*From afar*) We order you to drop your weapon. You're surrounded. (*The spectators break into laughter.*)

ZUCCO: Tell her to give me the keys to the car. It's a Porsche.

THE LADY: Idiot.

A WOMAN: Give him the keys, give him the keys.

THE LADY: Never. All he has to do is take them himself.

A MAN: He's going to blow your face off, my little lady.

THE LADY: Good. I won't have to see your faces anymore. Good.

A WOMAN: This woman's horrible.

A MAN: She's mean. There are so many mean, cruel people.

A WOMAN: Take the keys by force. Isn't there a man here who will look through her pockets and take the keys?

A WOMAN: You, there, who suffered so much when you were a kid, whose head the Germans put their foot on while threatening your mother, show us you have balls, show us you still have at least one left, even if it's small, even if it's all dried up.

A MAN: Lady, you ought to be slapped. You're lucky I'm a worldly man.

THE WOMAN: Well then look in her pockets, take the keys, and slap me after.

The MAN *approaches trembling, reaches out his arm, searches the* LADY*'s pocket, takes out the keys.*

THE LADY: Idiot.

A MAN: (*Triumphant*) Did you see? Did you see? Someone bring the Porsche here. (*The* LADY *laughs.*)

A WOMAN: She's laughing. She finds a way to laugh even though her child's going to die.

A WOMAN: How horrible.

A MAN: She's crazy.

A MAN: Give the key to the cops. Let them deal with that, at least. I hope at least they know how to drive a car.

The MAN *comes back running.*

A MAN: It's not a Porsche. It's a Mercedes.

A MAN: What model?

A MAN: 280 SE, I think. Very nice.

A MAN: Mercedes, that's a good car.

A WOMAN: Well bring it here, regardless of the make. He's going to kill everyone.

ZUCCO: I want a Porsche. I don't want to be made a fucking fool of.

A WOMAN: Ask the cops to find a Porsche. Don't argue. This is a crazy man, so he's crazy. We have to find him a Porsche.

A MAN: That, at least, the cops will know how to do.

A MAN: Who knows. They're keeping their distance.

They go toward the POLICE OFFICERS.

A MAN: Look at us, we civilians. We're more courageous than they are.

A WOMAN: (*To the* CHILD) Poor little one. Is that mean foot hurting you?

ZUCCO: Shut up. I don't want anyone to talk to him. I don't want him to open his mouth. Shut your eyes, you. Don't move.

A MAN: And you, lady? How are you feeling?

THE LADY: I'm okay, thank you, I'm okay. But I would feel ever so much better if you would shut the fuck up and go back to your kitchens and wipe your kids' asses.

A WOMAN: She's harsh. She's harsh.

A COP: (*On the other side of the gathering.*) Here are the keys to the car. It's a Porsche. It's there. You can see it from here. (*To the people*) Pass him the keys.

A MAN: Give them to him yourself. It's your job, killers.

A COP: We have our reasons.

A WOMAN: Reasons my ass.

A MAN: Me, I'm not touching those keys. It's not my job. I'm a family man.

ZUCCO: I'm going to kill her, and I'm going to shoot myself in the head. I don't give a shit about my life. I swear I don't give a shit. There are six bullets in the clip. I'll kill five people and then I'll kill myself.

A WOMAN: He's going to do it. He's going to do it. Let's get out of here.

A COP: Don't move. You'll piss him off.

A MAN: It's you who's pissing us off by doing nothing.

A MAN: Don't bother them. Let them do what they do. They have a plan, that's for sure.

A COP: Don't move. (*He places the keys on the ground and, with a baton, pushes them through the peoples' legs all the way to* ZUCCO's *feet.* ZUCCO *slowly bends down, picks up the key, puts them in his pocket.*)

ZUCCO: I'm taking the woman with me. Get out of my way.

A WOMAN: The child is saved. Thank you, dear God.

A MAN: And the woman? What's going to happen to her?

ZUCCO: Get out of my way.

Everyone scatters. Holding the gun in one hand, ZUCCO *leans down, takes the* CHILD'S *head by the hair, and shoots him in the neck. Screaming, running. Holding the gun pointed at the* LADY's *neck,* ZUCCO, *in the almost deserted park, goes toward the car.*

XI. THE DEAL.

In the lobby of the Little Chicago hotel.
The MADAM *sits in her armchair, and the* YOUNG GIRL *waits.*

THE YOUNG GIRL: I'm ugly.

THE MADAM: Don't say such silly things, little duckling.

THE YOUNG GIRL: I'm fat, I have a double chin, two stomachs, breasts like soccer balls, and my ass, thank God it's behind me, that way I don't have to see it. But I'm sure it's like two hams swaying with every step I take.

THE MADAM: Just be quiet, silly girl.

THE YOUNG GIRL: I'm sure of it, I'm sure of it; I can see, in the street, the dogs follow me with their tongues out and slime dripping from their mouths. If I let them do it, they would sink their teeth into my ass like they would any other meat.

THE MADAM: But where did that come from, silly goose? You're pretty, you're round, you're plump, you have curves. Do you think men like a dry tree branch they're scared will break if they hold it? They like curves, my little one, they like curves they can really grab onto.

THE YOUNG GIRL: I want to be skinny. I want to be a dry tree branch men are scared of breaking.

THE MADAM: Well, not me. Besides, you're plump today, you can be skinny tomorrow. A woman changes, in her life. She doesn't have to worry about that. When I was a young girl like you, I was skinny, so skinny, you could almost see through me, just a little skin and a few bones. Not even a shadow of a breast. Flat like a boy. It made me angry, because at that time I didn't like boys. I dreamed of filling out, I dreamed of having pretty breasts. So I'd wear cardboard breasts that I'd made myself. But the boys figured it out and, every time they'd pass by, they'd elbow me in the chest and crush one of them completely. After a few times, I put a needle inside one of the breasts, and it was a real tearjerker, believe you me. And then, you see, everything began to get rounder, to fill out, and I was very happy. Don't worry, my starling: you're plump today, you can be skinny tomorrow.

THE YOUNG GIRL: It doesn't matter. Today I'm ugly, fat, and I'm miserable.

Enter the BROTHER, *talking with a* PIMP.
They don't look at the YOUNG GIRL.

THE PIMP: (*Impatient*) It's too expensive.

THE BROTHER: It's priceless.

THE PIMP: Everything has a price, and yours is much too high.

THE BROTHER: When you can put a price on something, that means it's not worth much. That means we can negotiate, lower, raise the price. I chose an abstract price because it has no price. It's like a Picasso painting: have you ever heard someone say it's too expensive? Have you ever heard a seller lower the price of a Picasso? The price that's been chosen, in those cases, it's an abstraction.

THE PIMP: In the meantime, it's an abstraction that'll go from my pocket to yours, and the emptiness it leaves in my pocket, I won't find it as abstract as all that.

THE BROTHER: An emptiness like that, it fills right back up. You'll fill it back up quickly, believe you me, and you'll forget the price you paid faster than it's taking you to negotiate it. But me, I'm not negotiating. Take it or leave it. Make the best deal of the year or stay poor.

THE PIMP: Don't get worked up, don't get worked up. I'm thinking.

THE BROTHER: Think, think, but don't take too long. I'm going to have to bring my sister back to her mother's house.

THE PIMP: Ok, I'll take it.

THE BROTHER: (*To the* YOUNG GIRL) Your nose is shiny, chicky.

You really ought to think about putting on some more powder. (*The* YOUNG GIRL *leaves. They watch her.*) And so, my Picasso?

THE PIMP: I still think it's expensive.

THE BROTHER: She'll make you enough money that you'll forget the price.

Exchange of money.

THE PIMP: When will she be ready?

THE BROTHER: Don't get worked up, don't get worked up; we have all the time in the world.

THE PIMP: No, we don't have all the time in the world. You have the money, I want the girl.

THE BROTHER: You have her, you have her, it's as if you had her.

THE PIMP: Now that you have the money, you're regretting it.

THE BROTHER: I'm not regretting anything at all, nothing. I'm thinking.

THE PIMP: What do you have to think about? This isn't the time to think. So, when?

THE BROTHER: Tomorrow, the day after.

THE PIMP: Why not today?

THE BROTHER: Right, why not today? This evening.

THE PIMP: Why not right now?

THE BROTHER: You're getting worked up, you're getting worked up. (*We hear the* YOUNG GIRL'*s steps.*) Right now, okay. (*The* BROTHER *runs off to a room to hide.*)

Enter the YOUNG GIRL.

THE YOUNG GIRL: Where's my brother?

THE PIMP: He told me to look after you.

THE YOUNG GIRL: I want to know where my brother is.

THE PIMP: Let's go, come with me.

THE YOUNG GIRL: I don't want to go with you.

THE MADAM: Do what you're told immediately, you fat cow. There's no arguing with a brother's orders.

The YOUNG GIRL *and the* PIMP *leave. The* BROTHER *comes out of the room and sits down in front of the* MADAM.

THE BROTHER: I'm not the one who wanted that, Madam, I swear to you. She's the one who insisted, she's the one who wanted to come to this neighborhood and work. She's looking for I don't know who, and she wants to find him. She's sure she'll find him here. I didn't want to. I looked after her like no other older brother has ever looked after his sister. My chicky, my little love, I never loved anyone like I loved her. I can't do anything about it. Misfortune struck us. She's the one who wanted to, all I did was give in. I could never say no to my little sister. It's misfortune that's singled us out and that hounds us. (*He cries.*)

THE MADAM: You're a real piece of shit.

XII. THE TRAIN STATION.

In a train station.

ZUCCO: Roberto Zucco.

THE LADY: Why are you repeating that name all the time?

ZUCCO: Because I'm scared of forgetting it.

THE LADY: A person doesn't forget his own name. That's got to be the last thing a person forgets.

ZUCCO: No, no; me, I'm forgetting it. I see it written in my mind, and less and less well written, less and less clearly, as if it were erasing itself; I have to look closer and closer to be able to read it. I'm scared of ending up not knowing my name.

THE LADY: I won't forget it. I'll be your memory.

ZUCCO: (*After a pause*) I like women. I like women too much.

THE LADY: You can never like them too much.

ZUCCO: I like them, I like them, all of them. There aren't enough women.

THE LADY: So, you like me.

ZUCCO: Yes, of course, you're a woman after all.

THE LADY: Why did you bring me here with you?

ZUCCO: Because I'm going to take the train.

THE LADY: And the Porsche? Why aren't you leaving in the Porsche?

ZUCCO: I don't want to be recognized. On a train, no one sees anyone.

THE LADY: Am I supposed to take it with you?

ZUCCO: No.

THE LADY: Why not? I have no reason not to take it with you. You haven't displeased me since I first saw you. I'm going to take it with you. Anyway, it's what you want, if not you would've killed me or let me go.

ZUCCO: I need you to give me money to take the train. I don't have any money. My mother should have given me some but she forgot.

THE LADY: Mothers always forget to give money. Where do you want to go?

ZUCCO: To Venice.

THE LADY: Venice? What a silly idea.

ZUCCO: Do you know Venice?

THE LADY: Of course. Everyone knows Venice.

ZUCCO: That's where I was born.

THE LADY: Bravo. I've always thought no one was born in Venice, and everyone died there. Babies must be born all dusty and covered in spiders' webs. In any case, France cleaned you up well. I don't see a trace of dust. France is an excellent detergent. Bravo.

ZUCCO: I need to leave, yes; I need to leave. I don't want to be arrested. I don't want to be locked up. It scares the shit out of me being around all these people.

THE LADY: You're scared? Be a man. You have a gun: you'd make them all run away just by taking it out of your pocket.

ZUCCO: It's because I'm a man that I'm scared.

THE LADY: Well me, I'm not. With everything you've made me see, I'm not and I never have been.

ZUCCO: It's precisely because you're not a man.

THE LADY: You're complicated, complicated.

ZUCCO: If they arrest me, they lock me up. If they lock me up, I go crazy. Besides, I'm going crazy, now. There are cops everywhere, there are people everywhere. I'm already locked up in the midst of all these people. Don't look at them, don't look at anyone.

THE LADY: Do I look like I'm going to turn you in? Idiot. I would've done it a long time ago. But these jerks disgust me. You, I rather like you.

ZUCCO: Look at all these crazy people. Look at how mean they look. They're killers. I've never seen so many killers at the same time. With just the slightest signal in their heads, they'd start to kill each other. I wonder why the signal isn't going off, there, now, in their heads. Because they're all ready to kill. They're like lab rats in cages. They want to kill, you can see it in their faces, you can see it in the way they walk; I see their closed fists in their pockets. I recognize a killer at first glance; their clothes are covered in blood. Here, they're everywhere; you have to keep yourself calm, very still; you have to avoid eye contact. They must not see us; we must be transparent. Because otherwise, if you make eye contact, if they realize you're looking at them, if they begin to look back at us and to see us, the signal goes off in their heads and they kill, they kill. And if there's one who starts, everyone here will kill everyone. Everyone's just waiting for the signal in their heads.

THE LADY: Stop. Don't panic. I'll go buy the two tickets. But you have to calm down, or we'll be spotted. (*After a pause*) Why did you kill him?

ZUCCO: Who's that?

THE LADY: My son, idiot.

ZUCCO: Because he was a little brat.

THE LADY: Who told you that?

ZUCCO: You. You said he was a little brat. You said he took you for an idiot.

THE LADY: And what if I liked being taken for an idiot? And if I liked little brats? And if I liked little brats more than anything else, more than big jerks ? If I hated everything except little brats?

ZUCCO: You should've said so.

THE LADY: I said so, idiot, I said so.

ZUCCO: You shouldn't have refused to give me the keys. You shouldn't have humiliated me. I didn't want to kill him, but everything snowballed because of the Porsche thing.

THE LADY: Liar. Nothing snowballed; everything went wrong. You had your gun pointed at me. Why was it his head you blew off getting his blood everywhere?

ZUCCO: If it had been your head, it would have gotten your blood everywhere too.

THE LADY: But I wouldn't have seen it, idiot, I wouldn't have seen it. My blood, I don't give a shit about it, it doesn't belong to me. But my son's blood, I'm the one who fucking put it in his fucking veins, it's my property, it was mine, no one had to splatter my property all over the place, in a park, at the foot of a group of idiots. I have nothing left of my own, now. Anyone can walk on the only thing that used to belong to me. It'll be cleaned up tomorrow morning by the groundskeepers. What do I have left, now, what do I have left?

ZUCCO *stands*.

ZUCCO: I'm leaving.

THE LADY: I'm leaving with you.

ZUCCO: Don't move.

THE LADY: You don't even have anything for the train. You didn't even give me time to give it to you. You don't give anyone time to help you. You're like a switchblade you close from time to time and put back in your pocket.

ZUCCO: I don't need people to help me.

THE LADY: Everyone needs people to help them.

ZUCCO: Don't start to cry. You look like a woman who's about to cry. I hate that.

THE LADY: You told me you liked women, all women; even me.

ZUCCO: Except when they look like women who are about to cry.

THE LADY: I swear I won't cry.

She cries. ZUCCO *moves away.*

THE LADY: And your name, idiot? Are you even able to say it to me, now? Who will remember it for you? You've already forgotten it, I'm sure of it. I'm the only one who remembers it now. You're going to leave without your memory.

ZUCCO *exits. The* LADY *remains seated and watches the trains.*

XIII. OPHELIA.

Same place; night.
The train station is deserted. The sound of falling rain is heard.
Enter the SISTER.

THE SISTER: Where is my dove? In what filth have they dragged her? In what despicable cage have they kept her? What kinds of perverse and vicious animals surround her? I want to find you again, my turtledove, I'll look for you until I die. (*Pause.*) Man is the most repugnant animal of all the repugnant animals on earth. There's a smell men have that disgusts me. Rats in the sewers, pigs in the sludge, the smell of a pond where dead bodies rot. (*Pause.*) Men are dirty, men don't wash themselves, they let dirt and repugnant liquids from their secretions accumulate on themselves, and they don't touch it, as if it were a precious gem. Men don't notice it because they all have the same smell. That's why they spend so much time with each other, and why they spend time with whores, because whores, for money, put up with that smell. I washed her so much, that little one. Bathed her so often before dinner, and bathed her in the mornings, scrubbed her back and her hands with a brush, and brushed under her nails, washed her hair every day, clipped her nails, washed her completely every day with hot water and soap. I kept her white as a dove, I smoothed her feathers like a turtledove's. I protected her and kept her in a cage that was always clean so she wouldn't soil her immaculate whiteness with exposure to the filth of this world, to the filth of men, so the disease-ridden scent of men wouldn't infect her. And it's her brother, that rat among rats, that stinking pig, that corrupted male who dirtied her and dragged her in the mud and pulled her by her hair into his shit. I should've killed him, I should've poisoned him, I should've stopped him from circling my turtledove's cage. I should've put barbed wire around my love's cage. I should've crushed that rat with my foot and burned it up in the wood stove. (*Pause.*) Everything is dirty, here. This whole town is dirty and full of men. Let it rain, let it rain again, let the rain fall on the shit where she is and wash my little turtledove clean.

XIV. THE ARREST.

The Little Chicago neighborhood.
Two POLICE OFFICERS. *Some prostitutes and, among them, the* YOUNG GIRL.

FIRST POLICEMAN: Did you see someone?

SECOND POLICEMAN: It's stupid. Our work is stupid. Standing here like parking signs. Might as well go back to being traffic cops again.

FIRST POLICEMAN: It's normal. This is where he killed the detective.

SECOND POLICEMAN: Exactly. This is the only place he won't come back to.

FIRST POLICEMAN: A murderer always comes back to the scene of the crime.

SECOND POLICEMAN: He'd come back here? Why would you think he'd come back? He didn't leave anything, not one suitcase, nothing. He's not crazy. We're two completely useless parking signs.

FIRST POLICEMAN: He'll come back.

SECOND POLICEMAN: In the meantime, we could have a drink with the Madam of the brothel, and discuss the crime with the ladies, and walk around somewhere else, among all these calm, quiet people; Little Chicago is the calmest neighborhood in town.

FIRST POLICEMAN: There's a fire under the ashes.

SECOND POLICEMAN: A fire? What fire? Where do you see fire? Even the ladies are calm and quiet like produce vendors; the johns are walking around as if they were in a park, and the pimps are watching over their goods, as if they were booksellers making sure all the books are on the shelves and none have been stolen. Where do you see fire? That guy won't come back here, I bet you, I bet you a drink at the Madam's.

FIRST POLICEMAN: He certainly went back home after killing his father.

SECOND POLICEMAN: That's because he had things to do there.

FIRST POLICEMAN: And what did he have to do there?

SECOND POLICEMAN: Kill his mother. Once he'd done it, he never went back. And since there aren't any more detectives here for him to kill, he won't come back. I feel like an idiot; I feel like I'm growing roots and leaves on my arms and legs. I feel like I'm sinking into the concrete. Let's go have a drink at the Madam's place. Everything's calm; everyone's walking calmly. Do you see someone who looks like a killer?

FIRST POLICEMAN: A killer never looks like a killer. A killer walks calmly around everyone like you and me.

SECOND POLICEMAN: He'd have to be crazy.

FIRST POLICEMAN: A killer is crazy by definition.

SECOND POLICEMAN: Not necessarily, not necessarily. There are times when even I almost want to kill someone.

FIRST POLICEMAN: Well then, there are times you must be almost crazy.

SECOND POLICEMAN: Maybe, maybe.

FIRST POLICEMAN: Definitely.

Enter ZUCCO.

SECOND POLICEMAN: But I'd never—even if I were crazy, even if I were a killer—I'd never walk calmly around my own crime scene.

FIRST POLICEMAN: Look at that guy.

SECOND POLICEMAN: Which one?

FIRST POLICEMAN: The one who's walking, calmly, over there.

SECOND POLICEMAN: Everyone's walking calmly, here. Little Chicago has become a park where even children play ball.

FIRST POLICEMAN: The one who's wearing military fatigues.

SECOND POLICEMAN: Yes, I see him.

FIRST POLICEMAN: Doesn't he remind you of anyone?

SECOND POLICEMAN: Maybe, maybe.

FIRST POLICEMAN: It looks like him.

SECOND POLICEMAN: Impossible.

THE YOUNG GIRL: (*Seeing* ZUCCO) Roberto. (*She rushes toward him and kisses him.*)

FIRST POLICEMAN: It's him.

SECOND POLICEMAN: No more doubt about it.

THE YOUNG GIRL: I looked for you, Roberto, I looked for you, I betrayed you, I cried, and cried, to the point where I became a tiny little island in the middle of the sea and these last waves are drowning me. I suffered, so much, that my suffering could fill up all the caves in the world and cover its volcanoes. I want to stay with you, Roberto; I want to look after every beat of your heart, every rise and fall of your chest; with my ear glued to you, I'll hear the sounds of the workings of your body, I'll look after your body like a mechanic looks after his machine. I'll keep all your secrets, I'll be your suitcase for secrets; I'll be the bag in which you'll put your mysteries. I'll take care of your weapons, I'll keep them from rusting. You'll be my agent and my secret and me, on your trips, I'll be your suitcase, your keeper, and your love.

FIRST POLICEMAN: (*Approaching* ZUCCO) Who are you?

ZUCCO: I'm the murderer of my father, my mother, a detective, and a child. I'm a killer.

The POLICE OFFICERS *take him away.*

XV. ZUCCO IN THE SUN.

The rooftops of the prison, at noon.
No one can be seen, during the entire scene, except ZUCCO *when he climbs to the top of the roof.*
Voices of prison guards and prisoners intermingle.

A VOICE: Roberto Zucco escaped.

A VOICE: Again.

A VOICE: But who was guarding him?

A VOICE: Who was supposed to be watching him?

A VOICE: We look like idiots.

A VOICE: Yeah, you do look like idiots. (*Laughter.*)

A VOICE: Silence.

A VOICE: He has accomplices.

A VOICE: No; it's because he doesn't have accomplices that he always manages to escape.

A VOICE: All alone.

A VOICE: All alone, like the heroes.

A VOICE: We have to check the alcoves in the hallways.

A VOICE: He must be hidden somewhere.

A VOICE: He must be huddled up in a cabinet, trembling.

A VOICE: Except it's not you who's making him tremble.

A VOICE: Zucco isn't trembling, he's making a fucking fool of you.

A VOICE: Zucco's making a fucking fool of everyone.

A VOICE: He won't go far.

A VOICE: It's a modern prison. You can't escape from it.

A VOICE: It's impossible.

A VOICE: Absolutely impossible.

A VOICE: Zucco's done for.

A VOICE: Zucco may be done for, but, at the moment, he's climbing up the roof and making a fucking fool of you.

ZUCCO, *torso and feet bare, gets to the top of the roof.*

A VOICE: What are you doing there?

A VOICE: Get down immediately. (*Laughter.*)

A VOICE: Zucco, you're done for. (*Laughter.*)

A VOICE: Zucco, Zucco, tell us, how do you manage to spend not even one hour in prison?

A VOICE: How do you do it?

A VOICE: Where did you escape from. Give us the escape plan.

ZUCCO: By going up high. You can't try to go over the walls, because, on the other side of the walls, there are other walls, the prison's still there. You have to escape through the roof, toward the sun. There will never be a wall between the sun and the earth.

A VOICE: And the guards?

ZUCCO: The guards don't exist. You just have to not see them. In any case, I could take five in one hand and crush them with one blow.

A VOICE: Where does your strength come from Zucco? Where does your strength come from?

ZUCCO: When I move forward, I move fast, I don't see the obstacles, and, since I haven't looked at them, they fall on their own before me. I'm alone and strong, I'm a rhinoceros.

A VOICE: But your father, and your mother, Zucco. You shouldn't mess with your parents.

ZUCCO: It's normal to kill your parents.

A VOICE: But a child, Zucco; you don't kill a child. You kill your enemies, you kill people capable of defending themselves. But not a child.

ZUCCO: I don't have enemies and I don't attack. I crush other animals not out of cruelty but because I haven't seen them and I've placed my foot on top of them.

A VOICE: Do you have money? Money hidden somewhere?

ZUCCO: I don't have any money, anywhere. I don't need money.

A VOICE: You're a hero, Zucco.

A VOICE: He's Goliath.

A VOICE: He's Samson.

A VOICE: Who's Samson?

A VOICE: A gangster from Marseille.

A VOICE: I knew him in prison. A real animal. He could beat the shit out of ten people at the same time.

A VOICE: Liar.

A VOICE: With nothing but his fists.

A VOICE: No, with a donkey's jawbone. And he wasn't from Marseille.

A VOICE: He got himself fucked over by a woman.

A VOICE: Dalila. A story about hair. I know.

A VOICE: There's always a woman who will betray you.

A VOICE: We'd all be free if it weren't for women.

The sun rises, shining, extraordinarily luminous. A strong wind picks up.

ZUCCO: Look at the sun. (*A complete silence settles over the yard.*) Don't you see anything? Don't you see how it moves from one side to the other?

A VOICE: We don't see anything.

A VOICE: The sun's hurting our eyes. It's blinding us.

ZUCCO: Look what's coming out of the sun. It's the sun's phallus; that's where the wind comes from.

A VOICE: The what? The sun has a phallus?

A VOICE: Shut up!

ZUCCO: Move your head: you'll see it move with you.

A VOICE: What's moving? I don't see anything moving.

A VOICE: How could you think something's moving up there? Everything's fixed in its place since eternity, and well-nailed, well-bolted.

ZUCCO: It's where the winds come from.

A VOICE: We can't see anything anymore. There's too much light.

ZUCCO: Turn your face toward the East and it will move there; and, if you turn your face toward the West, it will follow you.

A hurricane wind rises. ZUCCO *falters.*

A VOICE: He's crazy. He's going to fall.

A VOICE: Stop, Zucco; you're going to wipe out.

A VOICE: He's crazy.

A VOICE: He's going to fall.

The sun rises, becomes blinding like the impact of an atomic bomb. Nothing else can be seen.

A VOICE: (*Screaming*) He's falling.

A SHORT BIOGRAPHICAL ACCOUNT[1]

One part of my life is dedicated to traveling, the other to writing.[2]

B-M Koltès

Bernard-Marie Koltès, born on April 9, 1948, is the youngest of three boys in a middle-class family, in the town of Metz, France. His father Édouard is an officer of the French colonial army, called to fight in Algeria, later in Indochina. In the absence of the father, Bernard-Marie grows a "passionate and unconditional love"[3] for his devout Catholic mother, Germaine, the intensity of which remains unwavering throughout his short life. At Metz, the young Bernard-Marie witnesses the bombings of Arab coffeehouses under General Jacques Massu's watch, the town's infamous military governor. Engrained in his young mind, these images grow into a long-lasting aversion to his hometown—and his father's values—as later portrayed in his play *Retour au désert*. A shy and introvert student, he repeats two years of middle school, unnoticed by his teachers, except one who considers his written compositions 'literary events' in and of themselves. He is an avid reader of Rimbaud from an early age. After high school, in 1967, he attempts—and fails—to pursue higher education in journalism, in the city of Strasbourg.

A first life-changing event occurs, in 1968, when he sees the legendary actress Maria Casarès performing *Medea*, by Seneca. The performance is so baffling it leaves an indelible mark on him. He decides to dedicate his life to the theater. Only a few months later, a second life-changing event occurs during his first trip abroad, for a summer job in Quebec, which leads him to discover New York while in transit. He will return to the American megalopolis throughout his life, considering it the mirror-opposite of his hometown, a place of diversity and hospitality toward outcasts. The need to

---

   1   This account provides a broader biographical context to the introduction's in-depth discussions of individual plays. It is difficult to overstate the significance of Arnaud Maïsetti's biography of Bernard-Marie Koltès, which came out with Les Éditions de Minuit in 2018. Along with the posthumously published interviews (1999) and letters (2009), Maïsetti's biography, and the *Dictionnaire Koltès* edited by Florence Bernard, out in 2022 with Éditions Honoré Champion, are indispensable supplements to Koltès' plays, for all interested artists, readers, and scholars.

   2   Koltès, Bernard-Marie. Interview with Michael Merschmeier (*Theater Heute*, no 7 /83). *Une part de ma vie : Entretiens*. Les Editions de Minuit, 2010, 34.

   3   Koltès, François. Preface. *Lettres*, by Bernard-Marie Koltès. Les Editions de Minuit, 2009, 8.

escape France becomes insatiable and, from a young age, Koltès discovers himself an avid traveler. Later, in a 1988 interview: "I find it essential to travel after your studies. You learn things that will remain useful your whole life. If you don't shove in the face of 18-year-old kids the small place they occupy in the world, they'll spend their lives thinking they're very important, and that their careers are very important. If you learn this when you're young, you won't forget it. For me, when I was 20, it called everything into question."[4]

In 1968, the cultural heart of the city of Strasbourg beats around *Le Centre Dramatique de l'Est* (CDE), a drama school Koltès applies to multiple times, but fails at the entrance exams. Unscathed, he puts together an independent theater group, directs his own stage adaptations of classical novels by Gorki and Dostoyevsky, and of the Song of Songs. Ambitious, he sends his texts to Maria Casarès, who fails to respond, but also to the director of the new *Théâtre National de Strasbourg* (formerly CDE), Hubert Gignoux. Impressed enough by the manuscript, Gignoux admits Koltès to the coveted drama school with no entrance exam, but in the "stage management" section as a pretext. Gignoux is an influential man in France's cultural world of the time. Thanks to him, the play *L'Héritage*—Koltès' first original text—is broadcasted on the national radio, France Culture, in 1972, with the voice of Maria Casarès; so is another original play, *Voix sourdes*, in 1974. But these small successes are short-lived: his screen adaptation of yet another new play fails to be fully produced, and his rewriting of Shakespeare's *Hamlet* will not be staged during his lifetime. Having wagered the entirety of his social identity on becoming a successful playwright, Koltès falls into depression, then into drugs to alleviate the pain of what he considers an inconsequential body of work. In December 1974, at the shock of his family and friends, he tries to kill himself—and fails.

After recovering, Koltès abstains from drugs: "I don't think there is any real difference in nature between the experiences of taking drugs and not taking them. Dope leads to a purely personal frenzy that is strangely similar to the frenzy you experience without it."[5] Nevertheless, drug-induced frenzy becomes central to his first and only novel, finished in 1976, whose equestrian title *La Fuite à cheval très loin dans la ville* is a direct reference to heroin. His suicide attempt will also be his last, and marks a period of transition. To believe Koltès' interviews, that period leads to his

---

[4] Koltès, interview with Emmanuelle Klausner and Brigitte Salino (*L'Événement du jeudi*, January 12, 1989), *Une part de ma vie*, 149.

[5] Koltès, interview with Alain Prique (reviewed by the author, *Masques*, 1st trimester, 1984), *Une part de ma vie*, 42.

now legendary monologue, *La Nuit juste avant les forêts* (originally titled *La Nuit juste avant les forêts de Nicaragua*), written in 1977. He calls this "play"—which subscribes to no dramatic convention—the beginning of his true work that will include six subsequent major plays. From this renewed corpus, Koltès purposefully—and anachronistically—banishes his 1978 stage adaptation of J.D. Salinger,[6] commissioned by a stage director whose collaborative approach proved to be antithetical to the playwright's solitary work ethic.

In 1976, the year Koltès finishes his novel, his father dies at the hospital from an unattended phlebitis. The same year, he is baffled by Patrice Chéreau's production of *La Dispute* by Marivaux. At the time, Chéreau was a rising star on the French stage, a collaborator of Pierre Boulez, producing worldwide. After attending *La Dispute*, Koltès ranks him among the artists he aspires to work with. In 1977, he travels to the USSR and Czechoslovakia. In a span of a few months, he writes *La Nuit juste avant les forêts* for his friend, Yves Ferry, who delivers the one-sentence monologue at the Avignon's Off festival in July. The stage set is rudimentary: a chair and a table. It will be Koltès' last attempt at staging his own work. He is particularly put off by the Avignon Festival, the overwhelming number of productions, the competition among artists, and the mondaine atmosphere surrounding the venue. His verdict: "Avignon is a sinister place."[7] In the meantime, he reads Marcel Proust, Mario Vargas Llosa, James Joyce, and Rimbaud again. In January 1978, he makes a decisive trip to Nigeria. His childhood imagery of an exotic Africa immediately falls apart as he witnesses, right at the airport, then throughout his trip, the gratuitous violence of white folks against black Africans. The murder of a black worker at a construction site managed by a French company becomes the premise of *Combat de nègre et de chiens* (originally titled *Pour Nwofia*). He begins writing the play the same year, not in Nigeria, but during yet another solitary trip, this time to Central America (Mexico, Nicaragua, Guatemala). It is a Mayan village, by the Lake Atitlán, that sees the birth of *Combat*. Writing and traveling increasingly go hand in hand. His inclinations are particularly toward countries whose languages are foreign to him.

In 1979, in Pigalle, Paris, he befriends Copi and Hervé Guibert, who take part in the "Front Homosexuel d'Action Révolutionnaire," a belated

---

6 Koltès, Bernard-Marie. *Sallinger*. Les Editions de Minuit, 1995.

7 Koltès, *Lettres* 294.

response to the 1969 Stonewall riots in New York. Although at home within the gay community, particularly in New York's late 70s and early 80s, partaking in the clandestine gatherings on the Hudson's West Piers, Koltès never participates in its political movement. He also refuses to consider homosexuality as a predominant motif in his work. "My homosexuality is not a solid pillar for my writing to rely upon. My desire, of course, but not my homosexuality specifically. Besides, to me the expression of desire seems to be the same for the homosexual and the heterosexual."[8] *Dans la Solitude des champs de coton*, whose entire dramatic tension relies on the mechanism of desire—while never identifying the object of desire—is a case in point.

While in Paris, he frequents the movie theaters almost on a daily basis, watching anything available at the box office, from Tarkovsky to Bruce Lee, from Jean-Luc Godard to American musicals. He is particularly enamored with films by Scorsese and Coppola, actors such as Brando, De Niro, and Travolta. Jim Jarmusch's *Down by Law* will later bear on his conception of *Dans la solitude des champs de coton*. Later in 1984, he drafts yet another movie script, this time inspired by Travolta, called *Nickel Stuff* (in his correspondence, he refers to it as *Saturday Night Fever N° 3*).[9] The script will be considered by Chéreau and Claire Denis, but will never be made into a film. His musical taste grows equally eclectic, ranging from Bach, whose fugues he says inspired the structure of *La Nuit juste avant les forêts*, to Bob Marley, who was the inspiration behind the character Abad, in *Quai Ouest*.

In the fateful summer of 1979, Hubert Gignoux sends the manuscripts of *Combat de nègre et de chiens* and *La Nuit juste avant les forêts* to Patrice Chéreau. After Koltès' death, Chéreau recalls a few decisive factors coming into play when reading the manuscripts. First, both men being roughly the same age, their worldviews were contemporaneous, while most French directors produced only the classics for convenience' sake. Second, Chéreau was intimidated by *La Nuit*, admitting he did not understand it, because the text dispensed with all the dramatic tools a director relies on: a clear-cut character, an identifiable situation, an evolving plot, etc. He also admits to being, at the time, averse to monologues as a genre. In fact, he did not stage this particular text until 2011, roughly 22 years after Koltès' death. In turn, *Combat* seemed more approachable, adhering to the dramatic conventions *La Nuit* dispensed with. Even so, Chéreau admits he did not understand all the aspects of *Combat* either, but still thought something new

---

[8] Koltès, interview with Alain Prique (*Le Gai Pied* February 19, 1983), *Une part de ma vie*, 30.

[9] Koltès, *Lettres* 482.

and significant lied in it, a new language worth unraveling. Lastly, Koltès himself contacted Chéreau, stating that he deemed nobody else worthy of staging this play, a request that did not fall on deaf ears. Koltès will have to wait about four years for Chéreau's production to see the light of day.

In the meantime, *Combat* is produced for the French national radio. In the spring of 1980, the early version of the play along with *La Nuit* are published in a book format. These two plays now circulate among artists in France's theater world. The following year, a stage director affiliated with La Comédie Française reaches out to Chéreau for works by contemporary playwrights, and leaves with *La Nuit* in hand. The text Chéreau did not want to stage is now fully produced at the Petit Odéon theater. The press chatters about a daring new voice, one article extrapolating that *La Nuit* exudes "a melodious homosexuality [...] seeking its place between Céline and Genet."[10] On May 11, 1981, to Koltès' chagrin, Bob Marley dies. The playwright returns to New York and starts writing *Quai Ouest*, his so-called "New York play," rooted in his experience at the abandoned warehouses on the Hudson piers.

In 1983, Chéreau is appointed as the director of the new Naterre-Amandiers theater. He decides to inaugurate his theater with *Combat de nègre et de chiens*. He states as his mission to showcase contemporary playwrights on a yearly basis, alongside classical plays. Subsequently, Chéreau produces Jean Genet (1983–1984), Heiner Müller (1984–1985), and Valère Novarina (1986–1987), among others. For the production of *Combat*, Koltès agrees to do something he will not repeat: he sits with Chéreau and modifies parts of the play to the director's request. By the time it is put on stage, the play has transformed from its earlier published version. At Chéreau's initiative, Koltès starts doing interviews with the press, but becomes quickly wary of how his words are being reported. He increasingly asks to review, at times change, the written transcripts. Following *Combat*'s production, Chéreau vouches to stage all of Koltès' future plays.

From the moment he devotes himself to the theater, in his early twenties, Koltès makes the decision not to hold a steady job, which he sees as a hindrance to creative work. As a result, he is constantly in financial trouble. Chéreau decides to provide him with a modest salary working in the new theater, in exchange for drafting reading notes on plays lined up for production. Although not studious in this task, Koltès is among the group preparing the second full production of Genet's *Les Paravents*—following Roger Blin's, in 1966, which provoked the ire of right-wing activists. In response to Chéreau's request to produce his epic play for a second time,

---

10   Maïsetti, Arnaud. *Bernard-Marie Koltès*. Les Editions de Minuit, 2018, 198.

Genet initially states that *Les Paravents* is too colossal a play to be staged again. Chéreau persuades him and, in 1983, Maria Casarès plays the role of Saïd's mother, as she did in Blin's production. A few years later, Koltès confesses in an interview that Genet is "the sole contemporary playwright who draws my interest."[11] He adds that the novels—more baroque and lyrical—interest him most, and finds Genet's plays too anchored in the post-war period. Critics never ceased to draw parallels between the two writers, especially regarding the motifs running through both works, and their overall rebelliousness. Although Koltès himself does not adhere to that genealogy, there is little doubt that his affiliation with the production of *Les Paravents*—an epic play against the Algerian war—left an indelible mark on him. On April 15, 1986, Jean Genet dies alone in a Parisian hotel room. Upon hearing the news, Koltès confides to a friend this quasi-patricidal thought: "Now that he is dead, I know that I loved him." Soon after, his reading notes on *Les Paravents* turn into a "prologue" for a never-to-be-finished novel (the text is published posthumously under the title *Prologue*). Its protagonist—a traitor—is depicted in the guise of Genet himself. More significantly, the answer to Genet's *Les Paravents* takes the form of *Le Retour au désert*, Koltès' own play about the Algerian war, later staged in 1989.

In 1983, he travels to Senegal, then to New York again, where he finishes *Quai Ouest*. Around that time, he realizes he has caught a mysterious disease, a virus that by the early eighties is offensively dubbed the "gay cancer." Until his death, in 1989, Koltès does not mention the disease in his published plays, or even in the posthumously published letters and diaries, and never does he speak of it in his interviews, unlike other contemporaries like Hérvé Gilbert. The word "AIDS" remains deafeningly absent from his corpus. It is so, except on one—revealing—occasion. In the handwritten manuscript of the monumental play *Quai Ouest*, at the bottom of a notebook page, while listing random thoughts about the direction the play should take, amid tentative lines intended for his characters, Koltès refers to the character of Cécile, the sick and begrudged mother suffering from a mysterious and unnamed illness, who dies at the end of the play (also played by Maria Casarès). In front of her name, he writes in cursive: "blood loss + AIDS." For the play's audience, Cécile's illness remains as mysterious as the epidemic was for the general public in the early 80s.

Like in the case of *Combat*, Chéreau's production of *Quai Ouest* is delayed and Koltès moves on to other projects. This time, he drafts a movie

---

11 Koltès, Interview with Véronique Hotte (*Théâtre Public*, November–December 1988), *Une part de ma vie* 126.

script called *Nickel Stuff*, imbued with American cinema, one that Chéreau and Claire Denis will briefly consider producing. 1984 is an important milestone for the author: his only novel, *La Fuite à cheval très loin dans la ville*, is published by Les Éditions de Minuit. His biographer, Arnaud Maïsetti, reports: "Thanks to the insistence of Alain Robbe-Grillet, Jérôme Lindon then published a novel he had rejected almost a decade earlier—without Koltès changing as much as a comma."[12] From that point on, all his texts (the two previously published plays included) will come out with this small yet imposing publisher, whose dramatic catalogue until then essentially boiled down to one single author: Samuel Beckett. Most of his later plays will be produced abroad, in translation, before Chéreau gets to stage them. Fed up with mediocre foreign productions and translations, Koltès personally sends the manuscript of *Quai Ouest* to the celebrated post-Brechtian German playwright Heiner Müller, who incidentally knew as much French as Koltès knew German: almost nothing. Müller promptly accepts the task. A couple of years later, the German production sparks critical outrage due to the sheer number of mistranslations, but Koltès remains adamant that his choice was the right one. In 1984, his travel destination: Egypt.

1985 brings a sense of urgency in his writing, fueled by the awareness that his affliction is taking over his body. In the spring, Koltès begins *Dans la solitude des champs de coton*—his second play inspired by the Hudson piers—while *Quai Ouest* comes out in print with Minuit. He travels to Brazil, deems São Paulo to be the "Latin New York." He is awestricken by the art of capoeira, considered as a synthesis of dance and martial arts, and in the context of his own popular culture, John Travolta and Bruce Lee. He is equally ecstatic to learn that capoeira originated as a clandestine art, among black slaves forbidden to bear arms, who learned to fight under the guise of a dance. Constantly at the brink of hitting the adversary, posed as a dance partner, an actual strike is nevertheless prohibited—even considered vulgar—but the imminent risk of the strike holds the spectator's attention. In a letter from Salvador de Bahia, written to his brother François, he confides "I am racking my brain" to find a way to bring the structure of capoeira to the theater.[13] *Solitude*, finished in February of 1986, may have succeeded in doing just that. Two characters, the Dealer and the Client, never cease to pick a fight from the beginning to the end of the play, threatening to strike each other in long poetic sentences, yet never landing a hit. Although the last sentence, "Then, what weapon?," may imply the fight is imminent—granted

---

12 Maïsetti, 245.

13 Koltès, *Lettres* 501.

it remains only a supposition, since the text ends with a question mark—the said fight would then occur offstage, and be therefore deemed too vulgar for the theater.

At the start of 1986, Koltès still awaits Chéreau's production of *Quai Ouest*, while having already finished with *Solitude*. In the spring, he is invited to write a short play to be staged at the Avignon Festival. The invitation is by Lucien Attoun, director of Théâtre Ouvert and the dramatic repertory for France Culture radio. The play will be part of a cycle of dramatic shorts by fifteen young playwrights, under the common title "Dare to Love." Only at the very last minute, he drafts *Tabataba*: a dialogue in the form of successive monologues, reminiscent of *Solitude*. A young man and his begrudged older sister, spending the evening hours secluded in their backyard, struggle with feelings of incestuous love, which they channel through an unexpected transient object: a beat-up Harley Davidson. When staged in Avignon, Attoun is so impressed he wants to tour the play, but Koltès insists—as did Genet for his monumental *Les Paravents*—that this brief play was meant to be produced but once. In April, Chéreau finally stages *Quai Ouest*. Critiques are unconvinced: Chéreau's colossal stage set stifles the actors along with the text. Unscathed by his failure, Chéreau immediately decides to stage Koltès' next play, *Dans la solitude des champs de coton*, without having read it.

In fact, *Solitude* opens as early as January 27, 1987, a mere six months after *Quai Ouest*. The Ivorian actor Isaach de Bankolé—who had played the silent Abad—is now the loquacious Dealer. Contrary to his other productions of Koltès, Chéreau will stage three different versions of the text (1987, 1988, 1995). During the first production, the play comes as an oddity to the French theater scene: it has precedence neither in form nor in content. Critics are bewildered, some confused as to what to do with this new specimen, others immediately bothered by it. Measuring the potential of the text—Chéreau always underscored the difficulty and the necessity of staging contemporary authors—he decides to give it a second shot the following year. Bankolé is now part of Claire Denis' new feature, *Chocolat*, and Koltès travels to Cameroun to meet both actor and director. Later, Denis will offer Koltès the opportunity to write a script for another project, called *White Material*, a task Koltès enthusiastically accepts, but will not finish before his death (Marie NDiaye will take on the task of writing the script, and *White Material* will come out in 2009). In Bankolé's absence for the 1988 production of *Solitude*, Chéreau decides to play the role of the Dealer. It will be the start of a rift between the playwright and the director. Koltès remains adamant that the role of the Dealer belongs to a black actor. In interviews, he will hint to his displeasure, without openly criticizing Chéreau. After Koltès' passing, in his 1995 production—the most celebrated by the critics and the public—the director commits a second betrayal. Again acting as the Dealer, he puts a great emphasis on homoeroticism between the two characters, which the playwright considered secondary to the play.

In July of 1987, stunned by the Boulevard actress Jacqueline Maillan, Koltès finishes writing an entire play for her. *Retour au désert* is set in the early '60s, in his dreaded hometown of Metz, at the height of the Algerian war. The play also stands out from his corpus because of where the action takes place: in the house of a bourgeois family—the stamp of Boulevard theater—while his other plays were purposefully set outdoors. Summer 1987, Koltès begins translating Shakespeare's *Winter's Tale*, commissioned by Luc Bondy. In July 1988, *Retour* is published with Minuit. In September, Chéreau stages the play in a private theater—a first for Koltès—and runs it through February of the following year.

January 28, 1988, Roberto Succo murders a police officer in Toulon. Italy, Switzerland, and France issue warrants for his arrest. The wanted-person posters can be seen all over the Paris metro stations. Succo is handsome, Koltès "falls in love." The media calls him "The Killer With the Eyes of Ice" and "Public Enemy No1." He is considered a cop killer, a kidnapper, a rapist, and a burglar. A few years earlier, in Italy, he had stabbed his mother, and suffocated his father—a police officer—with a plastic bag. Caught, he was committed to a psychiatric hospital, from which he escaped. In order to cross the European borders, Succo falsified his ID card, changing but one letter in his last name, from Succo to Zucco, which seemed to be enough to avoid being caught. In February, a 16-year-old girl named Sabrina tells the police her boyfriend, whom she knew as Kurt, looked eerily like the wanted person. She adds that he pretends to be a "secret agent" as a way to explain his ever-changing disguise. She leads them to Succo, who is arrested near Venice, by an officer who was a friend of Succo's father. The day following his arrest, Succo climbs on the roof of his high-security prison, undressing in front of the local press which hurried to the site, then walking on an electric cable, like on a tightrope: "Hey, you with the camera! Come here—I need to talk to you!"[14] Clearly, this was not an escape, but "pure theater," according to Succo's biographer,[15] a detail which certainly didn't escape the playwright.

---

14   Froment, Pascale. *Roberto Succo: histoire vraie d'un assassin sans raison*. Gallimard, 2001, 408.

15   Ibid., 409.

Breaking his ribs in his fall, the assassin is taken to prison again, where he suffocates himself with his pillow case. Never before did Koltès conduct such extensive research on a news story in order to write a play.

In June 1988, Koltès attends Peter Stein's production of *Three Sisters*, by Chekov, at Nanterre-Amandiers. Shortly after, he publicly expresses the wish that his next play, *Roberto Zucco*, be staged not by Chéreau, but by Stein. He personally mails the manuscript of his new play to the German director. At the end of November 1988, he travels to Lisbon to meet Claire Denis for the film project *White Material*. He feels his end is approaching, and still multiplies projects. Pierre Boulez offers him to write an opera—a genre largely foreign to Koltès—which the playwright eagerly accepts. He plans to translate a second play by Shakespeare. Most significantly, he starts writing a new play, this time for Maria Casarès, the actress who kindled his desire to write for the theater at the age of twenty. He always regretted not writing a text for her as the main character. He calls the play Coco, surprisingly inspired by Coco Chanel and the Book of Job. The character Coco is on her death bed, filled with disgust for her maid who cannot stop putting on lipsticks. Sadly, none of these projects will come to fruition: both his body and mind abdicate to the disease. As Bankolé testifies: "His writing had become spotty, like one's memory becomes spotty. He wanted to write, but he no longer could."[16]

Koltès wants to find a place where to die. He is reminded of Guatemala, the Mayan village by the Lake Atitlán, where he began writing *Combat de nègre et de chiens*, the play that lunched his career. Mid-January 1989, he arrives in Mexico, his luggage full of medicine. On February 9, he finally reaches Guatemala. In his letters from the first trip there, back in 1978, addressed to his mother and to a friend, he had already stated that, instead of being buried in the cold earth of a western cemetery, "I want to be buried here,"[17] in Guatemala. He tries, by himself, but is too frail to reach his beloved Mayan village. On February 14, he calls a friend to fetch him and bring him back home. On February 16, in a wheelchair, he attends the final performance of *Retour au désert*. Early March, Claire Denis asks him to Lisbon, and despite his condition, Koltès heeds the call. It is the wrong decision: he cannot produce what Denis asks of him. Reaching the end, Koltès calls his family to come to Lisbon. To his brother François, he writes a letter consisting only of the following words, in English: "In God we trust/ Do we?" His mother and brothers join him in Lisbon. Lying on his deathbed,

---

16 Maïsetti, 333.
17 Koltès, *Lettres* 395.

he says to his mother that he does not want to die. He is transferred to a hospital in Paris. Like Jean Genet, who passed three years before him, Bernard-Marie Koltès dies on April 15.

AMIN ERFANI

Amin Erfani is an author, translator of contemporary French theater, and scholar of avant-garde literature. His academic work focuses on 20th and 21st century French and Francophone literature; comparative literature; theater; psychoanalytic & critical theory. His translations (including of Valère Novarina & Bernard-Marie Koltès) have been published and produced on both sides of the Atlantic, and his literary work has appeared in various literary journals in English and French. He is a professor of French language and literature at the City University of New York.

Andy Bragen has held Workspace and Process Space Residencies with the Lower Manhattan Cultural Council, the Clubbed Thumb Biennial Commission, and a Jerome Fellowship. His produced plays include *This is My Office* (The Play Company), *Don't You F**king Say a Word* (59e59/ABTP), and *Notes on My Mother's Decline* (Playco/ABTP). Andy is an alum of New Dramatists, and has an MFA from Brown University. He teaches playwriting at Barnard College.

Michaël Attias is a saxophonist/composer and literary translator based in New York City since 1994. His translation of *Battle of Black and Dogs* was premiered at the Festival Koltés NY 2003 at the Ohio Theatre under the direction of Doris Mirescu. It was once again performed at Yale Repertory Theatre in 2010 under the direction of Robert Woodruff. Attias designed the sound and composed the music for both productions.

Anna G. R. Miller, Ph.D. is a translator, scholar, and teacher specializing in modern and contemporary theatre. She holds degrees in French from New York University, the University of Oxford, and Vassar College, and has lived and worked in Paris.

Marion Schoevaert is the Artistic Director of In Parentheses theater company in NYC. She has translated and directed French playwrights in the US, such as Michel Vinaver, Olivier Cadiot, Jean-Luc Lagarce, Violaine Schwartz. She is the co-producer of the Koltes Festival in 2003.

Theresa M. Weber lives in the mountains of Western North Carolina. She once lived in New York City where this *West Pier* translation was first completed in a café in the mid-1990s. She's a practicing lawyer and long-recovered denizen of the Theater, her most pertinent credentials being a friendship and collaboration with the incomparable Marion Schoevaert.

The Martin E. Segal Theatre Center (MESTC) is a non-profit center for theatre, dance, and film affiliated with CUNY's PhD Program in Theatre and Performance. The Center's mission is to bridge the gap between academia and the professional performing arts communities both within the United States and internationally. By providing an open environment for the development of educational, community-driven, and professional projects in the performing arts, MESTC is a home to theatre scholars, students, playwrights, actors, dancers, directors, dramaturgs, and performing arts managers from the local and international theatre communities.

Through diverse programming—staged readings, theatre events, panel discussions, lectures, conferences, film screenings, dance—and a number of publications, MESTC enables artists, academics, visiting scholars, and performing arts professionals to participate actively in the advancement and appreciation of the entire range of theatrical experience. The Center presents staged readings to further the development of new and classic plays, lecture series, televised seminars featuring professional and academic luminaries, and arts in education programs, and maintains its long-standing visiting scholars-from-abroad program. In addition, the Center publishes a series of highly-regarded academic journals, as well as books, including plays in translation, written, translated, and edited by leading scholars.

www.theSegalCenter.org

The PhD Program in Theatre and Performance, The Graduate Center, CUNY, is one of the leading doctoral theatre programs in the United States. The Faculty includes distinguished professors, holders of endowed chairs, and internationally recognized scholars. The program trains future scholars and teachers in all the disciplines of theatre research. Faculty members edit MESTC publications, working closely with the doctoral students in theatre who perform a variety of editorial functions and learn the skills involved in the creation of books and journals.

www.gc.cuny.edu/theatre-and-performance

The MESTC Publication Wing produces both journals and individual volumes. Journals include *Slavic and Eastern European Performance* (SEEP), *The Journal of American Drama and Theatre* (JADT), and *Western European Stages* (WES). Books include *Four Melodramas by Pixérécourt* (edited by Daniel Gerould and Marvin Carlson—both Distinguished Professors of Theatre at the CUNY Graduate Center), *Contemporary Theatre in Egypt*, *The Heirs of Molière* (edited and translated by Marvin Carlson), *Seven Plays by Stanisław Ignacy Witkiewicz* (edited and translated by Daniel Gerould), *The Arab Oedipus: Four Plays* (edited by Marvin Carlson), *Theatre Research Resources in New York City* (edited by Jessica Brater, Senior Editor Marvin Carlson), *Comedy: A Bibliography of Critical Studies in English on the Theory and Practice of Comedy in Drama, Theatre and Performance* (edited by Meghan Duffy, Senior Editor Daniel Gerould), *BAiT-Buenos Aires in Translation: Four Plays* (edited and translated by Jean Graham-Jones), *roMANIA AFTER 2000: Five New Romanian Plays* (edited by Saviana Stanescu and Daniel Gerould), *Four Plays from North Africa* (edited by Marvin Carlson), *Barcelona Plays: A Collection of New Plays by Catalan Playwrights* (edited and translated by Marion Peter Holt and Sharon G. Feldman), *Josep M. Benet i Jornet: Two Plays* (edited and translated by Marion Peter Holt), *Czech Plays: Seven New Works* (edited by Marcy Arlin, Gwynn MacDonald and Daniel Gerould), *Playwrights before the Fall* (edited by Daniel Gerould), *Timbre4* (edited and translated by Jean Graham-Jones), *Jan Fabre: The Servant of Beauty and I Am a Mistake* (edited and foreword by Frank Hentschker), *Quick Change: 28 Theatre Essays and 4 Plays in Translation* (by Daniel Gerould), *Shakespeare Made French: Four Plays by Jean-François Ducis* (edited and translated by Marvin Carlson), and *New Plays from Spain: Eight Works by Seven Playwrights* (edited by Frank Hentschker).

IN MEMORIAM: Daniel Gerould (1928–2012), MESTC Director of Publications
Martin E. Segal (1916–2012), MESTC Founder

www.ingramcontent.com/pod-product-compliance
Lightning Source LLC
Chambersburg PA
CBHW050830230426
43667CB00012B/1938